Table of Contents

Dedication

I dedicate this book with gratitude to the entire cast of characters I created in this life to further the evolution of my soul. My parents, siblings, ex-husbands, The Roman Catholic Church and all the extras to whom I bow for the important roles you have played in the production of my life the movie.

Sincerest appreciation for Archangel Michael, Yeshua Nazare, Sathya Sai Baba, Mother Mary, Melchizedek, King Solomon, Abraham, Enoch, Moses, my daughter Anastasia, Marcy Calhoun, Fredereka Farris, Chief Golden Light Eagle, Joao de Deus and the Casa Dom Ignacio Entities, and Sondra Sneed without whose love, joy and guidance I would not know myself to be the truth of who I AM.

Special thanks to Dr. Carl Gustav Jung, and John D. Spooner for your inspiration, generosity of spirit, and encouragement.

For those who see me as I once was . . . I have died and resurrected a million times, it is but your eyes that have not.

– Siobhan Nicolaou, *The Sword of Truth*

Introduction

This book is about my journey through the colorful pages of my soul and how I emancipated my body, integrated my emotions and freed my mind from the illusion of evil. Duality was my own personal hell on earth for much of my life, and unlike other modes of transformation, mine has taken place through the integration of the emotional body as a means of changing the perceptions of my mind, rarely the reverse.

The battlefield that was my childhood paved the way without missing a brick to the loving embrace of a much grander illusion. Leaving home at age fourteen, I steeped myself in a stronger concoction for another thirteen years.

On this trickier level of the playing field I was respected, protected, able to keep up with the dance, and smart enough not get trampled under hoof. Unlike my home where darkness was fed into my emotional body unknowingly and under the guise of love, in my new world I picked up this bigger, sexier more alluring chalice of greater power and drank deeply.

The taste of freedom found ironically in this new type of bondage was seductive and delicious, and all I had felt about myself as a child was validated in my experience. I consumed the illusion, played in it, laughed in it, cried in it, lived it, believed it, breathed it, slept with it, snorted it, supported it, and loved it. Years later, when I changed the program, the real dance began.

In 1987 at the onset of the harmonic convergence, my capacity for denial reached its limit and everything suddenly turned the deepest shades of black. Given the choice to live or die, I chose to live negotiating that life had to be different from what it had been.

Awakening was inevitable, although not knowing this, I reached for some answers in a new way trying to make any sense of things. Attending a meditation class for the first time, I opened the door of light within my mind and heart that revealed something greater than the darkness I believed was life.

The only greater ecstasy than complete and utter bondage is the complete and utter freedom from it.

- Siobhan Nicolaou, The Sword of Truth

The awareness of the light that lives within me, and the pain that kept me feeling separate from experiencing it, put me on my path to wholeness. My healing process set in motion twenty-seven years of an intense production of shadow play manifesting itself in hundreds of ways and in many disguises.

My divided mind tormented me until I integrated enough illusion to come to the consciousness that any "evil" in my experience is a reflection of my own inner demons. Demons became real when I became aware of my light; until then I had nothing to compare them to. In this new contrast my life became a fantastic exploration of my emotional baggage on my journey to the truth within the baggage itself.

Until the light, it seemed natural to live life in drama and pain with a false sense of normalcy carved out of the ingestion of society's wine. For decades after my awakening, it felt like the darkness and the light were battling over possession of my soul. I have experienced countless dreams of the devil challenging me, tempting me, teaching me, coaxing me, having sex with me, threatening me, talking to me. Many times I woke sweaty and breathless, yet always victorious tricking him and finding a way out. As I evolved, I came to stand my ground moving among the demons unheeded, protected by my entourage in and out of my dreams. Now I stand as the light and compassion within and among them all.

To myself I am whole and I am love. To my siblings I am an enigma. To the indoctrinated Catholic, I am Satan herself. To those I help, I am an angel. To those who want to stay asleep, I am their worst nightmare. To my lover, I am the deepest part of themselves. To that which is darkness, I am the light of love aflame within the essence of its unworthiness.

To Archangel Michael, I am a full time job. To my Guardian Angel, I am way too hard on myself. To my Mother, I am courageous. To my Father, I am a woman. To my daughter, I have immense strength. To God, I Am That I Am.

My journey to wholeness has been a road of unconventional stepping stones traveled without any help from traditional therapy. It is the continual trip down the yellow brick road of self examination that challenges me in every step saying "How bad do you want it?" It is not a path for those of weak mind or spirit. Freedom takes courage, commitment, and the desire to break free from blame, projection, and the illusion of separation. It is challenging, revealing, and most of all rewarding.

I have been judged in every way, by everyone, for every move I have ever made on every level as I have turned my back and made different choices for myself. I have walked away from what everyone in my life from birth has told me is truth and learned to listen inward.

Grief was my constant companion until I realized nothing can be lost or left behind and that in the deaths of my many loved ones, I grieved only a part of myself. There are no sacrifices in life other than that of the ego, and I have lost nothing through gaining the wisdom of my experience on the other side of my pain.

The only difference we are here to make is within ourselves, where all conflict begins and ends. Our veils are the film projected into the holographic creation of our life the movie. This book is an offering of love and inspiration for those who hold themselves and others in contempt consciously or unconsciously, whether in the past or present. May this book inspire you to love yourself above all, transmute and transform should you choose the path of wholeness and a life lived consciously.

I am living proof that one can integrate their way from any perceived level of darkness back to the source of light within it. I know now that I am love, and that I am loved, and I am at peace in the arms of my one, my all, my only self. It is only through love that your true purpose is revealed.

While it is true that one's perception must shift to exact a complete change in consciousness, there is a great deal of integration that takes place between awareness and lasting transformation, and it all begins and ends in the emotional body.

Those who believe wholeness comes solely by way of mind will only know half of the truth.

- Siobhan Nicolaou, The Sword of Truth

Chapter I

Starry Eyed

There is nothing in my childhood that can explain why or how I have become who I AM. It is only through healing and transformation that I have become that I AM, and even when I believe I have arrived at who I think I AM to be, I AM given the option to become more or more of the same. The key is love and knowing that who you are, and who you were, are always in the process of becoming.

- Siobhan Nicolaou, The Sword of Truth

Starry Eyed

My parents were born in the 1930's - a time when ignorance was normal and consciousness was nil. They did not know who they were outside of what they had been told by others, and raised me from their limited wisdom and capacity to love.

Grandma's Italian lineage took our roots from Rome the long way to California via Madera then Hawaii where she was born the last of eleven children. Grandma sang all the time, danced ballroom and the hula well into her 70's. She was feminine, full of grace, faith and courage leaving my paternal grandfather while my father was still a toddler in 1936. The man I embraced as my Grandfather was a caring man that she met and married shortly after her divorce, and she remained his wife for fifty years.

Grandpa was a foreman for US Steel working happily for decades ensuring quality of life for his family. The only things I knew about Dad's youth was that he got in trouble for stealing crates of tomatoes from trucks, he was a good athlete, and Father Gregory was his mentor. Taken under Father Gregory's wing at a young and impressionable age, he became the father figure my dad looked up to. His commitment to the priest derived from his patriarchal conditioning, fueled my father's disdain for the feminine. They remained closest companions throughout the priest's ninety two years and traveled the world for decades on Vatican lira.

Mom's German family had status in their East Bay community. Oma Steinbeck was born in San Francisco, moved to the East Bay when she was very young. The family owned a large meat company there for forty-one years. My Opa was a very tall, huge-handed man with a soft personality who died before I was born. Oma visited twice in my childhood, and always stayed at a hotel. She walked upright assisted by her cane, wore French lipstick and expensive face powder. She was classy and smart, sad and beautiful. Tante Donna was tall, shy and blue-eyed like my Opa, the opposite of my fair skinned, black-haired boisterous mother, who had brown eyes like her maternal grandmother.

Baptized Lutheran with a rebellious soul determined to evolve, my mother at age fourteen proclaimed her devotion to the Catholic faith and found herself placed in Catholic boarding school through college. She met my father while he worked the wood fire grill at a landmark diner in her East Bay town. Stopping in for lunch, mom's classy, sophisticated long lean looks met with dad's square jaw, olive skin, muscular build, and I surmise chemistry took over from there. She married my father right out of college, despite her parents disapproval and threats to disown her for marrying an Italian who they viewed as beneath her station.

Marie was born eight months and twenty-four days after the wedding, with Stephania a close second fifteen months later. Two years passed and I was conceived on the current of my parents' negative thought forms and emotions, on the tail of two lost pregnancies. My nature as an empath absorbed everything through feeling and the heaviness of the energy began veiling my soul. Then there was Grandma . . .

Staring off into the sky with starry saucer eyes, the adults around me bustled. The warm rays of the sun suffused my face while the subtle scent of narcissus wafted through my playpen in the early spring air. Five months old and not entirely in my form, Grandmas's playfulness captured my momentary attention. Her spirit exuded celebration and beauty, her vibrance permeated my auric field with *la dolce vita*. She was the motherly love I resonated with, and we were very close until the moment she passed thirty-seven years later.

Mom focused compulsively on daily chores, keeping order about with three small children dutifully performing one task after another. It was as if she made a pact with God that he would reward her at the end of her life for agreeing to suffer all the way and doing everything right. Children in those days were often considered a Catholic duty, a daily duty, not a daily joy.

Six months later, we moved to another house where my brother Matthew was born and fifteen months later Mark. The folks went through the motions of life without forethought or reflection, living a typical life like everybody else.

Known as a "good baby," it was my nature to be floating happily in other worlds rather than caring to engage those around me. My earliest memory of feeling the negative energy of my surroundings was at eighteen months as I steadied myself on the ottoman at Oma's. Dad dragged Stephania by the arm as she resisted his lead forcing her from one room to the next. The energy of fear stirred the moment of peace that surrounded me, my throat constricted and I let go, falling back on my behind.

Stephania, imbalanced from the time she was small, was challenging for my parents. Her condition worsened yet went unacknowledged and untreated; she inflicted physical and emotional pain on me throughout my childhood with hardly a reprimand. My energy responded by closing down, finding it safer to be invisible.

If you tell your mind to forget, it will, and when you tell it to remember it will do that too.

- Siobhan Nicolaou, The Sword of Truth

Chapter II

Die Hand Des Schicksals

Die Hand Des Schicksals

We never heard any intelligent dialogue or observed any healthy solutions concerning the family problems between my parents; democracy was absent in their militaristic style of parenting. We were given no sense of value or voice and were never encouraged to honor our body, mind, feelings or spirit.

By age three, mother's chores and punishments were enforced, and my toddler photos showed the weight of the emotional blankets in the sadness of my large eyes. She collected and typed her rules and regulations, organizing them in an old blue-green cloth covered binder for everybody's reference. There were chores and bed times for every age group. My parents were also great at making up punishments on the fly. Those never made it into the book, but created the sticky substance later used to form the bricks with which I built the walls around my heart.

Illusion was gaining momentum and preparing me to join the ranks of Catholic school. Too young and too sensitive,

I entered first grade at age four; we lasted through the school year, then moved for a third time.

The first of two houses we occupied for a two short years in that rural mountain town was at the end of a gravel driveway next door to Mrs. Taylor. Mrs. Taylor was a widow who had white hair and big blue eyes. She took fondly to us, especially Matthew, and gave us a Brach's candy caramel wreath for Christmas. Finding the flavor of raspberry particularly good, I searched for the shiny purply label when it was my turn to pick. Our house had wood and linoleum floors, our television screen had a green hue and sat on metal stand in the living room. Army tanks were the images that I retained from television at that time, along with the faces of Walter Cronkite and Captain Kangaroo.

My earliest recollection of a dream was in this house, a flying dream still so real.

> *I watched my shadow glide over the gravel about 3 ft above the ground to the end of the driveway, feeling the warmth of the summer sun on my back and the arid heat emitting from the rocks below. I felt free, like all was well and I was safe.*

Waking to a different reality entirely, I did what all kids do and covered up my feelings of stress with things that looked playful. Manifesting my greatest fear again, we uprooted and moved to a remote house that sat on a small hill overlooking an acre lot at the end of a dirt road. The vegetable garden was the view out the front window down the slope, with the chicken and duck coops right along side. The back and side lots were grapevines, pine trees and manzanita bushes as far as the eyes could see. My room, shared with my sisters, had cold cement floors and with bunk beds and a phonograph.

Not knowing how express myself, taught to be quiet, my repressed anguish manifested as bladder and kidney infections with alarming frequency. As this was wildly inconvenient for my mother, her words felt like arrows when she targeted me with the emotional brunt of her shame and disapproval. The folks never addressed my sadness, or their actions or tried to figure out why I was sick all the time, they only knew how to empower that there was something wrong with me, and all of it was my fault.

One of the few times I remember my mom in a space of peace was when she read us books each night before the lights went out. I studied her face, watching her lips as she read with clarity and expression. I noticed how her left front tooth ever so slightly overlapped the right, and how her lipstick had faded into varying shades by the end of a long day. She read us the Brothers Grimm (the unabridged not really for kids version), Aesop's Fables, nursery rhymes and a multitude of stories that I still remember today.

Dad, never adopting the work ethic of his blue collar family, didn't seem to believe in himself enough to create an economic solution to the ever increasing population of our family. As he hopped in and out of sales jobs, they scraped together what they could. The nuns from our parish brought us dinner on numerous occasions, and with it came the feeling of poverty instead of a memory of gratitude or prosperity. We bought groceries with food stamps at times over an eight year period until finally dad kept the same job for over a year.

There were five of us now with more moving parts and personalities to control, so I guess mom and dad decided it would build a stronger team if the pain were distributed more evenly. None of us initially realized that a non-admission of guilt to the question of "who did it" would bring us ALL to the belt, or the paddle, but it did. We stuck with that plan, putting the weight of the collective threat on the one singled out by the pack after all had taken his / her beating. For a while we figured we should cover each other's asses and suffer as a unit because there was always something wrong with something. We cried when mom and dad would try to break us down to give each other up, and we learned to be strong against tyrants.

My eldest sister Marie, burdened with so much responsibility, naturally heaped onto her pile the job to protect us and find ways to improve things- mostly at her own expense. I held my feelings under water until they drowned trying to carve a sense of stability and security out of life.

Getting hurt happened frequently. Without many regular toys, we were always coming up with whacky ways to stimulate our young minds and satisfy our curiosities. As day was breaking on a mild summer day, our slumber was interrupted by the commotion of Marie waking dad as he scrambled to his feet and bolted outside. Stephania, first on the scene, was holding up Matthew dangling from a rope he had tied around his waist before jumping out of the tree house. The only thing that seemed strange was noticing dad did not wear pajamas to bed.

I received my first communion in second grade, wore a white dress carrying a rosary, hands approvingly folded. Going to confession saying, "forgive me father for I have sinned" confused me not knowing what it really meant. Answering "no" to the questions given by the priest, he would get more general as if he had to find something. Feeling guilty and trying to do the right thing, I made something up to feel worthy of the penance. I was given a scapular and told to wear it like a press pass in case I should die so St. Peter would know to let me in. Viewing it as ridiculous through my six-year-old perception, and not completely convinced, I forgot about it until one day it resurfaced on my closet floor and I ground it under the ball of my foot just to see if anything would happen.

Mom, now pregnant with Amanda, got us moving on short notice to the wine country where she was born for a small wrinkle in time. The flood came in December, and I watched dad frantically stack the orange weave furniture and sandbag the doors. We watched as the red wagon floated across our disheveled yard. Mom got us organized, wrapped the baby and piled us into the Oldsmobile. My eyes were glued to the swift moving water on the road out the car window as we partially drifted to Oma's in the East Bay. Oma had beautiful things and a beautiful home. We ate cold cereal the one or two days we were there, and a smile broke across my lips savoring the Sugar Pops and gazing through the short, sheer, cheerful curtains out the window of Oma's breakfast nook.

In January, Mom made Marie fish-shaped birthday cakes out of the Baker's Coconut Book, and before she could blow out the candles and get too excited, we felt the possibility of another flood due to the torrential rain, putting a nervous damper on the party. The saturation of the land yielded a forest of rhubarb that grew alongside the fence that lined a cracked cement path on the side of the house. Mom made strawberry rhubarb pie, making a lasting impression on my post-toddler tastebuds. Dad hitched up the wagon after the flood and moved us to higher ground back to the Nor Cal pines and then the lower Sierra foothills to begin again.

Trying to soothe my emotions, I began chewing my nails down to the quick. My aura, continually shredded by uncertainty and trauma, stacked layers of emotion in various corners of my body and mind. Chewing my nails to blood was quiet and oddly comforting as the responsibilities of chores and family got heavier every year. My two older sisters passed the frustration caused

17

by stress down the pecking order taking the form of verbal abuse, intimidation or brute force if Stephania had something to impress upon me. The raising of voices was more commonplace now and being older I was beginning to hear my mother's words in a different way.

Our new house in Folsom was over one hundred years old and right above the main drag of the old west town. Some plants from the Victorian era like sweet scented violets and string of hearts were present in the garden. There was a huge fig and cherry tree, red geraniums and more snails than I had ever seen. Mom would send us out as her henchkint with small paper bags partially filled with salt to kill them, to "do something constructive" as she often said. There was a walk-in cellar with a few leftover canned pickles in old glass jars still sitting on the cold damp narrow shelf. The houses on neighboring streets had flowers planted along the outside of the fences with pink lilies so fragrant that the scent drifted sweetly for blocks in the soft clean air.

We kids slept upstairs in the dormitory divided by a single center wall, and we all got new beds. Each one of us got an official metal army cot, with US ARMY stenciled on it. It came complete with a three inch mattress and a matching foot locker. We were required to mitre the corners while making the bed, and mom often bounced coins to see if the bedding was tight. Our beds were stripped and remade every Saturday, and yard work was likely if the weather was good. All chores were inspected before we could play, and was very frustrating if I had to do something over. "doing it right the first time" was impressed upon me and how I adapted to make things easier on myself in one way and harder on myself in another.

Beginning third grade with my new uniform and Campus Queen lunchbox gave me a glimmer of hope. I loved my lunch box because Grandma gave it to me. It was pink, metal and created its own microclimate, so my bologna sandwich was a failure by late afternoon. I made peace with warm iceberg lettuce and the unique smell of hot tin and brown apple that hit my nose when opening the lid. Good mustard was my saving grace.

A small school, a small class with ominous reflections in my classmates reinforced my feelings that life was painful and most people in it hurt. I was depressed, always the youngest, skinniest most sensitive child and did not develop physically as the rest of the girls. Having the darkest skin in class after swimming all summer didn't help our relations either. Turning the negative projections of those around me inward, I was beginning to believe the inadequacy I felt. Turning seven years old and overwhelmed, I cried my eyes out begging my mother to put me in another school. Between my lips and her ears the words completely vaporized; she looked at me expressionless, lit another Virginia Slim and gave me the silent clue to carry on.

Mom pregnant once again this time with twins, veered my adventurous spirit happily away from the house exploring around our quiet Victorian neighborhood. The streets with no sidewalks were shaded by humongous trees surrounding the mansions that were just as big and just as old. Finding a bee hive in an old hedge, I looked at it closely watching the bees go about their business. My heart opened to the fuzzy tranquility of the honeybees. Imprinting the hive with my olfactory sense to preserve my delightful discovery, I picked up my steel horse from the dirt and pedaled home.

When the twins Sara and Luke were born, a baptism followed within months of their arrival and Mom invited the clergy over for coffee and cake at our house. Mom had towels called the "priest towels" which we were never allowed to touch. The edges of these special towels were thoughtfully crocheted, always folded neatly and brought out only when the priests came over. Sent to the bathroom to wash my hands before cake, I hastily reached to dry my hands almost touching the towels of "holier than thou." I could feel my mother's words like a spell on those towels and momentarily retracted my hands. Standing alone, hands wet, I chose to err on the side of caution and wiped my hands on the towel of nothing special. Relieved having let myself off the hook, I ducked out trying to mask the feeling of guilt for having the thought.

Manifesting allergies far worse than before, the energy held in my heart turned into asthma. Asthma became part of my experience after I encountered my first spirit with everyone dismissing it as my imagination. My attacks were sometimes fierce and scared the hell out of me when I was unable to breathe. Beside myself with terror and sadness, I tried to block my sensitivities completely.

A scratch test soon revealed I was allergic to darned near everything. Cigarette smoke, chalk dust, dogs, dust, cats, milk, and tree pollens of all kinds. My respiratory system, irritated by paint fumes and other harsh chemicals, sent me to Grandma's when dad had to paint. Mom and Dad continued to smoke and bought a dog they named Otto Edward Leopold Von Bismark Schönhausen for dramatic effect. We called him Biz for short. The joy of a pet was clouded by the burden he became to all of us kids who were given the responsibility for his care, and he lasted about eight months.

Chapter III

A Rock Feels no Pain

CHAPTER **III**

A Rock Feels no Pain

Fourth grade came at the time when schools did away with old math and I flunked with a capital F. Sister Augusta meant well and had such horribly buck teeth that it was distracting. Her saliva would foam as she struggled to form words through her protruding teeth. Coupled with my deep sense of hopelessness, I called it a wash and kept trudging forward trying not to stare.

Stephania was becoming more angry and aggressive at home, managing to extinguish any sparkle that lingered in the air. Mom, in response, added more rules and punishments using dad as her enforcer. Exercising our muscles of rebellion, we would cuss because it was forbidden. If we got caught, we had to scream our words high from the back porch in my mother's effort to reinforce shame. From the depths of my throat, I bellowed for the whole world to hear; but the words fell mostly flat on the deafened ears of Mrs. Mendez who lived next door.

Mrs. Mendez was a great woman with a house full of warm memories of those who had gone before her. The house had the original well on the screened-in back porch, boarded up since the dawn of pipes and plumbing. Like another grandmother, she taught me how to play card games like casino while we ate persimmon cookies on the front porch. She had a parlor with a fireplace and old photos of older times on the mantle. She wore a house dress with an apron, and always had a cloth hanky. She gifted us continually with an abundance of citrus, pomegranates and other great things from her garden's bounty. The laughs we shared echoed in my heart across her shaded front porch down the short stone path to the gate of her white picket fence. Her laughter was intoxicating and inspiring, always lending a lift and a sense of comfort to know she was right next door.

My creativity expanded beyond paint by numbers, water colors and spirograph, when I met an artist on Main St. who offered to give me art lessons. Art led me to the discovery of my soul showing me the abundance of it's brightest colors. Carol Mathis had a studio / gallery on Main St. She was the daughter of a famous artist, George Mathis, known for his lithographs of the gold rush days in Eldorado County. Carol was real and down to earth, wore cowboy boots, smoked cigarettes and created all day.

In the morning when mom put me out like the cat, I wandered down and hung out with her even if I had no class that day. I spent hours honing my water color skills, painting pen and ink drawings of various types of exotic mushrooms. Carol taught me the skill and art of using pen and ink which quickly became a favorite, and showed me how to use charcoal, pencil and oil pastels. Carol was magic with everything. She walked around and picked up any medium creating something spontaneous and spectacular. The smell of rubber cement still lingers in my mind when I imagine her affixing colored tissue paper to create layered cities and landscapes.

Business hours on Main St. were unpredictable except for a cafe or two, and no one was ever in a real hurry. Various types of "out to lunch" signs hung in the proprietors' windows while they shuffled in and out of the saloon for afternoon breaks. If time had moved any slower, tumble weeds would have formed in my mind's eye and rolled past horses tethered to hitching posts, slapping flies with their tails. Carol introduced me to another Main St. artist named Spence (over a bourbon old fashioned and a Roy Rodgers at the saloon) whose medium was oil paints. Visiting his gallery was euphoric, and the smell of oil paint mixed with turpentine brought me to the sensuality of the palette.

Spence put paint to canvas from sun up beyond sun down, and no doubt in his sleep. Quietly I watched him squeeze the silky paint onto the palette, announcing, each color by name as he mixed them to create other colors.

Many paintings hung in his gallery, but one stood out in particular. Mostly orange, red and gold, the devil stood in the foreground leaning back, smiling diabolically, watching a launched warhead rise through the clouds in the near distance. It was a huge conversation piece and one for silent contemplation. Spence paid me to model for a class on Wednesday nights, and I felt a ray of worthiness in his friendship.

Forming a sense of individuality and beginning to develop into the creative soul I was divinely intended to be, my new sense of self threatened those around me. I learned to keep myself small so others felt better about themselves and left me alone. Making it home at dusk, skipping up the alley with smiles in my heart, I would shut myself down before entering my house. Pausing for a deep breath, I closed my heart and bowed my head. With my joy completely suffocated I turned the handle and stepped through the front door.

Unsuccessful in relating to kids my own age, I continued connecting with the adults around me instead. They were not mean spirited and were much more interesting. Conversation topics included travel, and theorizing of all sorts which opened my mind to new and inspiring thoughts. Activities became more artistic, creative, soul connecting and I began learning so much about things of real interest to me.

Sister Loretta, my fifth and sixth grade teacher was an amazing soul. She truly loved her vocation, and her alignment with the Father, Son and the Holy Spirit spilled over into the many ways she made learning fun. She designed learning stations for us with headphones and other cool things you rarely saw in Catholic school. She was smart, resourceful and way ahead of her time. I was impressed that she constructed the Q&A board with alligator clips attached to the ends of wires. We touched them to the button heads of the paper fasteners, lighting a red or a green light indicating a right or wrong answer. Sister Loretta's class was my first look into my soul's history, teaching me in depth about the only thing in school that ever moved me enough to pay attention.

Learning the ancient history of the Romans, Greeks, Egyptians, Sumerians, Canaanites, along with the oldest names for their territories and the great rivers that ran through them struck deep cords of resonance. Words like Mesopotamia, Constantinople, Tiber, Nile, Tigris and Euphrates stirred and enlivened my soul. Studying about these cultures, so closely entwined, with their simple, extravagant and passionate ways of life, I connected with my ancestors in the civilizations responsible for birthing all knowledge of the highest order. They were a most creative, innovative, strong, spiritual and physically beautiful people.

Her classes kept a light breeze in my sails and distracted me from the ugliness and inadequacy projected from my emotions to my mind rapidly becoming solid beliefs about myself. Beginning to appreciate the human form in ancient sculptures and paintings, I noted the proportions and was stunned by its sheer magnificence. Deciding to be an archaeologist when I grew up, I never imagined it would mean unearthing the ruins of my past and integrating the pieces of my shattered self.

Marie, bound to a state of perpetual servitude, retreated into books for self preservation and something she could call her own. Marie, always interested in medicine and by her nature the ultimate caregiver, was a candy striper by age thirteen at the local sanitarium. The hospital was full of older patients with a variety of illnesses, both physical and mental. Marie read her patients books, fed them and found her natural place in the circle of life.

Stephania simmered in her discontent because I was asked to model for art classes and was being treated like something special. She was a menace I avoided constantly, but sometimes she appeared out of nowhere to blindside me. Beyond Stephania's shadowy presence, observing my parents punish my siblings was painful to me. Feeling their ways of control so deeply, sorrow stole my breath adding another ten obsidian bricks to the fortress surrounding my heart. The walls became so solid and high, they cast a shadow over my rainbow soul to become the black cloud that eventually blocked my light completely.

Sara and Luke were nearing age two when Oma died; Mom received her inheritance, and we pulled up tent stakes to buy a house across the river. We moved from a fun and inspiring neighborhood to a more rural setting with fields instead of art. Boredom without guidance in a less refined culture was my canvas, and I did the best I could to remain inspired within my new condition. Our new home had more rooms, but we still had to share them. Dad put in new linoleum and transformed the garage into a bedroom and laundry room. Mom dedicated Oma's beautiful furniture to the front room and forbade us to sit on her well-made comfy couches. A large painting by Walter Keane hung on the wall mirroring the sadness in my large eyes, and a dark dramatic painting of the crucifixion captured my now jaded perception of Christ in the world.

Matching the chill of what was becoming my heart, the heat was turned down to fifty-five degrees at night no matter how cold it was outside. Jumping into a cold cot each night found me completely under the covers blowing hot air around myself to get warm. Finding a position within my blankets that held the heat leaving a small hole to breathe, I remained as still as possible so not to stir the air surrounding me. Going to the bathroom in the middle of the night was resolved through trial and error. Wrapping myself in my blanket and running to the bathroom, I found my mattress was freezing upon return. Running to the bathroom without cover, left me too cold to relax enough to pee. Either way, I had to focus myself into relaxation, relief finally came with release of my bladder as the steam from my urine rose to warm my inner thighs. Most of the time I would just stay in bed in my one position and try to go back to sleep.

Dad took a job selling cutlery and kept the job for several years. With dad now a traveling salesman, mom had us to herself for long regimented days. Art classes went out the window and the threat of our father's retribution hung over our heads in mom's calculated attempt to keep us in line. Mom and dad struggled to come to terms with Marie and Stephania turning into young women, and searched for answers within their golf-ball sized sphere of consciousness.

Getting older and out-growing the pack mentality, we silently agreed it was every man for himself as we began breaking away from the collective pain and running for our lives. We knew how or how not to act by way of a look and other nonverbal clues. Finding it enough at this point to cover our own asses, when hell's fury opened its door to our brother, we stepped out of the way until the scorching wind passed.

Many people on the new block were giving parents and society the finger so to speak, there were black light posters on people's walls and some really interesting examples of living. Crazy daisies on sides of Volkswagen buses, macrame plant holders, bongs, and dinning tables covered in capsules being divided among the adults. The pungent smell of patchouly wafted onto the street in some cases and marijuana spilled out of wooden boxes on coffee tables. Long-haired kids ran around playing amidst this intoxicated version of peace, love and nothing better to do.

Music was bigger than television then. Everyone had a record player or a hi-fi and our house was no exception. When mom and dad weren't around, Stephania played Janis Joplin lining up with her mannerisms and music so she could strum her guitar singing Janis's songs while smoking at the neighborhood hangout. Mom forbade us to listen to our music when she was home and loved to blast Tchaikovsky's *1812 Overture* when she was in a good mood, marveling at the power of the canons. There were homes where the Carpenter's music took center stage; the melodies and lyrics melted into my mind as I lounged on soft new furniture in a quiet, nurturing home that felt so foreign to me.

Dad was considered the "fun" parent because he ate candy and shared, played with us outside, encouraged art projects and taught us girls how to cook. He often took me with the boys fishing and on the way to the river we stopped by the bait shop. He bought us starburst candy, orange soda, earthworms and brightly colored marshmallows for bait, then crammed it all into a small styrofoam cooler. Soda and candy was a rarity at home, and we piled into the truck tearing the wrappers off our candy with abandoned restraint. Fishing was a great way to be away from whatever mom was imposing on the girls, and eating candy and sipping sweet bubbles made it all the more glorious.

On outdoor adventures our manners could relax and I could eat my sandwich in peace not having to abide by the rules at home where mealtime was always tumultuous. We had to raise our hands if we wanted to speak. The seating arrangements were dictated by das field marshal and determined by our manners. If we relaxed for a minute by landing an elbow on the table, it was met with a jab from the tines of Mother's fork, and the repeat offenders had to sit next to her. It was so difficult sitting around our long table next too so much pent up energy while constantly being told to sit up straight and often subjected to my father's anger and opinions.

It was a rule that we had to eat everything that was put in front of us whether we liked it or not, and Stephania never could stomach the texture of eggs. Dad, fed up with her defiant claim came unglued and made her eat everything on her plate. Stephania fearfully complied and in turn vomited the eggs partially into his lap. He proceeded to yell, and throw a fit as she cried. Tears erupted around the rest of the table in response to the fear and anger that enveloped our beings. No one said a word; no one ever did.

At age nine standing in the field, I extended my right arm with palm facing out in front of me, moving it slowly left to right, creating an invisible shield of intention to push the pain away. Armoring myself with the lyrics from Simon and Garfunkel's I Am a Rock, I consciously sealed myself from the pain of life because a rock feels no pain and an island never cries.

Adults like Carol were my respite, so when she moved from Folsom to the Gold Country I visited. We went to her father's home / art studio, I made new friends and played in the river panning for gold nuggets. We ran around old cemeteries rubbing gravestones with black charcoal on paper, capturing the imprints of angels and other interesting images. Riding horses in the dry, dusty heat of the summer sun, I marveled at the size of the golden scarabs that emerged from the dirt at dusk on my way to the pavilion. Country tunes filled the air and the pampered campers danced under the starlit sky along the Coloma River. When summer was over, it brought me into the seventh grade when school became more pleasant than the energy at home.

Sister Gertrude was conflicted in her role as a nun and although she aspired to be hip and on the leading edge in the content of her teaching, she fell miserably short. Home economics class brought us to clean the convent and instruction in sewing. The class itself was derived from a Butterick "how to" insert with which it seemed she had little experience. Finding a bottle of Black Velvet whisky in the cupboard, I imagined it was for the priests and wondered how the sisters could be happy living such narrow lives.

In eighth grade I was a cheerleader, blue and gold, and somewhat enjoyed it, in spite of the lack of support I received from the other girls. Mr. Campo, my math teacher, was interesting and made sense to me. We connected in his ability to get me to understand math and our love for Hawaii and other traveling adventures. He gave me photos of trips to Waikiki and we shared a love for the ocean, Puka shells and anything beyond day to day life. Mr. Campo was another breath of fresh air in the otherwise stale content of Catholic school. His perspective was expansive and the positive part of my last year in parochial school.

The routine of my home life that summer was pleasantly interrupted by a call from Carol, who had married and moved to another place in the Gold Country and invited me up the summer before I entered high school. Mom drove me up to spend two weeks with Carol and her new husband who were live-in managers of The Vineyard House in Coloma. President Ulysses S. Grant had stayed there while visiting in the 1800's and gave a speech from the front steps. I stayed in the president's bedroom and felt pretty amazing getting comfy in the bed where he once slept.

A storage room upstairs was filled with treasures stashed there dusty for at least six decades. Outside everywhere were very old empty bottles of varying sizes, an some crystal door knobs that turned purple from their continual exposure to the light of the sun. Massive oak barrels used for aging wine sat out back, and antiques of all kinds could be found even among the rows of straggly vines of a once thriving vineyard. Carol sent me and my friends on very clever scavenger hunts, taking us half the day on a wild imaginative journey to claim the final prize. We rode horses and played in the river, making it hard to leave the divide that summer, as I knew in my heart it would be my last visit.

The waning heat of our August days brought me to the reality of high school and to finding my place among the student body. The folks believed I was better off at the Fair Oaks high school as it was a beautiful high school with more refined kids.

Mom arranged a ride with a preacher's daughter who was a couple years ahead of me and I had to walk across the damp, cold fog-filled field to get to her place. Agatha lived on the church grounds and was always wolfing down a bowl of cold cereal for breakfast as I arrived. Her house was quiet and sterile, and I couldn't help but notice her softer and easy going mannerisms.

Entering high school at age twelve had its challenges, mostly in the freedom it allowed me away from home. I discovered new neighborhoods with finer kids, better cars and opportunities to hang out in style. The Eagles "On the Border" spilled out the windows of the seniors' shiny waxed Mustangs onto the newly paved parking lot, and we spent days trying to change the water to wine. Two classmates met their maker burning to death in a car crash and sent an ashen cloud of grief over our otherwise jovial group. It was the second and third deaths I experienced among my friends. My marine biology and English classes were the only two of any interest to me, and the only two I ever attended. Second semester found me more interested in sunbathing along the American River rather than going to class, and I was transferred to my local high school sophomore year because of poor attendance.

As a witness to the constant turmoil between my older sisters and my parents, I knew they were making plans to leave home. The thought of having more responsibility for my five younger siblings and subsequent subjugation of my soul lighted my way out the door. I found solace in the field across the street often lying in the tall grass and watching the clouds go by, munching on minor's lettuce, climbing the giant oaks or crying to the depths of my soul. The earth always nurtured me unconditionally and held me in her arms of unwavering love, no matter what I brought of myself to the table.

My sisters continued acting out, climbing out the bedroom windows at night and hanging out with neighbors down the street. When Marie left home they hung out with different, grungier types of people. Stephania had a boyfriend which she spent most of her time with, while Marie went out with his brother, trading one family in ruins for another, striving to create anew.

I hung out under the stars with friends on balmy summer nights, sneaking out the window myself a time or two. Once while still dark, I laid down to rest in a spot of tall tender grass for a few minutes before I had to make haste to get home. I gazed silently at the mix of fading stars and blue beams of morning light, deeply inhaling the first breath of sunrise. The light blended blue and gold, with its long rays enhanced the beauty of the peach and olive orchards. Picking up speed, staying ahead of the cackling pheasants who signaled the dawn of each new day, I hurried down the path. Over the fence with but for a moment's pause, crouching behind the tomatoes, peering at the house to gauge any activity. Staying low to the ground, I made my way across the lawn to my window carefully removing the screen and climbing in. Burying myself under the covers, I tried to catch a few winks before we all had to get up and get ready for Sunday morning church.

Dad would make pancakes on Sunday, and then chores as usual. We didn't discuss our parents or their actions with others because we saw nothing wrong with the picture. If anything was talked about, it was in a laughing context. "Remember when Dad...?" and we would laugh sharing stories of past times we had gotten hurt at the hand of either parent or some other reference to pain. My siblings and I were allowed to fight and make fun of each other, we teased each other all the time. I made up names for everybody and laughed about that too.

The ability of my mind to deny what would have destroyed me before I was ready to face anything was nothing short of amazing. The effects of prolonged exposure to the negative energy at home hardened my attitude along with my perception, and I let it protect me and take control. I stopped chewing my nails to the quick by befriending the Marlborough Man and had a relationship with him that was satisfying for another fourteen years. Leaving fear and weakness behind, I summoned the demons of my brutal inner past and moved forward with an aura that spoke for itself.

The compressed emotions from years of accumulated anger began bubbling up beneath the surface of my denial. The energy swirled up from it's depths after mom and dad announced at the breakfast table one morning that they were getting a divorce. Mostly still around the table, we swallowed our feelings along with our words, then carried on with our various chores. We gathered our belongings with the pieces of our broken hearts and silently left for school.

I learned how to fist fight at home, and was told "never pick a fight, but if you get in one, don't come home a loser." I sought to keep the feeling of rage about their plan to divorce down, but that day I got into a fight, I didn't come home a loser, and I got a good look at a part of myself that I was barely beginning to become conscious of.

Mom who I never saw as courageous then, exchanged religion for spirituality and packed up the youngest three children to create a new life at a community in Nevada City. The word "guru" was totally foreign to me, and not understanding what it was about, I put it out of my mind.

Three months later, I watched my mom drive away with Sara and Luke and Amanda looking out the back window of the car waving us goodbye. Our family dispersed in seven different directions that day. My sister Stephania disappeared; Matthew and Mark lived with dad for a while, then Matthew shared an apartment with a friend and the beloved Antonuccis embraced Mark as their own. I hit the bricks with Marie at fourteen years old, staying with friends all over town.

Somewhere within the year that followed, I was at a bar shooting pool when a brawl broke out. Like a spaghetti western, bottles flew through the air, bar stools were taken up as shields, and fist fights ensued.

Although I was standing back and watching, not moved by it one way or another, the cops showed up too quickly and I was caught making tracks out the back. Taken downtown but being a minor, I was sent to juvenile hall. Wasting my phone call on my father, who told me to get my own ass out of trouble, I cried softly to sleep in my dormitory bed.

Annie was a guard who saw the light in me, though I had no idea it was there. She was a no nonsense gal who called me out of the lunch line the next day to ask me what I was doing there. She held up a mirror of light to me and I was touched by her genuine concern. The black cloud of "not me" quickly blotted out her sun, but I never forgot how for a second I remembered another truth about me.

"There is no love from an outside source that can heal you, it can only reflect what you are capable of doing within the self."

- Abraham

My court date arrived and Mom came down from the mountain quite unexpectedly, and unlike I had ever known her. In a cotton skirt with long graying hair, she sat and watched calmly as the court decided to release me into her custody. After taking me to lunch, she returned me to the wild and returned to her gentle life in the hills.

Chapter IV

The Principles of Lust

"The principles of lust are easy to understand, do what you feel, feel until the end. The principles of lust are burned in your mind, do what you want, do it until you find . . . love."

- Enigma MCMXC a.D.

The Principles of Lust

Turning fifteen and a big corner in how I wanted to live life, I found a pseudo sense of normalcy in a man from a different side of the tracks. Jimmy came from a good Sicilian and Irish family, was naturally well built with striking blue eyes and brown hair. He was educated, had a great job and many opportunities that come with being a respected family in the community. He was Romanesque in his love for rough contact sports, cleanliness, dietary preferences, and uninhibited sex.

Jimmy seemed to have it together so much more than other people I was around and I was trying to pull my life together. We shared a love for the same things including motorcycles, table games, outdoor sports, and alcohol. We were a great team and won almost every game we played against others. The competition between the two of us was healthy and stimulating and we began spending more time together.

Jimmy was my first real lover, and through him the second circle of hell became a realm we frequently occupied. In those days, everyone went out with everyone else and without drama, exclusivity or concern unless you were married and even then with the amount of barrier dissolving drugs around anything was possible and no one had any regrets.

Almost a year passed with a whole new life of recreation unfolding until one night on the back of Jimmy's bike, we made a left turn and a truck ran a red light and hit us. My body flew up to hit the window of the truck with my face, breaking my cheekbone. My leg broke in half from the impact, and I fell unconscious on the cold, gray street. Waking up a day later, I opened my eye viewing my cast encrusted leg and my immobilized arm in a sling, with no idea how any of it happened.

My seven-day hospital stay on heavy doses of Demerol kept me painless and seeing a diabolical gargoyle figure standing in my doorway each time I looked left. About five days into my hospital visit three or four doctors were buzzing around my bed. The light was bright and I couldn't see very well, my right eye being still mostly closed from injury, trying to focus on what they were doing and saying. Their words were muffled, I couldn't stand how it felt. I ordered them all to leave, and they left me alone, broken and crying for the first time in years.

After the doctors left, a blond-haired, blue-eyed male nurse came into my room and came close to the side of my bed. Looking right at my face, he gently ran his fingers through my hair and asked me what was wrong. I said "I'm not sure, but I just want it to be over." He reassured me, walked out and I never saw him again.

Doctors surgically inserted a thirteen inch metal rod into my right tibia with a threaded knob poking out of a two inch incision made just below my knee cap. The rod remained there for nine months before it was removed, and my cheekbone had to heal itself. Leaving the hospital with Jimmy in a floor length gown and robe, I gathered my strength to brush my long black hair, then crutch into the Club SoCal where we rolled dice for a brandy separator on the way home.

He bought a bigger house to accommodate his family for the holidays and our friends on the weekends, with much more space for personal pleasure. Jimmy was cited for being under the influence in our accident and wound up doing a short stint in a county facility. Things looked normal from the outside, I kept a positive attitude while we laid low to sort life out. That year, I got my first job to help out and picked him up for work furlough and began pulling things together. Before my seventeenth birthday, I bought property in Montana with part of my settlement and continued to look for the fun in life.

Never one to think things through and prone to aggression Jimmy smashed the windshield of a co-worker's car with a brick, because he owed him money. The same guy ratted Jimmy out to their employer about his circumstances which resulted in the immediate termination of his job.

Jimmy was scared and losing control. He had tons of energy, his temper was bad, and his frustration levels were running high. He had never not worked and had almost twelve years with the company when he was let go. He began to get jealous and would literally tear doors from their hinges in fits of frustration. He once grabbed a loaded shot gun pointing it at me. I sat down and surrendered thinking "well, this is it." He ejected the shells instead and threw the gun to the floor. I found myself surrendering to his rage much like I did my father's as a child by leaving my body almost to the point of black out.

Looking for a job with little success, Jimmy decided to sell drugs which seemed like a good idea at the time, but he didn't have the mind to play the game. He got enmeshed with some players in Southern California and like always I never bothered myself with the details. He was set up while we were on vacation and our home was looted. When we got home Jimmy just lost it and it wasn't long before I knew it was time for me to take a bow. That day came very soon, with my first attempt dramatic and weak.

The second and last time, I left letting him follow me to Luigi's house. Luigi was a friend of the family and I knew I would be safe there. Jimmy gave me crap until I ran up the steps. Luigi came outside onto the porch and wisely, Jimmy turned around and left. Staying between Luigi's and Marie's distraught for weeks, she gave me a couple of beautiful fur pieces to help me find the positive side of it all, and I decided while drying my tears that fur cures practically everything.

Chapter V

Angel Flying Too Close
to the Ground

Angel Flying Too Close to the Ground

On the wings of a messenger, it came that another close friend had died; my black velvet hood shrouded my tear soaked cheeks while Luigi embraced me. The heaviness of the hearts in attendance could have sunk the Titanic. When it was over, everyone dispersed in silence, but maybe it was just me.

Marie moved into the house next door and rented me her back room. Getting a job as a waitress in a donut shop, I spent time tending Luigi's house and stayed there in his absence. His friends came by, but I never said anything to them beyond "would you like a cup of coffee or something to eat?" As a good woman, I left the room when they gathered to talk and minded my own business.

One man I noticed particularly came over alone, and sometimes when Luigi was not home. He was different from his other friends. He handled his utensils like a European gentleman, had impeccable manners was thoughtful and quiet. He was a man of very few words but when he spoke it was after he deliberated every thought. Marius would stay and read or be with his thoughts as I carried on about the house, then he would go just as politely as he had entered.

"If you had not of fallen, I may not have found you . . ."

- Willie Nelson

A couple of months passed, and after determining I was not Luigi's girlfriend, Marius invited me to go to the coast with him. From the moment I slid into his car, we smiled at each other knowing this was it for us; we laughed aloud and headed west. Marius was the kind where no words were needed for me to know how to respond. When he would come by I knew upon his entry whether to go pack a bag or just make coffee. His had a presence hard to ignore when he entered a room, and my delight drew me to welcome him with a kiss every time.

Men were a perceived problem for Marius. Taking our relationship more seriously, he would come in and sit at the end of the counter behind a newspaper and wait until I finished work to drive me home.

Joe Federico, from Los Angeles, used to stop by the donut shoppe for a cup of coffee and a plain cake donut. Joe was in his sixties and had a band affiliated with a popular record label and used to comment on how I looked like Cleopatra, a Liz Taylor of sorts. He drove a beautiful Cadillac early model like a `55 with wings and told me more than once he wanted to take me to Southern California.

He wanted to introduce me to some people down there and to prove his connections, he brought Ernest Borgnine's brother into the shoppe to meet me one night and have a cup of coffee. Joe left a gold box with a pearl necklace in it for my birthday, along with a note. I never got the opportunity to thank him as I quit my job soon after. On my nineteenth birthday, Marius woke me gently from my sleep with a kiss, a dozen red roses and a fur cape, and shortly after that we were married.

My childhood joys recreated themselves in my life with Marius as did the reflection of never being good enough. He was his own man and in my new territory there would be other women. Telling him I never wanted to hear about it, I asked him not to push it in my face. Granting my wish in our early years, my respect and love for him only grew stronger. Unaware of how much more of my partners' energy I receive than the normal person, it strengthened my connection to him and whoever else he was connected too. To deal with my chaotic stream of internal emotion, I tried to approach his infidelity from a position of power rather than weakness. Somehow from this standpoint I thought it would it make it less hurtful and more acceptable.

Marius and I decided to move from the city to higher ground, so I put that in motion. Rolling hills and huge oak trees drew us to a small town just above the fog line and just below the snow line, and I found *cielo* on a ranch in the foothills.

My body and heart felt warmer up there and began to thaw a bit, through the nurturing abundance of nature now beneath my feet. My inner temperature was cold and angry; denial was working for me very well, keeping a tight lid on things for the most part. My focus was taking care of my husband, managing the business we created, attending business association meetings, and everything else a twenty-year old '50s style bride would do for her man.

We had a couple of fine horses and a ten acre spread with fruit trees, a big red barn, a huge natural pond fed by three tributaries that spilled over into a stream that ran beneath the thick blackberry bushes on the backside of the property. I planted a vegetable garden in an existing plot and it even had a couple of rows of grapes. All kinds of wildlife would come enjoy the beauty of this paradise, and I sometimes took the rowboat out to the middle of the pond to drift aimlessly in the sun.

Marius was romantic and brought home the most beautiful clothes wrapped in tissue and in boxes tied with a single ribbon. He loved to see me look good and I had only the best. Living between my Bally pumps and my collection of lizard and snakeskin cowboy boots, whether I was out with my horses, feeding the cows, planting flowers, or driving the feed truck, my nails were always manicured.

When spring arrived, we rode our horses out to check the herd, the cow's bellies plump with calves preparing to give birth. The hills were green and fresh around the ranch, the streams flowed and the air was invigorating. The ground, still muddy in low lying places where the water pooled from the long winter rains, marked the end and beginning of a new season.

Summertime brought us to the cattle drive, and for a few days Marius, the boys and I rounded them up to receive Levasole boluses and shots distributed with pistol grip syringes while running them through the squeeze chutes. A special chute was reserved for the castration of the young bulls, and I left the balls in the hands of the men. I relished riding my horse and the strong intuitive connection we maintained. I enjoyed the sound of thundering hooves, the excitement and skill of the horses and the bellowing resistance of the cows being rounded up and moved at our will. When the day was over, the dust somewhat settled, the horses groomed and put up for the night, the crickets and frogs chimed into the slow rhythm of the evening serenade.

Taking care of the ranch and business kept me too busy to notice when he wasn't home, but I looked forward to his return and the chance to slow down and savor our time together. Marius always came up with ways to improve the business, and taught me how to be organized, manage my time and about business itself. He was extremely resourceful, and we shared many aspects of a functional life. Marius had several rare qualities, but the one I enjoyed the most was that he was secure in himself. He was not intimidated by me, appreciated my insight, and always supported what I wanted to do to further myself as a powerful woman. For the most part we were a single impenetrable unit and I loved how that felt.

Marie moved up into my area with her husband and tried to be more involved with my life. With Marie around I was irritated and became more serious and mindful. Like a virus that I could not shake, no matter what I did I couldn't get rid of her, or the churning pain within me that was the source of it all, trying to get my attention.

My soul's expansion has been dramatic at times, taking me down roads that I have asked for consciously or not. In sixth grade after my introduction to ancient history, I stated for years "I am going to Rome and Greece before I die," and little did I know that dream would be the key that would unlock me from my cage and set me on my path to greater freedom. Now approaching the age of twenty-three my foot size grew from 6 1/2 to 7; my Bally pumps did not fit right anymore, reflecting other areas in my life that I was out-growing.

Though we had moved, I maintained my circle of friends in Sacramento, and we played softball and volleyball on the Sacramento City Twilight League and had all kinds of serious fun. Many of my friends were Greeks and lawyers, and Olympia was one of them. Speaking with Marius about going to Greece with her met with some resistance. He was aware something was changing, and though he couldn't quite put his finger on it, he took a chance and agreed. Delighted beyond measure, I got my first passport and planned my three week journey to Rome and Greece.

Having never traveled that distance on an airplane before, I had no idea what to expect. Wearing a classic black wool dress and a pair of patent leather pumps with white piping, I stepped off the plane onto the tarmac in Rome, got down on my hands and knees and kissed the ground. Olympia and I grabbed our luggage and a cab into the city. Stretching my cramping leg between the seat was met instantly by the roaming hand of the cabbie. Olympia smacked him repeatedly with rolled-up paper while raising her voice in protest. I retracted my leg and laughed, imagining myself in the scene of a Woody Allen movie.

We arrived at the Pensione Suisse, on the Via del Gregorianna near the Spanish steps and walked up the solid white unfinished marble stairs to reception. I wanted to take my shoes off and feel the marble against my skin. Quivering at the thought, I reached my hand out, gently sliding my fingertips across the moulding and soft colored walls on the way to our room. The beds were solid and comfortable, warm and feathered with quaint bedspreads and a nightstand between our twin beds.

Olympia and I ran around Rome discovering gardens, gates, fountains and statues touching everything with our minds, hands and souls. We visited endless sites, dined on the Piazza Navona, and stumbled across the pyramid we had no idea existed in this wonderful city. We tried being out at night but were over run by aggressive men, so we stayed in sipping warm Asti Spumante, enjoying our bouquets of roses, and scripting postcards home.

Our trip to Vatican City was a transformational experience quietly strolling into St Peter's Square with its massive circular driveway surrounded by angels and its curved and perfectly aligned pillars. Out of nowhere, ten buses full of tourists pulled into the square and descended like a plague of locusts onto the cobblestones. In the same moment, we looked up to see the little red carpet roll out of a window where Pope John Paul II popped out his head, raised his hand and blessed us in about fourteen different languages. The tourists suddenly ran around in a frenzy cramming themselves back into their busses while all the commotion left us mildly stunned. Not quite sure what had happened, we stood still as the feeling of calm returned along with the sunshine and the pigeons.

Wooden chairs with red velvet seats were being quickly set up on the steps, and the swearing in of the Cardinals was about to begin. Skirting past the clergy, we hightailed it up to St. Peter's Basilica and opened the door. Taking my first step in, I exploded in tears, completely overwhelmed by its vibration. My body, overcome with the energy encoded in this most exquisite construction, took me to the floor, as my heart opened wider than I had ever experienced before. I walked speechless in the presence of Michelangelo's living art and in energy of the many souls there that I felt in resonance. Olympia and I kissed the feet of the male statues and wandered through the vast, empty marble halls lined with extraordinary tapestries on our way to the *Cappella Sistina*.

We took the long way back to the pensione, strolling along the Tiber by the *Castella de Angelo*, in awe at this dream come true and inhaling the good Roman air.

When we stopped and walked into the Forum, I felt my back straighten, and the weight of an invisible garment pin my shoulders back. My head was instantly aligned, held high, and I sprouted a new pair of balls walking further into the ruins. Bending down on one knee and putting my hand in the dirt, I gripped a piece of a column in my fist that lay broken on the ground. I knew this dirt and paused, feeling my soul within the stone, I reclaimed it as I picked it up and placed it in my pocket.

Olympia and I wandered around our last days in the the city eating focaccia off of bread carts, sampling pastry and drinking liters of coffee. We made a wish and threw coins in the *Fontana di Trevi* on the way out of the city, taking our last breath of Rome on our way to Greece.

Olympia's Thia lived in Athens, so we visited her humble abode with unfinished marble counters and a walled-in courtyard where the chickens lived. Thia pinched our arms and told us we were too skinny, cooked us a lunch and made us eat. Fresh cherries and Greek coffee topped off this perfectly lovely meal and the exchange of hugs and kisses overflowed with love and appreciation as we all said our teary goodbyes.

It was election time and emotions were running higher than usual. I could feel the pangs of the vibrational war going on inside of my solar plexus walking around Syntagma which was towering with scaffolds and speakers that amplified the voices of the passionate demonstrators representing each of the political parties. Looking and walking obviously American, we made tracks out of the square as the sun set over Athens. People often stopped me on the street saying, "John Wayne" when looking at my cowboy boots; some asked me for autographs thinking I was visiting from Hollywood. United Colors of Benetton had outfits more befitting, so I bought some clothes and blended in with the backdrop of Hellas.

Olympia had a couple of cousins who served as our bodyguards as we enjoyed the special kind of endearing insanity that makes Athens so great. Knowing the ins and outs of the city, the boys, Kosta and Spiros took us on many adventures, some of them separately.

At the Acropolis, old women pushed carts with pistachios around the flea market at the foot of the hill. Jewelry storefronts were everywhere and Spiros, Olympia's body guard, negotiated prices for my diamond and sapphire trinkets and I began to sparkle. Kosta and I ran around Athens eating *tiropita* from pita stands and dined on a lunch of whole roasted fish and beer. We bought ice cream cones from a street vendor to sweeten our breath and shopped for his family, bringing bags of groceries and other goodies to his mother's house.

Being a woman of few questions, I attracted men that never offered any answers and naturally found myself in interesting situations. Kosta and I were on the move and stopped into a bar along the way back to the hotel. We walked in, looked around, and silently chose a seat. Before I had a chance to sit all the way down in my chair, a white tablecloth unfurled to the table. Pulling my DunHills from my pocket, I brought a cigarette to my lips. A lighter appeared instantly flaming for my convenience. I placed my cigarette box slowly and somewhat suspiciously on the table, responding with a polite nod.

An unsolicited drink was carried over on a tray and placed before us as the waiter backed away a good five feet before turning his back and leaving our presence.

Observing quietly around the room, inhaling deeply and absorbing the feeling of it all, I noticed a long piece of fabric hanging loosely at the entrance of a hallway. Exhaling the smoke from my cigarette, I watched the curtain move gracefully propelled by a gentle breeze from an unknown source to revealed a glimpse of several beautiful women with long black hair standing in the shadows.

A man slowly emerged from behind the curtain and meeting Kosta at the bar, handed him a paper bag. Kosta put the bag into his jacket. I rose from the table without a word, extinguished my cigarette and walked out behind him.

We opened the door to the blinding light of the afternoon sun and ran off to meet up with Olympia and Spiros for a meal. In the morning, Olympia and I departed on our ferry from Piraeus to Serifos once Apollonia in the Aegean Sea. The ferry was crowded, especially downstairs where the Greek grandmothers pushed the children ahead in the lines and into the seats they were too old and too slow to reach before the people ahead of them. Olympia carried a big tote filled with wine and snacks and we found our seats on the top deck. Saturating my senses in the color of the sea, I stood at the bow letting the warm Mediterranean air infuse every cell as I gazed deeply into the dark sapphire blue water. As we got farther and farther away from land and water surrounded us completely, everything felt suddenly insignificant. My past was gone, my future uncertain and all I had was that moment and in it all things felt possible.

Arriving on Serifos, we walked down the pier and noticed an octopus and huge starfish on the white sand some twenty feet or so through the still crystal clear water. Greeted by a three wheeled truck with barely enough room for us and our suitcases, we were quickly whisked off to our hotel and unpacked. Serifos is Olympia's ancestral home and we paid our respects to the graves of the elders and visiting her familial home high up on the hill. Men with their donkeys were a regular sight, carrying tools and goods in colorful woven baskets hanging on their backs in perfect equilibrium.

We kept our Amstel in the cold shallow water along the shore while we sunbathed and daydreamed for hours. Grilled lobster and *horiatiki* were plentiful, and there was no doubt in my mind I had died and made it to heaven. Greece felt like I had imagined it in grade school and I was moved to tears on the night of the full moon walking up a hill toward the village, as I turned back to look out over the sea. The air was still and quiet, broken only by the sound of a distant *bouzouki* as the moon and the stars sparkled in the water's reflection. It was easy to understand how the Gods and the myths were born in the mix of all this. Deeply inspired, listening in the stillness for their voices, I never wanted to leave.

Olympia got a neck cramp a few days later and that turned us back in the direction of Athens. Walking into the market to purchase our tickets, the man in charge refused to sell them to us. Greeks being masters of the argument and often just for the sake of one, Olympia and the proprietor squared off. He wanted to settle things by letting her go in exchange for leaving me behind. Olympia argued louder and stronger until he finally gave in, mumbling under his breath as he handed her two tickets back to the mainland.

Returning to Athens we got her neck straightened out, and after a couple days of rest, we were buying plane tickets to Santorini. Arriving on the island, we took a bus up the long road into Thira that dropped us at the top where we threw our luggage into a tiny truck that banged its sides sporadically on the whitewashed walls along the narrow alley on the ride to our hotel. We laughed at the sheer madness of it all and marveled at the evening sky. We had a great room on the side of the hills, realizing the view from anywhere in heaven is amazing.

The full moon was waning upon our arrival, yet still so much bigger than I had ever seen it lighting up the Aegean sky. We filled our mornings with coffee and shopping, afternoons were full of sun, swimming in the clear blue water over the black stones of the lava beaches. At night we watched the drunk tourists try to dance at the local bouzouki club while inhaling the local cuisine.

Back in Athens, where there were telephones, I called home to let my husband know we were staying a few more days, and we hustled down to change our tickets. Having the opportunity to relax before our flight back to the states, we walked the city by night; strolling past a theatre and decided to take in a movie. We entered the lobby of the theater, grabbed a few snacks and took direction to walk through the rear doors. Opening the doors without thinking anything was too strange, we found ourselves outside under the stars of the Athenian sky. There were rows of folding chairs set up on the dirt and gravel where everyone was smoking and talking. Olympia and I blended right in, deciding there is little funnier than an American movie voiced over in Greek . . . We ran around Athens our last night smoking cigarettes, playing backgammon, eating late, and sucking down Amstel suds like there was no tomorrow.

We were shocked to sobriety on the 14th of June learning that Flight 847 with our original flight path from Athens to London was hijacked and on its way to Libya. An international incident was under way. Boarding our TWA flight leaving Athens three days later, we arrived in America safely with skin tanned the color of the Apollonian hillside.

Greeted with a nervous hug laced with sighs of relief when I returned home, the buzz of "what ifs?" and with "how would we haves?" percolated through everybody's brain, and I found myself at the center of an upset.

"I knew someday you would fly away, for love is the greatest healer to be found, so leave me if you need to

58

I will still remember angel flying too close to the ground."

- Willie Nelson

Having made it clear before I left that even if he granted me the trip it was no guarantee I would be staying, he wasn't sure which way the pendulum would swing. It was good to be home, but nothing would ever be the same.

An indiscretion Marius had with someone in my home while I was on this trip set off alarms too painful to deal with. The heart wrenching depth of my husband's betrayal showed me how badly I was betraying myself and became the fatal blow that ended our marriage. Unable to find it in my heart to let it continue, I made my point then let it go. Life went on like normal for a short time, but something in me had changed; not my love for him, but my desire to keep going in his direction. Gathering my guts with my cup of coffee, I spoke to him standing in the kitchen, telling him I wanted to leave his life but not him. His way was his way, and knowing I could never ask him to change, it made my next move abundantly clear.

Speaking with my brother Matthew, we agreed to get a place together and found one in Fair Oaks. I commuted up and down the hill to work at our business for about three months, sleeping at a friend's place on the divide until I just couldn't anymore. Marius and I both cried as I stepped up into the truck and drove my life away.

Bound by the cords of our unfinished past, Jimmy and I reconnected. With both of our lives in limbo, our neediness found its way back to a visit trying to find closure. He came over one night and as it was getting late, Marius knocked at the door; my brother woke up and we were alerted. Jimmy hustled into Matthew's room and made it over the balcony and down the fence staying close to the shadows along the walk, as I opened the door and my husband stepped into the living room.

Sensing the room, he by passed the couch and slowly walked to the window. He pulled back the curtain just enough to peer out, looked around for a minute, accepted my offer for coffee, then looked over his left shoulder down the hallway as he came back and sat on the couch. Thinking I would die from a heart attack before he was able to get to the bottom of his cup, I miraculously lived, and as always he left as calmly as he arrived.

Not feeling comfortable about what transpired, figuring I would do what adults do, I asked him for a divorce. Tying up loose ends at the house, I introduced the topic and opened the floor for discussion. Feeling the energy in his lack of response and the look in his eyes, we arrived at a mutual understanding and I dropped it.

Looking for any work to remove myself from Marius' life, I took a job as a 7-Eleven cashier close to the apartment. Working in this capacity was a way to get the ball rolling, my shift was the graveyard and I worked at night and until 3 a.m., which drew an interesting clientele. An angel disguised as a young woman named Jill came in to buy her beer almost every night after work. She was a bartender for an extremely busy restaurant and lounge down on the boulevard. She was energetic and friendly, always laughing with her raspy voice and joking in her rough sort of way. One night she made her regular twelve-pack purchase and out of the blue said she thought I had what it took to work where she did and encouraged me to apply. Hired on the spot after my interview, I showed up the next day and immersed myself in volumes of information to integrate a whole new career.

Reconnecting with my brothers, who I was always closer to growing up, felt wonderful. Being back around their sense of humor and around the part of my family that was career and family-minded gave me a sense of stability and accomplishment.

My little brother Luke was out growing living under the same roof with our mother. Luke was sweet, humble and ultra sensitive. He worked at a gas station, mowed lawns and touched every heart he met. Matthew was the handsome professional, methodical, complex, still-waters-that-run-deep type. Mark was the energetic business man, comedian, jock, inventor, and mechanic who knew moving parts like nobody's business. His true to Roman genes kept him at the gym and running around in joy as the excitement of his new ideas exploded from the unceasing expression of his brilliant mind and heart. Luke was taller and more beautiful than either of them, and I called him the Adonis of the three. Black wavy hair and fairer skin, Luke was sixteen years old with a size thirteen shoe and still growing.

Luke, after fighting with mom and breaking down, sobbed as I lay next to him on his bed holding him in my arms. I told him it would be okay, and that we would help him. The boys made plans to get him down to Sacramento to be with us and pulled together resources to give him a strong start. We were all very excited and it all felt so right, and Luke beamed with the light of gratitude and hope.

Business was good and getting into a new life with new friends, things got social. There were rehearsal dinners, weddings, parties, after party parties and I never missed one red carpet, step in my stride or drop of wine. Irreproachably infused in my denial, life seemed normal when measuring my value with society's yardstick. Life was moving along quite normally as normal people live. Winning sales contests at work, stripped from lifting weights and playing racquetball, I believed I had gotten a new life, but internally my darkness continued to smolder, and my demons brought me to self-inflicted patterns of abuse.

I occasionally spent time in the Bay Area visiting grandma, and had her to our apartment for visits too. One of her neighbors and friends, Virginia, had us over for coffee. Virginia was a very interesting Polish woman who wore a two-carat Alexandrite solitaire that I admired. Not being a common gem, I was intrigued by its size and complexity of colors. Virginia also read palms and she asked to have a go at mine. She looked deep into my palm and expressed her reticence in relaying what she saw. Allowing her to continue, she foretold the death of someone I knew that involved blood, lots of blood. After leaving I looped the information through my cerebral cortex intensely for weeks. I was more careful driving and imagined it could be anybody I knew. A few months passed and her words drifted to the back of my mind, occasionally resurfacing for review.

Matthew was focused on his career and his fiancee Rose, seeming fairly content. Luke was spending more time with us and commuting to work instead of staying at mom's. It was summer, spirits were high, the beer was cold and we shared the best this time of year has to offer. Luke came by the restaurant for a prime rib dinner with the boys and they were making final preparations to move him down the hill.

Remember man that you are light and to light you shall return.

- Siobhan Nicolaou, The Sword of Truth

A week or so had passed and Grandma came for a visit. We had coffee and breakfast and were getting our showers and hair together when I received a phone call informing me that our brother Luke was killed in an automobile accident. The accident happened on the highway 80, the truck hitting a boulder managing to spin around hitting the opposite wall of rocks and ended up facing north east when it stopped. Luke lay broken across the lap of his buddy who cradled what was left of Luke's head as he bled out almost completely onto the rear floorboards of the truck. Luke was barely alive when they got him to the hospital and died shortly thereafter.

Going into complete shock, I walked around breathless, blank and irritable. Losing all care about anything, not able to be present for grandma, I took her to our cousin's house and drove up the hill. Luke passed away two weeks before he was to celebrate his seventeenth birthday with his twin Sara. My heart over flowed with a familiar pain, but death had never before hit so close to home and never so deeply. Luke's death was unreal, and gave way to driving my truck off the road out into the middle of a field tearing up the grass with my tires, getting out and screaming at the sky for God to "come down and fight like a man"!

Taking a week off work, the family gathered its train wreck at Mom's house. My father barely held back his tears and my brothers wept, losing a piece of themselves while trying to be strong for the rest of us. Immediately going into resistance, I reached for my only known coping mechanism and dove deeper into a bag of white powdered "I don't care."

We received Luke's ashes within three weeks and set a date for their disbursement. About two hundred people showed for a separate memorial which was a testament to how sweet his young life had been to so many. Mom moved back to the Bay Area, not being able to withstand the reflection of the pain on the faces of the small Sierra community.

Going back to work was difficult, trying to keep my emotions in check. There was gossip about my relations with my manager and it was time for my review, and we all agreed I needed a change after two solid years with the company. I left two weeks later with my "excellence in service" pins, and the memory of my brother's face when I hugged him goodbye for the last time at booth 51.

In October the family converged to hike Luke's ashes up to the mountains, climbing in a staggered fashion. We scaled those beautiful hills into the Tahoe National forest where each of us took our turn and said our final goodbyes. I retained some of his ashes and created a small altar around them at home. Stephania was not there and we never told her about Luke's death, not knowing how she would react if we did, so we divided the portion of her pain amongst ourselves and carried it for her.

Stephania began to show up at our apartment barefoot and in need of a bath in the months that followed Luke's death, asking to stay with us claiming her windows were boarded up and the rooms were hissing from an over abundance of cockroaches. Matthew gently responded by getting her something to eat, driving her to a motel and paying for a couple of nights. The severity of her condition prevented us from being able to accommodate her. She was in need of medical supervision at the very least, and we did the best we could trying to contact her case worker for advice.

Stephania had been living in Sacramento for years, with our paths never crossing. She was diagnosed with a mental disorder by age twenty-four, was a full blown junkie living on disability and in an apartment in deplorable condition. The first and only time I went to her apartment, I borrowed a gun carrying it in plain view.

Cautiously I stepped out of my car, locked and loaded. The air that surrounded me was damp and layered with feelings of poverty and despair. I walked up the stairs across the tar-papered surface of the walkway measuring the weight of each step by the strength of the boards beneath my feet. Looking down at the complex pool, I saw a refrigerator a bicycle and other debris had long since acquiesced, sunk to the bottom and covered themselves with green slime. The doors of the apartments were held by frames of decaying wood and the paint was peeling from neglect reflecting the faces of the junkies peering from behind their curtains at the sound of my approach.

Her apartment showed signs of being occupied by more than one person, though she lived alone. Various nefarious objects strewn about the living room floor were treated as if invisible, and her furniture was badly stained. A poster of Marilyn Monroe hung on the wall and she had but a few other sticks of things she called furniture. Mom and my brothers alternated bi-weekly shopping trips for groceries, televisions, and clothes for them only to be stolen by the neighbors. It got worse over the years with more frequent calls by mom to Stephania's over loaded case-worker who offered the little help she had available.

I sat uncomfortably on a wooden chair while we spoke for a short time. Graciously declining her offer of anything to drink, I tried to pretend I felt nothing. My sister was visibly broken, her soul had mostly vacated her form and had given over to whatever wanted to step in and occupy her shell for the time. Handing her an envelope filled with cash, I made my visit short reading her energy and eyes shifting as my cue to leave. It was comforting to see she had a roof over her head; clearly there was nothing more anyone could do. Pausing outside the door to catch my breath and cover my solar plexus, my heart ached in tear-filled prayers.

Just under five months after Luke died, mom called me barely able to speak. Her words were slight and squelched from the tightness of her throat yet she managed to tell me Stephania was found dead in the bathroom of a public park in the dregs of North Sacramento. Stephania died from a single gunshot wound to the head, her body laid there for a week before being found. The small German 22 caliber handgun was recovered by her side, and her death was ruled a suicide. My brothers went to identify her body, and I took down all pertinent information, paying a visit to her case worker who handed over her file. Ordering a copy of her autopsy report, I read the report thoroughly, and became satisfied with their findings of suicide.

A small memorial followed, and the glacier began to melt from the top of the mountain of grief overwhelming my every sense. The dams of denial broke for mom whose heart was forced open for reconciliation through the deaths of our beloved Luke and Stephania. The pain that welled up in her chest brought her to her knees and she drowned in unfathomable grief. The gardens that always flourished at the hands of my mother, died upon the deaths of Luke and Stephania. Her heart torn open and turned to dust, she had nothing to give a garden for the next seven years.

Matthew's plan to marry Rose was coming to fruition, and I was losing my roommate. Never living with anyone but a mate or family, distraught and overwhelmed, I emotionally reached for what seemed the easiest option - not the smartest but the easiest. I rented the upstairs room with a bathroom from a hispanic woman and her white alcoholic husband. She was fairly new to Northern California and I met her through friends we had in common at the restaurant.

Mixed race couples were not common in our part of the world then, and I saw how awkward and sad it was observing her go to such great lengths to look and act like a suburban housewife. The family lived downstairs, cooked food foreign to me, and played with their small dogs. Their space was cluttered and dirty, much like the pain churning on my insides.

The room and bathroom were private, though I replaced my door handle with a locking one to keep everyone honest. Christa seemed cordial enough, had a lover on the side, stayed out all night placing the responsibility of her youngest daughter on her oldest daughter who lived at home with her boyfriend. The house had five bedrooms and a beautiful pool surrounded by what must have been a gorgeous garden before they moved in and let it go to ruin.

My new job was atop the highest building in the city that boasted a 360 degree panoramic view, and I added the art of French table side cooking to my resume. Commuting downtown, I spent less on rent though it equalled the amount I spent weekly on cocaine and alcohol. The money was not as consistent as the steakhouse and, feeling the pinch, I sold a fur to pay my rent and secretly thought about dying.

My denial kept me away from my true feelings while maintaining a couple of steady relationships and juggling a few purely physical ones. Sex was the putty that served to fill in the cracks of my broken heart making sure the wall stayed strong. No one knew the relationship I had with cocaine, my personal tragedies, my past or present pain. I never focused on it or discussed it with anyone. I began to cry when alone, opening the flood gate of emotions not expressed for almost a decade. Trying to detach from the deaths of my siblings, I managed to move forward with a smile on my face and focused on the joy of spring, my favorite holidays, and the weddings on the calendar.

Stumbling across a Greek club just over the river from work, food was served hot until 2 a.m., and flowed with my late night schedule. There was live bouzouki and belly dancing on the weekend and we danced, broke plates and reveled in old world simplicity. Friendships came easily with the owners and waiters who were all Greeks, as well as most of the patrons. Everyone was treated like family rotating through each other's tables all night and visiting.

I was introduced to a man named Thanasis, who was known to pick up the microphone and sing the old Greek tunes while everybody clapped and danced. He was humble, spoke the wisdom of everything in moderation and was always a gentleman. I considered him a friend, said hello when at the club and met him out every once in a while for a casual scotch and a few laughs.

Summer got off to a great beginning when Matthew married Rose, bringing the family together in celebration rather than pain. It was small and lovely and I was so happy to be in the wedding of my brother. Weddings always brought light to the dull gray veils of standing still, and when Olympia announced her plans to marry Robert, I anticipated her big day, and added another bridesmaid dress to my collection. Their wedding was beautiful, and the reception so posh and well executed that the reception hall looked as though we had missed a turn somewhere and walked through a portal into Vienna. Nothing beats the blues like a big Greek wedding.

As the end of the year approached, things slowed down to an uncomfortable pace leaving time to end relationships that needed to go. As the layers of my life continued to peel away, I was left emotionally raw with nothing to give to anyone and barely a breath for myself. The awakening that began for me surrounding the suicide of my sister was her death's gift to me. Dipping deeper than the bottom of a bindle, I found enough value within me to decide I did not want to succumb as she had. Negotiating with my heart that life had to be different, knowing life filled with this much pain was not worth living, the devil threw down the gauntlet. I picked it up as God's loving hand extended the ray of light needed to give me the strength to keep going. My mind began discovering ways to be good to myself, and I began reaching for things that would nurture instead of hurt me. New habits replaced old ones and I quickly began freeing myself from the bondage of chemically induced happiness.

Weary from the battlefield of my earliest years, I sat coughing dry dusty ashes from all that was disintegrating around me. Having hit hard pan at the bottom of my emotional pit, I learned that a renowned psychic was living my same neighborhood. Deciding to do something radically different, I signed up for a series of weekly classes. Meditation, visualization and intuitive development were her focus, working with people like me who are ultra sensitives. My energy, always fast and intense, blew out Marcy's portable stereo the first time I came charging through her front door as the energy tried to adjust.

Marcy spoke to us about levels and told us that all of our thoughts were valid even though at the time they might make no logical sense or have any point of reference. She encouraged using the intuitive process to put the pieces of our puzzle together as we learned to keep our emotions out of the way. She took us on a meditation journey through the levels of a pyramid, and I found the imagery especially easy for me. The light shone brightly within these realms that I had no idea were within me. When I opened the door it felt like a hand grabbed me, quickly pulled me through and closed it behind me.

About a week later, I noticed the lock on my bedroom door had been messed with, though nothing I could see had been touched in my room. I did not completely trust the people I lived with and placed my jewelry in a temporary safe spot in a false bottom of a large wastebasket in my bathroom. I left town for a few days believing all would be safe. Waking at home to the distant sound of the brakes and the back-up beep of the neighborhood garbage truck, I got up to use the bathroom. Through bleary eyes of the early morning, I glanced at the wastebasket, noticing it had been emptied with the bottom compromised. Losing my mind, I ran down the stairs screaming at Christa asking her who had been in my bathroom. She said her son had emptied my wastebasket. My heart dropped to the floor in blended rage and disbelief.

Trying to keep my cool, hearing the garbage truck a block away from the house, I ran out the door onto the street before realizing there was no way to recover my jewelry even if they were telling the truth. Distraught, knowing that it was all out of my hands, hell's revenge boiled in my heart, and despair flamed about me. Crying, head held in hands, feeling my anger seeking to overwhelm me, I controlled myself channeling it into a poem instead of making their life a living hell, and I allowed the light of peace to become my intention instead.

A step up for me in dealing with my emotions responsibly, the light within the darkness of my anger shone through and I knew I had to make a move and leave that house. An emotional week then passed and I carried the few pieces of my jewelry in my gym bag. While at the club eating dinner after work, my thoughts were pounding me to get my bag out of the truck to change clothes, but something kept me absolutely glued to that chair. About an hour passed and I forced myself up to go out to my truck. The lock on my passenger side had a slit across it as if a screwdriver was jammed in by force to bypass the lock. My gym bag was gone and so was the last of my jewelry, leaving my feelings muddled and indescribable.

The winds of change began whipping about me with such force I had no choice but to stand still trying to maintain my balance until I got clarity and guidance as to my next move. As the dust began to settle it condensed, took form, and ran me out of the main chamber of the inner sanctum. The hounds of hell were close on my heels as I made fast tracks for the narrowing exit. The course that was laid out in front of me changed with every stride. Jumping the hurdles and climbing the walls, I tucked and rolled through the ring of fire landing on my feet on the other side facing a new direction. A black streak up my leg revealed the only visible wound remaining, showing layers of more subtle shadows that would soon emerge from deeper places. The obvious wounds were easy to heal and it felt so good getting beyond the drama and emotion leaving it all behind. As I began to settle down moving in a lighter direction, the "devil" showed up in the inner world of my dreams:

January 1988 Dreamtime

I entered the red dirt cave through two boulders slightly blocking the entrance. My feet took flight making my descent into the chamber effortless. The reddish dirt walls with gray rocks cast off heat. It was arid with no plant life. Sitting on a rectangular solid mass of stone was Satan with my departed sister Stephania perched on his left knee. He was a huge being with human and animal features. He was rugged, and smelled of the earth. I could feel the heaviness of his presence and was intrigued by the size and slight twist of his long pointed horns. His piercing eyes

71

followed my wide cautious movements inside his subterranean lair. I was looking for the exit. Stephania beckoned me. I smiled and kept my distance, gliding through the air with slow seductive movements as if I were playing the game. Keeping them mesmerized with my dance, I unexpectedly darted up to his face, swiped two fingers of blood from my leg, wiped it quickly on his tongue and ascended instantly out of the cave.

Attending Marcy's final class, I spoke with her about the circumstances surrounding my jewelry. She told me I had shed the dark cloak that I thought had always protected me and I was vulnerable, not knowing how to protect myself otherwise. She gave me tools and opened my eyes to the light at work. Bringing light into my life created the first contrast I ever consciously experienced. Before the light, everything was dark, false, all normal with glimmers of joy. The invigorating victory in my dream propelled me forward, moving me out to the center of the dance floor where I quickly learned a few new steps.

Chapter VI

Dancing with Mrs. D

Prepare now for what you will inevitably meet face to face. For it is not about the part of yourself you will discover, but your ability to respond when it looks you in the eye.

- Siobhan Nicolaou, The Sword of Truth

Dancing with Mrs. D

I regrouped and stayed with mom in Palo Alto, for the first time since my siblings' deaths. Her house was simple and monastic; she meditated and chanted all the time and stayed focused on her work. Buying a deck of Animal Medicine cards, I learned more about myself, reading their wisdom and taking time to reflect. I created a small altar on my dresser, placing objects there that made me feel loved and protected. Still oblivious to the source of my guidance, choices were offered to me that would further my growth. Turning down several prospects for marriage over the few months that followed, I had to be hoodwinked into moving forward.

Finding a job as a cafe manager almost immediately, I immersed myself in work, looking forward to finding my own place and reinventing myself. Thanasis, my Greek friend, graduated from his law school and went back to his parent's house for a few months before moving out to the East Coast for a year to obtain a specialized law degree. He called, and like usual saw each other for drinks or coffee. One night when we went out for a casual dinner, he said he had eyes for me and that he wanted to start a family now that he was guaranteed a job with a firm when he got back the following summer.

Not thinking of Thanasis in this way, I was taken aback. He was good looking, really intelligent and had a solid life he was pulling together, but I was reticent and pulled away when he would get physical or clingy. Thanasis asked me to marry him, and to appease him I told him yes, but that I wanted to wait until he got back from Florida, attempting to create a little space between the yes and the wedding. He was adamant about not having sex before we were married, and that being a first, I interpreted it as an honorable gesture.

He left for Florida and we both got busy. Not more than a couple of weeks passed and he called, telling me how much he wanted to marry me, insisting he did not want to wait. Thanasis flew out, came over in a suit and spoke with my mother. We had a meal at mom's house and she raised her glass in approval of our union. Giving my notice to the cafe, I got my things in order in preparation for a move to Florida.

Thanasis was reassuring, and the nicest man that I ever dated, which served to calm my ambivalence. We drove to Matthew's house to offer Thanasis' intentions for my hand and ask for his blessing. We stayed the night and drove the rest of the way to Reno looking for a chapel and ran into a law school buddy who stood in as our witness. With a few words and the slip of a thin gold band, it was done. To further celebrate this momentous occasion, he decided we should drive by his family home with a bottle of champagne and break the news to his folks. He pulled up alongside the curb and suggested I wait in the car, as I had never met his parents.

The lights in the house were visible through the drawn white curtains of this modest family home. The fast movement of shadows behind the curtain indicated an upset, and soon after a young woman pulled back the curtains and peered at the car. Thanasis' father reacted to the news of our nuptials by turning over the dinner table onto the laps of his family and the floor of his house. His mother Antigone wailed and yelled, while his sister ran around hysterically. The front door flung open and the screaming drama of a heated argument rolled across the lawn and off the sparking tongue of Antigone. Thanasis jumped in the car and slammed the door. He was upset and tearful, but assured me things would be fine. We stayed at my mother's house and left for Florida the next day.

Not knowing Thanasis's financial situation or anything about his family, I had never asked believing it was none of my business. I later discovered his parents paid for everything, though he had student loans, he was still at their mercy and we would soon be feeling the twist.

Arriving in Gainesville in the first week of September, the thick, damp air of the South added to the eeriness of the Spanish moss that hung low from the gnarled branches of the massive trees. Gainesville wreaked of swampland ignorance; it was hot, sticky and grossly humid. We lived in a ground level cinderblock studio apartment that I affectionately referred to as "cellblock 31." The entrance was accessed from inside an open ended cement corridor with a single light bulb hanging from a cord in the center. The soda machine stood under the stairs at the other end of the breezeway, representing the only clean and shiny piece of metal I could see for miles. The weather-beaten cars in the parking lot showed varying degrees of rust, while pollen and leaves coated the windows.

Inside the apartment, the kitchenette was about eight feet from the foot of the bed, and I could not bleach the bathroom enough to kill the mold that seemed to grow back with greater force after every shower. Cockroaches are a part of life in the South and often the size of garbage trucks. The rainstorms were constant, intense and mostly quick to pass like the phone calls Thanasis received from his entire family.

Obsessed with the belief that I was not Greek, Antigone begged me to divorce her son, and made threats that left Thanasis in emotional turmoil. I empathized, stayed strong, tried to acclimate to my new conditions and comforted his sobs. Antigone was beyond furious, and after a week of negotiations with no chance I was leaving, she cut off all financial support.

The food in the South was awful and on our limited budget, we filled our bellies with fifty cent oysters and pitchers of beer. My mom sent us small checks so we could by a pizza now and then, and I bought a few cheap kitchen utensils and began to cook.

In my walks through town, I tried to get my head around a people who would name a doughnut shop Krispy Kreme or a supermarket Piggly Wiggly. Thanasis and I made love with the intention of having a baby and in the sweltering heat of a lunch break, I felt the moment of conception and remarked "it is done."

Two weeks later, the end of my EPT stick turned blue and I received a letter written by a woman we knew from the Mediterranean Club. She wrote she was surprised to find that he got married after having asked for her hand right after graduation. We briefly discussed the letter, his response made no sense to me, so I let it go and chose to move forward instead. We were married, we were in it together, the past was the past and we had enough to deal with. I suppose Thanasis believed he was being clever, but he too was hoodwinked for his own spiritual growth.

Having sold my truck in California for next to nothing, I took some of the cash and bought an inexpensive, mildly beat up car. It was an older green Oldsmobile and a little bit rusty like everything else. We stood back laughing while lubing the hinges with olive oil to keep the doors opening freely. Finding a job as a restaurant manager, I watched the streaming footage on the bar TV showing the destruction of the 1989 Loma Prieta earthquake. The phones were down but we got through long enough to determine my mother was scared but fine, my sisters were on the freeway but safe, and grandma was shaken not stirred.

Thanasis finally came out with the truth about ten weeks into my pregnancy that his folks were in Greece arranging a marriage in the village while we were getting married in Nevada. From that moment I interpreted his "niceness" as part of his deception, and I took control of my emotions to make the best of an interesting situation.

The holidays were fast approaching and soon I would be literally and figuratively in the face of his whole family. The news of a grandchild was kept under wraps until the end of my first trimester, and we were not sure how his family was going to take it. Before Thanksgiving, we called to give them the news.

The word baby resounded through the head of Antigone and with it the chance she would have her prized possession, a grandson. Not just a male, but the first grandchild of that generation. Antigone extended her basket of razor filled candy sending me a gift of gold earrings hoping they would make the barbs easier to swallow.

The purse strings from Thanasis' home loosened up with the news of a child, and my doctor's advised I fly home before the third trimester. We discussed where it would be best for me to stay, and with my mother's house not being an option, I expressed my concerns about his suggestion to stay at his folks.

Letting God take the wheel, I made my only priority taking care of myself and the baby growing inside me. For the first time I witnessed the crippling grip money had on children raised to be dependent on the family. How it can be used to manipulate and further personal agendas, keep everybody under control and create the illusion of wellbeing.

Staring out the window I watched the ground fade as our plane ascended through the low hanging clouds knowing I was not going back to Florida with him. A tear rolled down my cheek as I straightened my neck on my pillow, and six hours later, we were greeted at the airport by the Greek squad. Thanasis' father and uncle were standing by the car that was parked alongside the curb with the trunk and the rear door open. Not understanding anything being discussed, I stretched my legs, and gazed out the window thinking about what an efficient buffer the language barrier was. Feeling the tension in and around my body, I focused on relaxing as we pulled into the driveway.

The atmosphere in the house was tense and unsettling. Antigone greeted me with lip biting, thumb rolling nervousness undone for a moment by the gesture of an awkward hug. Glykeria ignored me beyond the initial introduction and Thanasis' father having little to say, kept mostly to himself. Antigone tried to contain her true feelings, but seethed beneath the thin veneer of her strained polite facade. Observing the family together in the same room was as strange as it was telling. Interactions between Thanasis and his sister were interesting, while Antigone exercised control in every move and every word. Being back around Antigone affected Thanasis' personality. He stood by his mother's side as she berated me and I began to see another reality emerge from behind the veil.

Members of his family came by at random times willing to embrace our new family and left trunks of gifts around the tree. I focused on the colorful ribbons, the beautifully wrapped packages and the blinking lights until grandma called and we went out for some Christmas cheer.

Thanasis caught a flight out to Florida right before his class resumed, and I sucked it up carrying on thinking of nothing but my baby and keeping my stress levels low.

My mother was unapproachable on many subjects, especially those pertaining to female bodily functions so she never offered support with my pregnancy. My new doctor was old school Italian who had eyes as black as night and a stone cold demeanor. Olympia gave me a book on what to expect, and I could not relate to the process. Dreaming several times I gave birth standing up with ease, I felt it couldn't be as complex as I had read. Antigone hosted a baby shower for all the female relatives and a few from my family showed up. The party was full of coffee and pastry, small talk and gifts bearing all shades of blue. I never wanted to know the gender of our child and believed that our baby would be a boy.

Thanasis' family spoke mostly Greek, but I felt the gist of their words in their expressions and the tone of their voices. Whether Antigone invited relatives for coffee, or she was invited for coffee, in fact, wherever there was coffee, she waved her pinched fingertips in their faces. Spitting crumbs of *paximadia*, trying to get them to see things her way, she raised her voice and burned them with her little black eyes until they caved in. The relief of righteousness filled her face, giving her enough wind to walk the length of the kitchen, gather her words, turn around, and begin again. I was polite and excused myself to my room trying to keep the feeling of peace around my unborn baby when the women gathered in the dining room to gossip and eat sweets.

Four weeks before my due date I was socializing less, the baby was growing more, and Thanasis made his way back to California. Antigone was always upset and created problems about everything. My family may have been messed up, but this was all kinds messed up. Her old world way compelled her to meddle in the entire family's lives and decisions, not just her own. She must have believed I too would succumb to the force of her will, but I kept the peace, and was sure somehow she would not be the one left standing in the end.

Everything in Antigone's world looked as though it had to do with appearances and she spent lots of time trying to keep them up. She gifted me gold necklaces and rings to make it look as if everything was okay between us when she wasn't behind the scenes causing trouble. Thanasis made the mistake of saying "what more could she do?" Shortly after that, she leaned on us to get married in the church before the baby was born. Antigone made arrangements three weeks before I gave birth and we jumped through the hoops down the Orthodox aisle.

She cooked three days for the wedding feast, and squeezed the family into her backyard to celebrate our officially blessed union. It was a good time, a beautiful day and even though I thanked her, she wouldn't give up trying to make me feel bad at how much work she did in preparation. No one asked for any of it; she never realized how she was the source of her own suffering, which was a powerful truth I would only come to know myself some years later.

My due date was fast approaching, and I received a call from my dad who I had not talked to in seven years. He was passing through town on Father's Day so we decided to go to the Oakland Hills to the Knowland Park Zoo so we could visit and I could get some exercise. Pulling into the parking lot flooded me with joyful memories of days spent at the zoo with Grandma. I was delighted it was still peaceful and astonished that nothing had really changed.

The lift chairs hung by the original small hook that barely seemed to grip the left side of the cable, taking us high above and around the park. The shiny red airplanes suspended by long sturdy arms of good German craftsmanship still whirled the excited children around in circles in the air. The snack bar area and the picnic tables were as I remembered. The snack bar offered the same treats with the exception of a veggie burger now added to the menu. In some ways, I felt I hadn't changed either, getting the same bridled feeling as I did as a child studying the petting zoo. Somehow children walking around in the mishmash of meandering barnyard animals with an untethered billy goat in a small space spelled chaos and injury. You still couldn't bribe me to go in there.

Larger animals roamed in big patches of land with lush foliage, and the giant tortoises I was allowed to ride as a three year old were still slowly walking around, only rides were now forbidden. Abundant shade of the massive Eucalyptus trees made viewing the elephants from the bench on the hill calming, as a gentle breeze softly evoked memories of a simpler time. With five hundred twenty-five acres of open space, the zoo winds around a series of hills that challenged my legs and strength carrying forty extra pounds uphill. We strolled by the monkey cages, dredging up the same feeling of disgust I had for them as a child, and a few of the monkey's faces were marked with the scars of their long years behind the wire.

Dad and I spoke little that afternoon; though he hadn't changed, our experience was different with my being a woman and soon to be mother.

Three days later at the stroke of midnight I went into labor. Never having menstrual cramps, I had no point of reference; the pain wasn't bad, just constant and cramping. Continually adjusting myself in bed, unfamiliar with what was happening, I got up and knocked quietly on the bedroom door of Antigone. She grabbed her robe and came out into the hallway half smiling in a glad-to-see-me-in-pain sort of expression. Her attitude made me wonder why I bothered, and I went back to bed. The "cramps" continued for hours but were no big deal, though I found it impossible to get comfortable. Calling my doctor a little later, I gathered my things to head to the hospital.

My doctor confirmed I was fully dilated and ordered me to lie down even though it was really uncomfortable. I wanted to walk around or stand, but they would not let me, and not understanding I had choices, I surrendered. Lying down prolonged everything and when my doc was fed up with it, he broke my water which sent me down the rabbit hole of hard labor. My pain level shot through the roof sending my mind set straight into "no %^&*()+# way," and "God could have done a MUCH BETTER job with all of this."

Thanasis, trying to be helpful made me want to throttle him confirming my belief that most men do not belong in the delivery room and should be out golfing and smoking cigars until it's over. There were several nurses in and out of the room that seemed like extras on a movie set, doing nothing to get me focused and settle the chaos that was whirling around me. Antigone was vocal and pacing outside the delivery room, where Thanasis would run out to feed her updates about my progress.

After a few intense hours of pushing in and out of the birth canal, and a bit of old world hardware, he pulled her out weighing in at almost nine pounds. Surprised for a second to see she was a girl, I watched as she took her her first breath, cried and looked right at me. Before the nurses had the chance to get Anastasia into my arms, I could hear Antigone yelling in the hallway at Thanasis, insisting he name our child after her. We had names picked out for both sexes and I trusted him to handle it. He gave in to make peace in the moment and signed the birth certificate according to her wishes. In no shape to get up off of the table and do anything about it, I let go and gathered my strength.

My brothers came down to the hospital overjoyed with the news of a little one. Uncle Mark held Anastasia with the same love and teary-eyed adoration he had for his daughter born the previous year. Mark's daughter now had a cousin and my daughter's birth foretold a dream soon to manifest in the life and heart of Matthew. Uncle Matthew brought Anastasia her first dozen roses, so she could say the first roses she ever received were from him and we all basked together in the warm glow of parenthood.

Anastasia and I slept side by side until the next day, when we were given the option to stay or go home. Feeling my strength and fire coming back, I insisted we leave immediately. Still not quite in the position to go toe to toe with Antigone, she knew I would and that was probably the biggest source of her fear.

Speaking with Thanasis on the way to his folks house, I was adamant about moving as soon as possible having very little patience left for his family's crap. We pulled up into the driveway; Thanasis opened our door and I walked slowly, feeling a little weak. The front door was opened by his father and I stepped up in over the threshold. Antigone dropped an iron bar across my foot, took Anastasia from my arms and performing some kind of ritual, stepped on the bar with both feet. Taking a small spoon of honey, she placed it on Anastasia's mouth. I was so stunned I couldn't move; Thanasis piped in yelling something in Greek, I took my baby back and never let

Antigone hold Anastasia again. I woke the next morning with my old sense of self returning, and she began to see from the look in my eyes how transparent she was becoming and how thin my patience was wearing.

Having no real money of our own kept us tied to the family purse, sending us after the delivery of our child to live in a family house an hour and a half east of the bay. We moved in with little more than a bed, baby furniture and kitchen necessities. A few weeks passed and the family started dropping by to welcome Anastasia, walking through her room while she slept. Her crib was adorned with icons and envelopes of money; some left gold coins and silver dollars. By the time the procession was over, she netted a fair amount in spendable cash. Without my knowledge or any consideration, Thanasis and his mother took the loot and bought my living room furniture in a design she approved of.

The house was a 1940's style home in an older neighborhood with crab grass growing unkempt onto the mostly cracked sidewalks. Thanasis, a new lawyer, and I a new mother, were both focused on finding our feet and holding them steady in our new worlds. Anastasia's room adjoined our bathroom and to make things work better I put a bed in her room to breast feed and change her through the night without disturbing Thanasis. Anastasia most often ended up next to me in bed and we relaxed into post-rest healing from the trauma of childbirth.

His parents had family that lived all over the town which brought them down on most weekends, it was emotionally draining. Everything they did was offered with the words of trying to help, but that never seemed to be the case. No amount of cash or gifts intended to get us ahead seemed to do that. The emotional scenarios Antigone created each week lasted almost to the next

Saturday right before she showed up again. In the interim, my focus was the joy of motherhood and cooking.

Yia Yia and Papou, Thanasis' paternal grandparents lived a few blocks from our house and they never gave us any grief. Yia Yia slipped me crisp one hundred dollar bills from her apron pocket, saying nothing more than "take it." She cooked like a fiend from the plentitude of Papou's garden and made the best Greek coffee this side of Athens. Pita filled with feta and vegetables lined the countertop all the way to the stove, which always had a simmering pot of something wonderful making the house smell like love. From dawn until dusk, Papou managed his whole lot which was an impeccably planned array of vegetables, herbs, flowers and fruit.

Papou was a tall Greek at about six feet two inches with beautiful blue eyes. He was a gentle, industrious and simple man that grew enough from his garden to keep five Greek households overflowing all spring, summer and fall. Papou happily filled our baskets with the best ingredients for Greek cooking life has to offer and my old world soul had so much appreciation for this beautiful gift. Not a single weed was found anywhere among his healthy and thriving plants. He never used spray and would go out of his way not to kill an ant. He possessed a great understanding of the plants and a respect for balance and harmony in nature.

Papou planted fava beans in the early spring, cutting the plant down to the top of the roots at the end of the season to plant his tomatoes right over the top of the under-turned soil.He knew the fava plant and roots contain huge amounts of nitrogen so he took the plant cuttings and turned them over in his compost. His tomatoes were truly God's perfection, their flavor and sweetness enlivened my body to my cells. I observed him many spring and summer days for hours as he made his way slowly around his garden of Eden. The vibration of his bounty was a testament to his knowledge, wisdom and his humble connection to his indwelling spirit. The families gathered around a long picnic table to relax in the shade of the breezeway. Papou took his breaks here, and even in his broken English through sips of wine and cigarette puffs, we managed to connect just fine. It's wonderful how no words are necessary when communicating over a plate of *horiatiki* and *fassolia*. The purity of food speaks directly to the heart of understanding, and at these times our communications were never misinterpreted.

Soon there was talk about the baptism and Greek couple we knew from the Mediterranean club asked to be the *Koumbaroi*. Planning was easy. I had little to do with it other than invites, the food and the cake. Antigone did not act out among people who were not her family, so she stayed mostly in check for the day.

Greek baptisms can be unsettling to an infant as they are anointed with olive oil and dunked under water three times. After each dunk, the child is held high in the air for all family to see while being blessed in the deep voice of the priest. The baby is anointed again in Myrrh, a lock of hair is cut, then the baby is wrapped in a sheet, given communion, dressed for the after party and circled around the altar with a candle three times. We were lucky to have an ex-Catholic priest who sat her in the fount and poured the water over her head and *Koumbaroi* who were loving and nurturing. I managed to get through the day almost completely unscathed until Antigone noticed her name was not on the cake. My posse dominated this blessed event, and we threw a great party. The following week, I tucked all the jewelry Antigone had given me beneath the utensils I borrowed from her for the occasion, and gave it all back to her.

Things settled down somewhat after that, but becoming my very sensitive self after two years of not having controlled substances coursing through my veins, I was feeling everything again. My body responded to the lack of pollutants by purging what I held within me for so many years. Manifesting yeast infections for months, I spent a fortune trying to kill them with over the counter creams. My desire to know why came with the inner strength propelling me forward as it always had in the combat zone of my life. It was a strength I called on constantly; yet was unconscious of its origin.

Being a mother is one of the greatest gifts God gave me. I had no clue what Anastasia's soul would awaken in me. Her big beautiful eyes with extra long eyelashes looked up to mine and I saw a beauty and innocence so precious she moved me to tears. Anastasia was an easy baby, with sparkle and wonder reflected in her eyes straight from the light of her soul. I watched her sleep on many occasions, her eyes moving rapidly beneath the surface of her closed lids. She was fully engaged in dreamtime and broke out laughing on numerous occasions.

With the clearer mind and clearing body, my advanced psychic ability was coming to the forefront for the first time since I was seven years old. It began drawing people, visions, words and awareness to me in a variety of ways. A fellow classmate from Marcy's group, spoke about how his denial had broken concerning his childhood and the profound effect it had on his life. In the perfection of my still pretty solid denial, my response was "guess I was lucky I had a good childhood," and I thought him a buffoon.

Not long after that, images of dismembered bodies began to surface in my mind to the point I was thinking it was official- I really was crazy. Not knowing what to do when they came up, I imagined the body parts put back together on the main body with rolls of hospital-sized gauze, trying to do something healing and positive.The visual clips continued for another two weeks, then stopped. Within days of that, a story on the news spoke about two trash bags filled with body parts that washed up in a nearby waterway and it suddenly made sense. Things of that vibration appeared to me psychically, living on the level of the lower astral my whole life. I continued to deal with my daily life keeping my visions to myself, and as dreamtime began opening up to me again, I gathered clues of the changes that were being made for me in the subconscious realms.

April 16, 1991 Dreamtime

I was in Marius' and my house in the country. Some folks at the end of the road wanted to tap into our electricity. It was at that point It came to my awareness about the "row of tapes" Marius had on these shelves in the living room. Each of the tapes belonged to a person and was wired to an electrical system. I told the people I could not let them take the electricity because I was not sure how Marius had things wired. I was thinking of the tapes. They also wanted me to watch their dog and I said no.

May 16, 1991 Dreamtime

I dreamt of Michael Corleone, his wife and the rest of the family. The Godfather wanted the family to hang on to the old way and rebuild the empire. Michael spoke to him gently and understandingly.

He simply told his father everybody was always in fear and that was no way to live.

The children hated their parents because their life was so controlled. Michael planned to keep

90

what had been valuable and build on that. Michael's wife, Kate, began to take down the old structure, some sort of room with dark wood paneling and as she was removing the old screws; she realized that the holes lined up with the new wood and she did not have to go through the work of creating new holes and unnecessarily damaging the new wood.

May 20, 1991 Dreamtime

Had a dream I was pregnant and gave birth to a baby boy I named Michael Anthony. It was a painless birth. A friend of the family told me I would get big like my sisters and with my hand I gave her words back to her. I hardly gained any weight with my pregnancy and after delivery immediately had a flat stomach. I hiked and swam at the beautiful Angels Camp, the water was clear and only Angels of light were there.

Anastasia and I strolled over to Papou and Yia Yia's for fresh air and coffee on our lazy mornings and occasionally drove up to Sacramento to visit her *Koumbaroi.* Sometimes we would stay the night and spend time around their Land Park neighborhood. Thanasis never wanted to go anywhere or socialize, but he never stopped me from doing my own thing.

"United we stand, divided we fall."

- Aesop

His parents' vindictive attempts to create upset between us was straining our marriage, and things had to change, we had to be unified. Unfortunately his folks were so unhealthy, we agreed we would not let Anastasia be around them and he promised me he would never take her to see them.

Trying to gain a foothold in a financial situation I couldn't figure out, I made the decision to go back to work. Working away from home was a short-lived effort, as I received feelings of the gut-wrenching kind telling me he was meeting his folks with our daughter. Asking his Yia Yia point blank, she confirmed my greatest fear, and I quit my job, called forth positive change and let everything go but my daughter.

We celebrated Anastasia's birthdays without inviting anyone from his immediate family, and it would be a matter of weeks after her second that I told him I was moving up north. I made it clear that he could come with me or stay there, but that I was not doing his family for another minute. Thanasis reluctantly agreed. We found a great house in Sacramento across the park from Anastasia's *Koumbaroi*. We enjoyed the massive sycamore in the front yard that shaded us on the hot summer days, until into the balmy summer evenings we were cooled by the gentle delta breeze.

In an effort to move forward in our new life, we agreed that his parents were not welcome in our home or to see Anastasia. I suggested we each seek counseling, more determined than ever to find freedom from the pain of dysfunction, and I asked around for suggestions.

Referred to a psychotherapist, I made an appointment, feeling very strange and not knowing what to expect. The whole idea scared and empowered me equally. Walking into her conservative office, I was welcomed by the receptionist and told to have a seat, to which I remained glued until I stood up for our introduction. The doctor had long thin straight kind of greasy hair parted on the left, held in place by a straight plastic hair clip. I looked at her face and saw a young woman who was educated but lifeless who sadly smelled of mothballs way before her time. She was calm and poised, asked me a few questions, and I began my story.

She looked at me and jotted a few notes. As I continued, she tried to hold her mouth closed but her eyes could not hide her disbelief. The letters behind her name went right out the window . . . I became strong and passionate, thinking this was the place to speak with the energy of my true feelings. At one point when perhaps I didn't sound enough like a victim, she paused to tell me that if she believed I was in danger of harming myself or someone else, she would notify the authorities and would do so without my knowledge. This is the law, but not knowing that at the time, this was a deal breaker. Not comfortable at the hands of anyone who had the power to make that kind of call, I clammed up immediately. She did not seem to be able to relate to my pain and did not have enough confidence in her skill set to help me, or in my mind, she would have not played her fear card so precipitously. In any case, it may have been the intensity of my words, the fire in my eyes and using the word "hate" that made her hackles go up. I felt unsafe and stood up in tears, told her we were finished, paid for my appointment and never went back.

> *"Can't find the reasons for your actions, or I don't much like the reasoning you use. Somehow your motives are impure, somehow I cannot find a cure. Can't find no antidote for blues."*
>
> *- Dire Straits, One World*

Marie and I reconnected after about seven years, both on the wave of seeking. Newly divorced, she cleaned up her life for the most part and got her own place in the hills. She went back to school, started collecting birds and became a licensed massage therapist. Marie's early love for medicine and helping others drew her practice to a chiropractor's office and she worked there helping people with her nurturing magic.

Driving back from Marie's apartment in Jackson, I noticed that about every four miles there was a dead owl on the side of the road which I recognized by the type of feathers. Knowing by way of my medicine cards that owls are the Native American totem for being able to see beyond "deception" and psychic gifts, I took this as a sign. Feeling/seeing the energy behind and within circumstances always gave me the inside track, and showed me my course of action or non-action and that led me to the truth of the situation. Honoring my intuition as much more than merely street smarts, it became clear that being "psychic" was all in the language that is used to define it.

My ghost encounter as a seven year old terrified me, and with no validation I blocked it for self preservation. As a child, I was wide open and subconsciously told myself I did not want to see, feel or hear the energy that made itself known to me. With that simple yet powerful declaration, I denied the psychical counterparts to all of my senses in certain situations, insulating myself from anything I did not have the capacity to deal with at the time. Being older with a much better understanding of my gifts, I understood I had been using them all along but now less afraid to admit it.

Pulling to the side of the road to reclaim that piece of myself, I took a whole owl wing home and placed it on my altar. Opening the door to my higher consciousness again, the subtler levels came back sometimes as a welcome feeling and sometimes with the agony of doubt. Still living so much in the world of illusion, when what I saw and felt about an experience didn't match, I wanted to believe what I was seeing more than what my feelings were trying to tell me. The conflict between my mind and my intuition made me feel the discord in conflicting information. Learning how to trust myself while drowning became a bold act of strength and empowerment. Flooded now with so much information simultaneously, it took a little time to to sort through what I was experiencing. I tested the waters and asked for clear signs about some things and got them in striking ways that left me beyond the shadow of a doubt.

With fresh air and inspiration kindling my action forward, I felt wonderful but still a neophyte, I was hanging onto the hope I could change my husband. In our home I did everything except our taxes. There were times I felt so confined and so responsible for everything that I needed to escape and I did partying with my *Koumbaroi*. But repeating old patterns wasn't the answer, and I saw how I could lose sight of my goals and refused to go down that road with Anastasia. Deciding to focus more in my own direction, I discovered more tools that nurtured and helped me deal with things in a balanced way instead of escaping.

"Ask and it will be given to you, seek and you shall find; knock and the door will be opened unto you."

- Yeshua Nazare

The next door of awakening came as a suggestion from Marie. She introduced me to Frederecka and paid for the session. Fredereka was a "conscious channel," a therapist and the first person I ever met quite like this. She channeled a being named Ciage, and imparted wisdom to clients this way. Fredereka closed her eyes . . . her body twitched a little as the two energies aligned.

The energy noticeably shifted in her office while her hands moved in front of her toward me scanning my energy field and "they" began to speak. They pointed out blocked energy within my auric field while giving an accurate reading of what it was related to, and asked me how they could help and what was troubling me. Frustration, blame and anger rose to the surface of my tongue, explaining my marriage and how Thanasis could not even chew correctly. The bone of contention between Thanasis and myself was the fact that he could not remember to close the shower curtain, and I could not figure out what HIS problem was. Fredereka/Ciage informed me that the amount of control I exercised in my life was directly proportionate to the amount of fear present in it as well.

Not able to hear or understand, I went on not getting what they were telling me. Feeling justified because I was right, not hearing myself or feeling my tension, I reiterated HE COULDN'T CLOSE THE SHOWER CURTAIN!!! How could that be MY problem?

After a few minutes, Fredereka reached her arm out, touched my wrist, softly looked into in the wideness of my eyes and said, "it is you." My eyes shifted right then back to meet hers. I could feel the sense of bewilderment in my eyes . . . she calmly repeated herself . . . and before I could rewind and exhale words of resistance to defend my position again, the veil dropped and a shift in consciousness occurred. In this epiphany, the dam of my denial broke and she continued to speak. Fighting to hold back tears in the recognition of her words, I experienced the depth of truth and humility for the very first time.

Clarity gave way to a greater understanding as she helped me put some pieces of the puzzle in place that had not fit until then. She was not judgmental and could relate to my pain. Fredereka's own personal quest for wholeness was continuous and fueled her passion for helping others. Fredereka had attended Werner Erhard's EST workshops years earlier and taught a softer form of workshop called

"A Gift, from Yourself to Yourself ," and I signed up with anticipation.

As a brilliant therapist, Frederecka got me to see how my mind was hooked up, how it was wired and by whom.

In the workshop series, there were seven of us whose stories varied vastly, and together we peeled the layers of the onion a little more every week. One gal spoke of her father as the ringleader of a dark sort of coven and how she had been abused as a child. I felt silly in comparison telling the story about when my mother took my favorite stuffed animal (my lamb) and threw it away. My lamb story was the tip of my iceberg; this gal had been trying to get through her levels for years. I learned so powerfully to not minimize or compare my pain with the pain of others. It fascinated me to see that what could destroy someone could leave another virtually unscathed.

As the weeks progressed, my mind learned to identify and discuss the feelings that created the basic assumptions I had taken on about myself as a result of what happened around me as a child, and how they repeatedly played out in my life. At the same time, my feelings were pushed farther and farther down as my mind gained in strength and became savvy of the process. The extent of the emotional healing was shallow in depth, but the awakening that was happening seemed miraculous. While taking her class, the light bulb had been switched on in my mind. I understood what she conveyed and it brought me a tremendous feeling of hope. My brain was creating new neural pathways firing up different parts that until then had been in the dark.

In and out of meditation, my mind was rapidly connecting the dots and integrating the information of my new found awarenesses. Quickly absorbing the dynamics around who, why, and how I developed a more clear understanding. The more I practiced meditation, the more

I found a way to get beyond my stormy layers and into other realms without using chemicals. For the first time, I could see and explain how the onset of motherhood set in motion old patterns of doing things right and being uptight about things that really didn't matter, like shower curtains not being closed and smudges on the coffee table.

"Learn how to see. Realize that everything connects to everything else."

- Leonardo Da Vinci

Meditating with white light gave me blissful peace in the moment, while dramatically heightening the activity in the mental and spiritual bodies. Holding my light in these realms without being grounded gave me no stability and overwhelmed in the highs and lows of either mental bliss or emotional catharsis. Studying my newly discovered stories with my mind, only allowed me to understand and figure things out rather than realize what was actually keeping my mind's motor running. My mind was illuminated, but I was still split having not yet acquired the tools that would keep me on a steady middle ground.

Fredereka was a hypnotherapist working toward her clinical certification. She asked me if I would be her client through her twelve-week training, and I happily pulled up a chair. Learning how to let the mind go in meditation helped in undergoing hypnosis, but I was aware of what was happening the whole time during our sessions as I answered her questions with an ideomotor response.

It was easy to allow things bubbled up from the past in a state that by-passed my conscious mind and reached into my subconscious from a place of deep stillness. It was in these sessions I recalled my sister Stephania almost killing me on the couch; I physically felt my air passage begin to close, and the fear of death I associated with it as I gasped for air. Frederecka had me change the scene by rescuing my inner child and I felt the relief in the moment that followed. It was strange remembering that day, that I had remembered the incident prior to that session once years before while vacuuming and how I had put it out of my mind just as quickly as it surfaced.

Hypnotherapy strengthened my ability to access my deep subconscious, and things were changing for the better. Smoking was my last chemical crutch, but I was smoking lighter cigarettes, smoking a lot less and asking for help. After my hypnotherapy sessions, relaxing became easier and I was able to let go, feel safe and deepen my meditations. Reaching a level of self nurturing that was perceptible, I woke up one morning and never smoked another cigarette. It was a great victory.

Finding myself more mellow and open, I reveled more in the joys of motherhood. Things that may have mattered before became less important and I was not so hard on myself in the matters of the mundane. Much to my surprise, it all got done, and the energy of the rigid structure began to soften. Beating myself up constantly about every little thing wasn't what fueled me anymore.

Fredereka offered a channeling class, and having been so intrigued and moved by what I felt in the transmissions given in her sessions with Ciage, I signed up. Wanting to experience this as my own reality, I found it was very helpful learning how to move the emotions over and how to allow. Each week we listened, meditated, and opened to channel. We used white light to protect ourselves from "dark energies and dark entities," and she encouraged us to use the same technique to protect ourselves all the time.

The class revealed the emotions that blocked my ability to channel and as I learned how to move them over, things shifted quickly. I found it fascinating at the end of the series to notice how the beings that came through for each person were so different based on their resonating vibrational frequencies.

When my portal was opened, a pale blue light of immeasurable proportions appeared. Humility poured from my eyes and I wept in the profound vibration of Archangel Michael. His presence filled the room, and left me utterly speechless. The following week I channeled a being named Octivar who appeared about 5 ft tall, was light blue too with no distinct features. His energy was joyful and wise, with a light-hearted approach in answering others' questions. When Octivar came through, my voice changed and I gave my form to his energy swaying my body and moving my hands with gestures from another world.

From this time forward I became consciously aware of Michael around me, so I began asking for his help and guidance. He is my best friend, who holds me constantly, firmly yet lovingly gripped in his right hand with the immensity of his energy. Participating in these classes altered and amplified my electromagnetic field and we experienced problems constantly with all things electrical. All my appliances went down one after another and light bulbs began to blow. The electric seat belts that automatically buckled us up when the ignition of the car was turned on began behaving erratically, moving up and down at will. Upon having them checked out at the dealer, they found nothing wrong. After a couple of months all strange electrical activity stopped.

The constant conscious use of the white light in my meditations pushed my feelings further into the subconscious, as my ego took hold with this knew found perception and I began to deny my darkness once again. My life did not reflect completely the truth of my knowledge; the separation of my mind and my unintegrated feelings could be heard in my words now with "us and them, good and bad, right and wrong." Until the awareness of light within me, there was no judgment of anything as right or wrong. There was no forethought, only pure ignorance with nothing until then to compare it to. Living inside and out a completely ignorant "innocent" existence, my life could have been summed up as the destruction of life itself under the guise of living the good life.

Contrast continued to show up, as Thanasis' father paid us an unsolicited visit with gifts for Anastasia. Thanasis sent him away and reiterated our desire he not return. Seeing signs of unification, things felt like they were turning around. I shared my findings about my classes with Thanasis and my excitement over feeling the relief of the acknowledgement of my past pain. I tried to impress upon him the value of doing the work. I also informed him he had to get healthy for Anastasia and that it would also help him gain strength for battling his parents. Something in him shifted with his decision to see a psychologist who was a colleague of Fredereka and he went to get some help. He did great and had awakenings of his own. He shared things with me that had now made sense to him about his childhood and he began to get stronger.

He wrote his family a letter letting them know he was individuating, remembering, and seeing a counselor and healing. A few months later he shut the door on it all when he had to take responsibility for his part in the drama. Like most of us do at times, he hung onto blaming his folks and chose to stop there. Antigone regained his sympathy and soon after she would meet him for lunch when he was at work. Thanasis' steadfast philosophy of everything in moderation made seeing his mother once a week seem harmless. My perception saw it as the kind of poison that accumulates over time, kills your quality of life, creates disease and guarantees a slow and painful death. After quitting smoking, I cleaned up my diet even more in my pursuit to become healthier in spirit, mind and body. Not sharing the same ideology, Thanasis left me alone, hid behind his newspaper, and probably thought of it as another feminine whim.

We argued more as I took on his need to heal his family issues. Knowing that patterns not made conscious have a life of their own, I would not take that chance with him. I couldn't get him to care; he saw no point. There were conversations with my family members that only empowered the drama and made me see how much I needed to make my own decision. Not wanting to leave and break up our home, yet knowing I had to, brought immense feelings to the surface of my heart and I waffled between guilt, grief and assuredness.

One day four simple words occurred to me that set me free of it all. The words in my heart rose to proclaim "it's not your problem" and I got that it really wasn't. It was between Thanasis and his family and my only responsibility was a healthy happy life for me and my daughter. The energy changed in that moment. I let myself off of the hook and everything fell into place.

When I told Thanasis I wanted to file for divorce, he left it to me. Meditating and praying for guidance, I began to ask about an attorney. The good thing about having good friends that are attorneys is they always have good attorney friends and I was given a referral. Being practical, money conscious and not quite sure how attorneys operate, I decided to get the most help possible for the least amount of cash, and began the task of getting my terms written and organized first.

Sitting alone quietly at our dining table, I thought of every possible category included in a divorce and wrote them all down. Then under each one I broke them down to the very last detail while pausing during the process and tuning in. Completing my papers I was prepared and made an appointment to meet with Brandon my new attorney.

Presenting the pages to Brandon, retainer in hand, I told him I believed I had covered everything and asked him to simply fill in the blanks with legalese and make it as painless as possible. Inspired by Spirit and feeling the power of "make my day," I moved forward fearlessly. Brandon looked at me, taken aback, and said he would look everything over and get back to me.

The papers were drawn up within two weeks and I went to the firm to pick them up. Reaching across his desk to take the papers from his hand, Brandon looked at me in disbelief and said "do you really think he is going to sign these?" I responded with a simple "we will see." Reading every page I initialed each one thanked him again and headed over to Thanasis' work where we had a notary prepared to seal the deal after he signed the documents.

The bright sunlight poured onto his desk at the office. Thanasis took the packet and read through the pages. Finally, he initialed every page and called his secretary over to notarize the agreement. I said nothing beyond asking secretary to make him copies. I sipped a cup of water, thanked my angels and waited for what seemed like an eternity to get my copy back and leave. Sliding into the car dizzy and breathless, I regained my composure, fastened my seat belt and quietly drove away.

Two months after we celebrated Anastasia's third birthday, we moved to Palo Alto and stayed with my mom until we found our own place. I enrolled her into the Palo Alto Montessori School and began looking for work. My body was going through a major release of toxins on a physical level and I was taking cleansing herbs and chose to go vegetarian.

My confidence and energy levels were high, feeling victorious and free from Thanasis' agonizing family, I was happily a single parent, knowing I did the right thing. I was really excited to be back in the bay area where I could create a beautiful life for both of us. Mom was accommodating, but not all that happy at first, having to explain to those who inquired that I divorced the lawyer she was so happy I married.

I toned and meditated twice a day to break up the ascetic energy I felt confined by within her home. Mom drove the right car, wore the right clothes, had all the right bumper stickers, wore Birkenstock sandals, wrapped herself in vegan ism and all things spiritually correct, but from what I saw she only allowed herself to live a very one pointed life of what encompasses the totality of a spiritual being.

Sara lived with mom too and I was concerned about Sara's depression. She had done little with her life but work since the passing of her twin and no one knew what to do. When not at work, she stayed in her "cave," accompanied by her best friend, the family dog, a grumpy beagle fox hound named Sadie who shared her emotions. Anastasia was a bright light and having a connection with Sara from when she babysat her when small, and the warmth and laughter of a child began to melt her heart.

Mom, Sara and I attended Reiki classes level one and two that were offered by two of her students that she held in her living room on two separate weekends. Receiving the level one attunement, Sara opened up and reclaimed more of her power and resurrected more from her grief. Within a day of the level two attunement, Sadie began convulsing and died. The vet discovered Sadie had a brain tumor. I mourned and blessed her, thanking her for staying by Sara's side until she rediscovered enough strength to open and move forward again.

Mom's sense of order was tested by the whimsy of a toddler, and we chuckled knowing this. Anastasia arranged mom's rocks and shells from various baskets into organized formations on the vast living room carpet and made huge nests from the strips of mom's shredder. She raised her voice being distressed when her smoke alarms would go off and on because our energy fields were trying to find harmony, and when they did it stopped. My vibration raised her roof and when the energy settled down, we were all able to enjoy the freshness of the San Francisco peninsula air and the smell of the rich earth that nurtured the roots of all the flowers and vegetables that made up her once again abundant garden.

Los Altos would be the little slice of heaven Anastasia and I settled into, and I took a job as a banking officer for a major bank in Palo Alto. The branch manager was a smart, capable and supportive woman. We all had a good time, but the industry was at the beginning of practices that would change banking forever and make me question my own integrity.

The social aspect was my favorite part of the job and I liked connecting with people, having lunch with my big clients while encouraging them to diversify. For the most part I liked the challenge, but it sucked the light right out of my life, putting me in a very uncompromising routine. Striving to maintain the natural order of what became my unnatural life, I was up at 5:30 a.m. to shower, dress and make breakfast before waking my toddler from her sweet slumber. I meditated in my suit across the living room putting her in front of Barney for thirty minutes before we left.

At 6:30 p.m., I walked thru the door kicking off my pumps and, stripping myself from the confines of the daily grind, walking down the hallway then tossing my suit onto the bed. Dinner, bath, Star Trek-The Next Generation, and story time were finished by 8:30 p.m. so I could meditate and be asleep by 9 o'clock. My structure became similar to the one that almost killed my spirit completely as a child, and my frustration turned into anger and impatience with everyone and everything. I became rigid, fixed and closed when dealing with Anastasia, and all fun seemed to vanish.

I was not born to drive in rush hour traffic.

- Siobhan Nicolaou, The Sword of Truth

The words of my mother automatically sounded from my mouth toward my daughter in the way I handled situations with her and it felt awful. Hearing my words, I would look over my shoulder to see if my mother was standing there and made a conscious effort to change them. Fear and doubt raised the old pattern of doing things right and became the whip with which I scourged myself, and reinforced my feelings of unworthiness.

My stress levels and intent to cleanse brought candida back into my life. I met a woman who used ear coning as a way to support the cleansing process of the body. Ear coning was a relaxing treatment which was really good for me and it drew out mountains of yeast from God knows where. The first piles of white powder were one inch high and within about three days my ears would fill back up. Some sessions my ears required two cones each, which was not typical.

Feeling abundantly clearer and more relaxed, my psychic awareness blasted my clairvoyance open making my meditations and visions more intense. The Akashic records opened up to me like never before and fine tuned to my mental frequencies, and it became effortless to retrieve information about myself and others. Archangel Michael, always with me, became an even stronger presence, I could feel holding me in and out of meditation.

106

The opportunity to awaken further came through a man named Michael Genzmer, who I met at a meditation gathering one Sunday afternoon. Michael, a six foot six inch tall lean mass of crystalline knowledge, worked for NASA yet was very down to earth. Drawn to each other immediately, he was much more than I could ignore and we carved out time to meditate, share and have lunch in Saratoga. His energy triggered many awakenings within me, teaching me much more about energy and its capacity to travel when directed through time and space.

With Michael as an adept, we spent time playing around in each others auric field using different techniques, merging our chakras which enabled us to connect in dream time and real time in the most profound ways. Visions and visitations of his energy to my home were common occurrences. Spiritual egos (being some of the biggest) created competition and power plays between us through our unhealed insecurities. We danced a short lived two-step playing out the extent of our gifts, recognizing we were puffing our feathers. Michael and I welcomed all emotions that came up between us by finding their place of origin and healing ourselves along our timeline. Transforming the energy between us cleaned up the unexplained feelings we shared in the present. Giving it a rest after about seven months, he faded into my dream time that showed me how far we had come.

March 03, 1994 Dreamtime

Michael and I were Native American males in a cave with a small fire burning, clothed in dark ceremonial hides and feathers surrounded by darkness. In the low light of the fire I painted his face with symbolic markings. Three on each cheek and a cross in the middle of his forehead.

There were owls, but mostly ravens present. I handed him a live rattlesnake. It was the initiation to be bitten by the snake and transmute the poison. The rattler struck and bit him on his left arm between the wrist and his elbow. As the poison entered his bloodstream, he felt the pain and began to convulse.

He got up and left the cave to transmute the poison alone. The rest of us remained and prayed to great spirit and to his animal totems to help him to the other side. Some time had passed in prayer and meditation and when we emerged from the cave he was there in a white hide and a white owl feather was dangling on the left side of his hair. It was a sign he lived, transmuted the poison and transformed . . .

March 10, 1994 Dreamtime

At Michael's house on the back wall was a two-sided fireplace with polished brick. There were large pastel colored salt rocks, opaque not clear in the shape of huge potatoes sitting upright in copper wire holders. There were many candles too. Everything was situated around the hearth with low steps and the floor beyond that was a juice bar of sorts. We were all guests there and there was a man who directed us as to the way everything was done. We walked thru the bar and removed our clothes and took a shower. We were presented with a deep hot bath. There were many bath salts available for our pleasure, but the aqua blue stuck out in my mind. Then the guide had us in a boat and we paddled slowly out into the night. He said to keep our voices down as we came around one corner where there was a huge Pharaoh's head shaped structure because there were two Egyptians sleeping twenty feet under inside. We paddled onto another pool of water, bathed some more and after we were anointed with oils, there was incense smoking everywhere. I felt a soft pastel glow feeling inside when we bathed, but when we were outside it was cold and dark. As we left I asked the guide if we should tidy the bathroom and he said "no, purchase a robe and that will pay for the clean up." The robes were white.

My job became more demanding by bleeding into Saturdays. The frequency of energy in my life raised so dramatically, it began tearing me apart. Sundays were Thanasis' visiting day with Anastasia and Monday it was back to the soulless routine. Corporate America, neither fulfilling nor supporting my quality of life, suffocated me in its grip. After another year of trying to fit into their mold, I submitted my letter of resignation and turned my focus to raising my daughter effectively.

Falling back on my food industry experience, I took a job at a restaurant in Menlo Park working as a waitress at lunch so I could be present for Anastasia in the evening and weekends. Life simplified, fell back into balance, and I rented a room to a young man who worked for an insurance agency. Terrence had a great attitude, he was easy, clean and lived off of espresso and joy. He had a great sense of humor and was like big brother to Anastasia.

Our Los Altos home, adjacent to a curiously empty lot, inspired a massive vegetable and herb garden. The side entrance covered in ivy we called the "secret garden gate." I spent many joyful hours there teaching Anastasia how to plant seeds and how to loosen the soil around the roots and bless each plant before placing them in the ground. She was a natural at gardening, and like with everything else needed little direction.

We planted zinnias and sweet peas, Roman and German chamomile and countless other plants and herbs that blossomed bright colored flowers. I taught her the properties of each herb, and we enjoyed the blossoms of the nasturtiums and borage, tossing them in our salads adding vibrant color and nutrition. Tomatoes were so abundant that salsa parties were imminent by August's end. Indian summer slowed the ripening of the fruit, leaving us with the perfect variation of pink and green to make fried green tomatoes while watching the movie. Anastasia was so creative and clever, she made faerie forts beneath the trees and faeries themselves out of different blossoms and leaves, gathering shapes and textures from the unlimited resources of the garden. We created a divine space that yielded tons of joy and brought us home to our hearts.

Running into into Michael at a meditation, he showed me a flier announcing an upcoming talk with the man's picture on the front. Looking at the picture chuckling I said, "I know this guy" and agreed to join the group for the talk when Gary came through town. Gary was clear and concise, soft yet masculine and I found the vibration of truth in his words. My mind tried to understand, but it was not with the mind I understood.

The talk was followed by a meditation of a different and grounding type keeping us in our bodies and using golden light. Placing my name and address on a mailing list to receive fliers for future events, I hugged Gary and bid everyone goodnight. Dream time immediately picked up the slack.

June 03, 94 Dreamtime

Mick Jagger came to me in a dream and told me about a meditation technique.. He had certain stones for every chakra and demonstrated how to place them. He had records, 45's, that played music for the meditation. He said it was about using the will, I told him I didn't choose to use my will and the dream blurred into the sunrise.

Feeling called to higher work, and knowing what helped me so powerfully in my process, I took advantage of my time and resources taking evening courses at the Palo Alto School of Hypnotherapy to obtain my certification as a hypnotherapist. Inducting myself helped me retrieve soul memories beyond the work Michael and I had done.

June 05, 94 Dreamtime

Finding myself in many lives on the battlefield as a man, mostly wearing armour, I saw myself in France fighting like hell at the end of a long battle, beaten up and bloodied. One of the last men standing, I staggered over to a tree letting myself fall against it to prop me up. Sliding down the tree and resting at the roots, I looked around at all the carnage. My sword, barely glinting in the setting sun, slid from my grip. I wept and roared, releasing the last of the air remaining in my lungs. Feeling the loss of my comrades, knowing we had fought and solved nothing, I rested in pain as my breath became slight, my lungs filled with blood, and I died. It showed me in my last breath that nothing is ever accomplished in that kind of battle, and wars are fought through the egos of men, especially the holy ones.

Having a stressless routine, life settled into a colorful rhythm for the first time ever. I was excited and happy going to bed at night because the joy of tomorrow just couldn't come fast enough. My eyes opened every morning to the sound of the chirping birds, the glorious smell of coffee and the light of a new day.

Chapter VII

Angels and Demons

Angels and Demons

Working as a waiter, polishing the utensils to the music of Ottmar Leibert's *Barcelona Nights* brought the feeling that some sort of magic was stirring that I could not define. Undoubtedly knowing I was where I belonged, I showed up eager everyday. Wearing Grandma's wedding ring as a deterrent, no one asked any questions. I kept to myself, did my job and left.

There were many regular customers, and one in particular came in often to have lunch with people from his office. Introduced to me by my boss Areti one afternoon as Dubhlainn, he came in often with men his age, and younger associate lawyers of the firm of which he was a founding partner. He was beyond arrogant, and deciding I didn't like him, I did my best to ignore him. Four of them came in for lunch one day, closing the check at 2:30 p.m. and they were the only people left in the dining room, which was now closed to prepare for dinner service.

They went through cocktails, three bottles of wine, Gran Marnier, then coffee. Sensing my enthusiasm as I prepared to leave, Dubhlainn waved me down to open another tab so they could continue to drink. He looked at me, following my walk across the room with his Irish blue and gold eyes and my boss without question made me stay. After two more rounds, he paid the bill and they left, leaving me a reasonable tip but little time to run my errands before picking up Anastasia. The next day he came in to have lunch and I told my boss Areti that he was rude, I did not want to wait on him and she gave me a pass.

I observed Dubhlainn frequently saying inappropriate things to others that left them too speechless to offer a response, and was amazed that people said nothing. One day as I was hurrying around the floor during an unusually busy lunch, Dubhlainn walked in with an associate from the firm and the only table left was mine. Areti looked at me, and knowing what had to happen, I took two menus and walked them to my table.

Dubhlainn always thought he was funny. He spoke with a brogue and loved being Irish. I treated them with every professional courtesy, making it almost through the entire lunch without some kind of remark. Crumbing his table, Dubhlainn stopped me and asked if the diamond ring I was wearing was because I was married or was it a keepsake from my previous marriage. The word "prick" ran through my otherwise unoccupied mind and I turned, positioned both palms on the table with straight elbows, leaned in looking him straight in his eyes and replied "one day we will meet on equal ground, and then I will be sure to tell you." His dumbfounded lunch guest could not believe his ears . . . Dubhlainn did not respond beyond a piercing look back. Taking the completed check from my apron, I placed it flippantly on his table and walked away.

Areti answered the phone while I was finishing up my cash-out at the end of my shift and called me to the phone. It was Dubhlainn asking to speak with me she said, shrugging her shoulders and handing me the phone. "First, he said, I want to know why you threatened me; second, if you found my glasses that I believe I left on the table?" Responding I said, "I was as threatening as you were rude" and that if he wished to discuss things further we should agree to meet in the parking lot when he came to pick up his glasses. Pressing the button to hold, I checked the table for his glasses. Finding nothing, I received the distinct impression he knew there was nothing there. He thanked me for my effort when I told him I did not find them and we concluded our conversation by saying we would meet another time.

He was not so obnoxious after that phone call and we both settled down, but he knew how to ruffle my feathers and he liked that. Dubhlainn made the point of giving me his card identifying himself, and told me to call so we could meet for coffee after I told him I didn't drink.

Not giving it another thought, I focused on the excitement of buying our Star Trek The Next Generation costumes that Anastasia and I would wear to the convention in San Jose, and about what to prepare for the Montessori potluck on Halloween night. Construction paper bats and pumpkins hung about three feet up on the fridge and pumpkin carving became our joy.

Holiday parties were keeping us busy at work and preparations for Thanksgiving and the enthusiasm of the children kept the holiday mood elevated. Paper hand turkeys and overflowing cornucopias soon replaced the pumpkins and bats on the fridge, and life felt more like the party I knew it to be.

Saturdays and Sundays we often drove to Half Moon Bay to eat breakfast at the Main Street Grill, watching Vasilli flip blueberry pancakes and scramble our eggs while singing to the tunes of the old juke box. Then as the fog above dispersed and rolled out to sea we drove down the pumpkin dotted coastline to San Gregorio and back through the hills of La Honda and the redwood forest of Woodside, landing us back in the sunshine saturated valley. Harvest time was at its end and the garden received some last of the season attention as we cut back the herbs, pulled out the last of the tomatoes and turned the ground for the winter.

Dubhlainn, almost three decades years my senior, was very conservative and married longer than I had been alive. I expected nothing more than to straighten him out, and I called. We agreed to meet day after Thanksgiving, at the British Bankers Club in Menlo Park. The BBC was an amazing place. It boasted two authentic Egyptian statues that stood ceiling to floor facing each other across the room. The ceilings were at least forty feet high, all dark wood with a circular velvet sitting bench in the center of the room surrounded by small elegant dark wood tables, old lamps and upstairs was a cigar smoking loft with card tables. There were countless paintings of distinguished men, original stained glass lamp shades, and a long beautiful old onyx bar.

I rushed in the entrance coming straight over from the gym, feeling as though I walked into a different time reminiscent of a fabulous men's club somewhere in London. My tennis shoes, black spandex pants and a sweatshirt kept me somewhat in real time as he stood up halfway from the seat of his chair to greet me before I sat down across our small wooden table.

He was a couple of glasses of wine down and offered me one but I asked for coffee instead. Reiterating that I did not drink he replied "oh no, not one of those." Ignoring his comment, I leaned back in my chair and sipped my coffee. I thought it peculiar that he was out Friday, the day after Thanksgiving, knowing he was married with a family yet in no hurry to leave.

Dubhlainn asked me if I wanted something to eat and I thankfully declined. He ordered something for himself and taking his wine glass by the stem he leaned forward, looked at me and said "you know you have great eyes." Trying to make sense of his advance, I focused to keep the conversation on point. He was very charming. We exchanged some superficial information about our lives and interests. I shared my interest in all things metaphysical and spiritual and the hypnotherapy course I was beginning. As he began to share his love for golf and travel, his energy field was knocking me over and I had to block what he was saying to "shield" myself. After a while, his lips moved without producing an audible sound, and I squirmed a little not quite sure what I should do next.

He asked how my holiday was and what my plans were for the weekend. Commenting vaguely in reference to having a happy Thanksgiving, I mentioned my birthday was over the weekend. I cut the conversation short while reaching for my handbag, letting him know I was on my way to pick up my daughter and thanked him for the coffee.

Dubhlainn extended his arm up, twisting his hand to alert the waiter for the check, and said he would walk me to my car. Our cars were parked in the garage below the street and we descended the stairs. I turned, unlocked my car and turned back to thank him when he took his shot at a wet kiss. I declined by turning my cheek to him and thanked him again. I sank into my seat, closed the door and waved goodbye as I left the garage.

Sunday, I woke with enthusiasm on my birthday and opened the front door to fetch the paper. Much to my surprise there was an arrangement of flowers on the second step. I picked them up, admired their beauty, and opened the card that accompanied them reading, "Happy

Birthday," Dubhlainn. I looked around, but no one was there. . .

"How did he find out where I live?" I thought, wondering if he followed me home from the restaurant.

Monday morning began like normal driving Anastasia to Montessori at 7:30 a.m.. My mind drifted recalling what had transpired at the BBC and the flowers, finally having time alone to process my feelings. Continuing in the silence of my morning routine, at 9:00 o'clock a knock at my door took me from the serenity of my feeling bubble into the narrow focus of my mind wondering who? What? Opening the front door, Dubhlainn stood on the other side bearing another arrangement of flowers. Asking him what he was doing, I invited him in out of the cold not feeling threatened, only curious as to why he felt so familiar to me and why he was so persistent.

Offering him a cup of coffee brought me to know he drank tea and I rifled through the cupboard to find some. Sitting on opposite ends of the couch, I asked him questions about himself and studied his handsome face, his salt and pepper wavy hair parted on the side and distinctive blue eyes. Taken in by the sound of his voice, my walls were softening and I let myself feel his energy. After a few minutes I began laughing, placing my hand in front of my mouth, apologizing for the interruption of his midstream sentence. I shared with him that I was watching his clothes turn from a suit and tie into the black and white garb of a Catholic priest, that it caught me off guard, and that somehow it suited him. Dubhlainn found that quite interesting, continuing that he had been in the seminary for three years in Ireland but left because he knew he could not keep the vow of celibacy. Time passed quickly in our conversation and I asked him to leave so I could get ready for work.

His energy anchored a presence in my home that morning that revealed itself almost immediately. Manifesting as two beings wearing black hooded robes with no faces, they always appeared together around the corners, always at a distance but I sensed them strongly, and saw them clearly. Never resisting but rather observing the energy, I let it be and waited to discover their meaning.

Tea in the morning became frequent and made for intriguing conversation, adding a bit of wind to my sails. After a few weeks the energy built and one morning it gave way and we found ourselves surrendering to our desire, and once engaged we were hooked.

All kinds of vibrations based in realities of the past drew us to each other for this experience and the energy picked up momentum. The demons that had not made an appearance for a almost three years popped up to remind me they had never really left. Our coupling flooded me with feelings, visions and dreams from lives spattered along our timeline. I gained great insight to the issues yet unintegrated and the pain and healing that was about to begin.

I cleared his energy from my body after each physical engagement after seeing what was all around him, but it was not enough. The dark presence of his hooded buddies got more intense, and in resonance attached themselves to my aura. All I knew in life and spiritually to that point was the separation of "good and evil," and saw all of what he revealed as his and not mine, as something definitely outside of myself until I dug a little deeper.

Journal Entry / Realtime

Regressing myself in meditation I touched on a lifetime in Europe where he was a priest, he molested me as a girl from age seven until I was well into my twenties. I observed us in the sacristy as he sat in a chair dressed from the

121

waist up and I sat naked facing him on his lap. He was gentle, kind and through my youth I believed he loved me. In the beginning it was playful and exciting, it was ours and only ours, he possessed my innocence, my soul, and as I got older he felt more threatening. He visited my parents at my home and when I would get back from school, he would be there chatting with them in the kitchen. I felt scared and intimidated not expecting to see him. His energy smothered me, he was everywhere, his look, the tone of his voice, kept me in check. His shame created my shame and as I became a woman he remained my only lover. At the end of our time together I got pregnant and when I consulted him he walked away. I went to the rectory. He ordered me to leave and refused to discuss it with me. In that moment the curtain dropped for the first time and I could see I had been lied to and there was no love. I meant nothing to him.

This cellular memory showed me the vulnerability of a child, how easily they are led, formed and beguiled. It showed me the "nicest" people are most often the worst and the word jumbled up spells "incest," revealing the secret levels of manipulation and control.

My dreams of Mick were peaking as I was getting to know my inner darkness and I was given many interesting looks into the windows of my soul.

January 10, 1994 Dreamtime

I dreamed that Dubhlainn and I bought a house in England. I was concerned about the lack of fresh fruit for me to eat. Everything felt so old and musty. I went to Mick Jagger's house and Jerry was really pissed off. She always thought she could control Mick, but she of course was

*shocked when she realized she couldn't. I wanted
to see him so badly but he locked himself into an
obscure part of his house where no one else was
allowed. One of his daughters had showed Jerry
the door one time and where the key was. Jerry
led me to the door and told me Mick had told her
that she would never have to go in there. She
unlocked and opened the door for me, then left.
The full sized door opened to reveal a small
crawl space that led to a laundry room. The
crawl space was full of old laundry. I
remembered knowing somehow that he never
washed any of his clothes. He only wore his
clothes once throwing the dirty ones on the floor
to be eventually discarded. I was wearing my
long floor length black brocade fitted coat with
poodle fur collar and cuffs that I affectionately
referred to as my "Mick coat" and I crawled
hands and knees through his clothes and mess to
the door. A light was on and I stood up. The room
was absolutely crammed with stuff. And there I
saw Mick, dancing around smearing blood on his
face while making faces in the mirror as if he
were practicing for a show. He saw me there and
got a little bit upset. He called to have me taken
away by two old men, butlers. When Mick
grabbed my arm, he stopped and by my energy
he recognized me. He sent the men away and
hugged me. He started to cry as we embraced. I
kept saying over and over that I just wanted to
make sure he was ok. . . . The timing seemed
interesting this being someone I had no logical
reason to be dreaming about, but he continued to
occupy my dream time.*

My meditations were not as long as before Dubhlainn was
taking up more of my time, coming by a few mornings

each week so my energy was now divided to include another person and his entourage. My efforts to align with my soul were being overshadowed by the darkness that vied for my attention and I felt the need to get away and gain clarity.

Trying to get some space, I drove to Half Moon Bay and got a room for Anastasia and myself at the Half Moon Bay Links resort where we watched television, ate candy from the mini fridge, swam around the hot tub, treated ourselves to dinner out and relaxed. When I went to check out, our bill had been paid, Dubhlainn had paid our bill. . . which meant he was somewhere nearby on the coast.

Out of nowhere, Gary called asking me how I was doing and if we could have lunch while he was passing through town. He told me that I was being cloaked by Dubhlainn's energy, and I knew exactly what he was saying. After my conversation with Gary, I told Dubhlainn that I was cutting the relationship off. I had come too far and life was better than I had ever known it and I was not sacrificing it for anything.

He was married, he had other resources and he needed to leave me out of that circle. Anastasia did not know Dubhlainn existed and I kept it that way for obvious reasons. Determined to remain aligned with my path, I was pulling material together for classes, offering channeled readings, seeing a couple of clients for hypnotherapy and handwriting consultations and wanting to turn it into something more.

The night following my decision to let Dubhlainn go, I had another powerful dream.

February 13, 2004 Dreamtime

I had a dream that Dubhlainn and I were with someone he considered an authority figure like a cult leader and another "brother" . They were engaged in a ritual . I was lying on an altar, arms held firmly in place. Dubhlainn was watching on the right while another brother stood watching from the left. The "leader" said to the guy on the left "go get the clothes." Before he returned the leader asked me "do you prefer black, peach or white?" I said "I would like white and "he said "well we don't have white" and he handed me a black dress and said "you will be seen wearing this, or you will wear it on your cheek" displaying an extra large safety pin intended as the fastener.

"One does not become enlightened by imaging figures of light, but by making the darkness conscious"

- Dr. Carl Gustav Jung

The two beings in that dream felt like the two that had taken up residence in my home since Dubhlainn came on the scene. Dubhlainn kept his own hours as executive administrator for his law firm after practicing law for many years as a partner. I did not understand how he managed it all, including his wife Deidre who never seemed to be a problem.

My spiritual life kept moving forward, and Gary invited me for an afternoon to have lunch at a house high on a hill in the South Bay with his family. The house was Mediterranean style with large clay vessels overflowing with flowers, a pool and terra cotta tiled roofs. It was a beautiful and peaceful place.

Oh ewige Nacht wann wirst du verschwinden? Wann wird das Licht zu finden meine Augen? (Oh eternal night when will you disappear? When will the light find my eyes?)

- Tamino in The Magic Flute, W. A. Mozart

Before lunch I had a reading with Gary. I explained that even though I had accomplished all of this therapy and felt better in many ways, I still had a black cloud over my head that I couldn't seem to shake. His reading was extremely accurate, speaking of energy within me and pulling things out of my aura that were deep and relevant. He saw things about my childhood he could have not have heard anywhere and offered a metaphysical antidote using energy that I could integrate over time.

While viewing my aura he mentioned the white light source went around my soul star directly into my crown. He encouraged a switch in meditations and gave me a tape using the tool of grounding and golden light. Gary further explained that the beings I channeled in my sessions were regulating the information imparted to me, wanting me to realize that the information I was continually seeking outside of myself was within me. I left the reading touched and altered, having sat in his aura for an hour while he spoke the truth of his message which resonated with me so deeply.

Jennifer, Gary's wife made spaghetti and salad for lunch that we shared with their adorable baby boy just under a year old, happily eating his pasta in his high chair next to us at the table. Jennifer was elegant and Venusian with her facial bone structure strong but soft, her energy feminine and light filled. She wore her blonde hair twisted up in a clip, knew the depth of her beauty and was not the least bit conceited. It was love at first sight for all of us in the purest sense of the word and we chatted, finishing lunch, and I made my way back to the valley.

Gary's words streamed through my consciousness in the weeks that followed, yet I had huge resistance at the thought of using his meditation tape. Queuing it on my stereo I hissed at it more than once walking through the living room to the kitchen. This was one of those rare instances when truth struck so deeply that I could not ignore it, and knew I HAD to DO it period. Giving up all I knew to date in order to do something completely different essentially from the ground up, my ego had to rumble before surrendering.

My meditation now was to begin at the base of the spine rather than the top of my head and thinking about that for the first time, it made sense to begin at the first chakra not the seventh. Gary spoke of my mental clarity, but mentioned that my unintegrated emotions were lying dormant beneath my solar plexus in the dark and that was why my life did not completely reflect the truth of my knowing. This was true in many ways, so I listened. He went on to say that the guilt I embodied was immense and to my core, and that at times I felt guilty for being alive. Jumping to my own defense immediately and halfway glaring at him, I said "I don't do guilt, I can justify everything I have ever done"! The vibration of his compassionate words generated a crack in my armor that I tried to conceal as tears bubbled to the surface.

Gary told me that I ran my masculine energy making the conscious decision to wall myself off from my feelings all those years before, and my healing processes to date had been mental or emotional. He encouraged me to rediscover the gifts and beauty of the feminine feeling again. Gary also told me that grounding my energy would give me the ability to manifest my projects and that the sacral chakra of creative power united with the throat chakra of creative expression was the way to the creation of all creations. Gary explained that the golden light is the appropriate light in this dimension for meditation because it lives within all levels of self. This tool allowed me to seep beneath the solar plexus and into the denser vibrations of my emotions where I would unearth all that was hidden creating the lower experience of my reality.

If someone wants to dig up dirt, all they need is a shovel.

- Siobhan Nicolaou, The Sword of Truth

Feeling more than hearing what he said, I wanted to experience what he was saying as part of my reality before I accepted it as truth for me. As Gary suggested I re-aligned the white light source to go through the golden light soul star then into the top of my head. It was a very new experience for me and I did it until the white light finally surrendered.

Meditating daily using his tape was different training my mind into silence through grounding. My meditations at first were purely a mental projection of the images following the guidance of the tape. It took a solid eight months before I had a breakthrough, and then I began to feel the light move within me.

The meditation gave me deeper insight and expanded my awareness the more I used it. I was thrilled to have such and adept teacher able to guide me through each phase of this awakening. I checked in with Gary for a reading about every eight weeks. He would talk to me about my progress, how the light was flowing nicely and encouraged me to stay with it. My roots of light grounding me from the base of my spine were small and shallow, and he said to expand them, deepen them and spoke to me of the subtleties and nuances so I learned to become aware of my energy and how to be present in my experience.

The golden light brought up things almost immediately, beginning with my head manifesting sinus infections that would go away with the help of antibiotics, then come back again. Gary looked at my aura explaining I had a dark blue egg shaped energy in my third eye. He said the blue egg was an energy ready to release and that I simply needed to forgive myself. It was related to lifetimes as a shaman and my misuse of my abilities and my awareness of it. Removing the egg in meditation, I indeed felt my aura "plump" as he said I would, accepting the light of my gifts and letting go of the guilt associated with their misuse. Once I filled the gap with the golden light, my sinus infection cleared and never came back.

Practicing grounding meditations, I became much more creatively productive and rooted in myself. Gary shared with me the next level which is the process of transmuting the denser energies in the emotional and physical bodies back into the light of the soul. I discovered how to get the mind to serve me instead of work against me and truly began to transform my life. My saving grace each day was taking the time to practice staying grounded beyond meditating and transmuting my emotions.

"If you want to know the secrets of the universe, think of it as energy, frequency and vibration."

- Nikola Tesla

Tumbling all the way down the rabbit hole of my soul's history, unlocked the awareness of what I was truly seeking.

The most valuable soil is derived from the richest of composts, and the process of turning rotting garbage into gold requires the courage to pick up the shovel with the strength and stomach to turn it over again and again.

- Siobhan Nicolaou, The Sword of Truth

The archeologist I always wanted to be came to life as I dug through the muckiest layers of parallel lives showing me the parts of myself responsible for the creation of my life I experienced as shadow. At times it made me physically ill, and the darkest hours of soul searching took me to the bottom of what seemed an endless pit, but my desire to be free kept me at the depths stripping me raw, my wounds torn open, painfully cold and covered in dirt.

It was hard to face the parts of me that loved to be feared and worshipped by the many who placed my ego high upon the pedestal, and I was often the best of the worst. At times it was hard to imagine any light within the darkness, but the deepest part of my being was steadfast, knowing light was within it somewhere.

Retrieving countless lifetimes played in extreme darkness, some in a pit and others on the highest levels of the spiritual ego's blinding light, I learned how love is absent on both sides of the same coin. From an indulgent Pope to a black magician in England, an interesting cast of characters made their way to the stage.

April 03, 1994 Dreamtime

Weighted by layers of aggrandizing vestments, large rings and hat designed to reinforce the illusion of separation between the church and the people, I stood under the weight of it all. Peering from a small window over the ignorant masses, I prepared for my appearance praying for the correct words and at the same time the redemption of my soul.

Mick Jagger's soul who seems to have wizard-like qualities matching mine, was drawn to me in resonance. The seemingly unforgivable parts of my soul's past where we shared this dance showed up in my dreamtime. I dreamed of Mick sporadically until 2005.

April 10, 1994 Dreamtime

I saw myself as a woman in a black hooded cape that swelled in the breeze as I swiftly made my way up to the sanctuary where we often gathered. A place encircled in the undulating green hills of what felt like England. I placed my infant son on the gray stone altar and drove a knife through his chest and waited to feel the surge of power and new abilities I was promised by the grand master (the soul of Mick) for sacrificing his life. Nothing happened, and in awakening to the fact that nothing was going to happen, I became overwrought with anger and expressed my feelings of betrayal and disbelief. When my denial broke, my guilt became so heavy and unbearable that I took my own life by drinking poison.

Experiencing the deep feelings of the overblown ego's madness hungry for power at any cost left a gaping hole in my heart from the conscious awareness of committing such a heinous act. Until it was integrated, I had always been neurotic about not keeping any kind of poison in the kitchen under the sink. The thought of poisons around food triggered a subconscious feeling of fear and foreboding of an agonizingly painful death. When I came to know why, it fell away and was never an issue again.

Reclaiming the light within each shard of darkness, I integrated the conscious awareness of the deed itself. Like a modern day sin eater, I felt the amount of responsibility it takes to possess the whole of knowing. Deciphering the subtleties and nuances of the consciousness of evil allowed me to see / feel the truth behind all my past, present and future intentions. Along with greater levels of integrity in my thoughts, words and actions came the realization of the amount of awareness, brutal honesty and self examination required to work for God on the highest levels of service.

Forgiveness of the most separate and murderous self enabled me to completely let go of the judgements I had accumulated regarding Antigone. No longer seeing her as evil incarnate in how I believed she "killed" her own children more subtlety to gain control over their lives. Tuning in to her in meditation, she stepped forth and I spoke to her with my heart finally able to forgive her for everything she put me through. Antigone was one of the largest reflections of the part I deemed most unworthy of love, and our dance was a huge gift in the light I claimed on the inside of that darkness and the other side of my own pain. For the first time compassion filled my heart with her in the center as I now had full knowledge of the levels of her personal pain in the depths of my own madness.

Life, determined to match my willingness to "leave no stone unturned," began heating things up between Dubhlainn and me. He would not go in to work until late morning sometimes leaving the house as I ran off to work myself. I asked him to make some important changes so our relationship could be healthier and he began to work on himself, taking some transformative steps in his spiritual evolution. We also had dinner out quite often and as I witnessed the changes in him that were necessary for us to move forward, I decided it was time to introduce him to Anastasia. Dubhlainn was quickly impressed with her ability to learn things so quickly and thoroughly, and his sense of humor and easy going nature went over very well with her. The more I grounded and ran golden light, the more my reflections changed as my vibration increased. Dubhlainn drew closer to me to enhance my joy while not being responsible for it, and life opened up even more.

My roommate Terrence moved out to live with his girlfriend after her graduation from college and my desire to generate more income got me looking around for a better job. I took a job at the most unique place in the redwoods between the valley and the ocean. It was the eccentric owners creative space and he put everything he had into making it the most fun restaurant anywhere. Seamus was tall around 6 ft six inches tall and the most interesting person I had yet met.

Seamus was a man balls to bones with a masculine ruggedness reminding me of the dirt and marble part of my soul I pocketed at the forum in Rome. Knowledgeable about so many things, he was wired in a way that few are and it was remarkable talking to him and comparable to a mild trip on psilocybin. Jumping on board the team at the restaurant was fun, intense and lucrative. I met some very interesting and wonderful people and I oozed with creative juices just being in that space.

At the restaurant everyone was greeted by a larger than human sized statue of liberty holding a huge overflowing ice cream sundae for the torch. The children made a beeline to the floor under the ledge by the front window. Huge rubber and resin sea turtles, lizards, iguanas, Komodo dragons, and other reptilians waited to be grabbed and taken over to the tables. Rare treasures and nonsense from all of his adventures hung on the walls ceiling to floor and he loved nothing more than being surrounded by the unlimited expressions of himself.

He wired a buffalo head that was mounted on the wall behind the bar so its eyes, ears and mouth moved. Seamus spoke to the children from a tiny remote microphone he kept in his front pocket. Knowing all of their names, he rounded the corner as the children climbed onto the barstools balancing on their knees to get face time with the buffalo head affectionately known as "Buck." The

133

innocence in the questions and the widening wonder in their eyes brought a sweetness to the hearts of the children. The magic of Buck was real, creating a memory much like Santa Claus for Anastasia which faded over time as she grew, but remains a joyful memory forever.

Harvest by Neil Young filtered through my empty head as I whirled in and out of my station. The weekends were insane with hundreds of breakfast guests and serious bicyclists that gathered in the redwoods to eat before dispersing to partake in the beauty of coastal northern California. Hot Jeremiah's Pick coffee flowed endlessly from our vessels with sausages and silver dollar pancakes bursting out the kitchen doors. Milk shakes and Seamus fizzes filled the soda-parlor styled glassware and met with smiles spanning ear to ear almost as wide and tall as the life sized Elvis painted on black velvet hanging on the back wall. I was loving my new job and had a connection with Seamus that further opened the pipeline to my soul.

Dubhlainn was happy I got a better job and drove out for lunch from the office to eat the clam chowder. Things were coming together nicely and life was flowing well for everyone. In a morning of blissful sharing with Dubhlainn, "I love you" overflowed from my lips, breaking the cardinal rule when seeing a married man. He said nothing in response, kissed me on my forehead, straightened his suit, adjusted his neck tie and said goodbye as he left to go to the office.

The air left my lungs, my stomach shrank with anxiety wondering if what I said was a deal breaker. We were so enmeshed I felt I could not bear his rejection. Life seemed strange and empty in the three days he did not reach out or come by the house. When he finally came by all felt fine, but with no good morning kiss I did not know what to expect. Preparing his tea, I carried it into the living room, holding my thoughts, words and feelings in as tight as I gripped the handles of the silver tray.

Dubhlainn put his arm around me, letting me know he knew the risk I took and produced a small black velvet box from his pocket handing it to me with a smile. My eyes welled as my mouth dropped open to find a channel set diamond band that sparkled in the ambiance of the dimmed living room lights. I slipped it on, thanked him excitedly and never took it off.

Dubhlainn found himself staying late in the evening after work, and I asked him how Deirdre felt about all of it, having wondered about what he said to his wife. He made it plain he wasn't going to tell her but if somehow he got caught he would come clean. Those fateful words would soon catch up with him as the three of us went to the Main Street Grill for breakfast one magnificent Saturday morning. Anastasia was eye deep in fresh raspberries, real maple syrup, and fluffy french toast dusted with confectioners sugar all about the time three young women walked in and stared past our table. They stopped and settled in a booth two rows down and directly behind us. Aware of the astonishment that appeared on their faces, I asked Dubhlainn what that was all about. The three young women were the best friends of his daughter; they all lived in the same area up the coast and went to college together. The proverbial cat was out of the bag and it was a matter of days before hell came down around his ears. He was not one to focus on the drama and what transpired between them over the following weeks, I will never know.

We went out and bought our Louis XVI bedroom set and I prepared our room for its arrival. When we went to his house to pick up his clothing we were surprised by a king-sized flat sheet draped over his side of his massive walk-in closet with a message written on it in black indelible ink that said R.I.P. Dubhlainn. To make Dubhlainn feel more at home, I let down my resistance and agreed to hang his father's Papal award encased in glass bestowed upon him by Pope Pius the XII on the wall next to my side of the bed.

January 2005 Dreamtime

That night I dreamed a Pope and I had sex while he wore a white and gold vestment with the award pinned on it to his right. I watched the pin slap back and forth with every deliberate thrust into my loins, but I never saw his face.

As easy as he seemed to take it all, that Catholic thing called guilt rose to the surface to smack him in his face. He was not the man most people thought he was, while others on the inside who had witnessed his philandering and arrogance for decades were happy to see it catch up with him.

Dubhlainn was coming clean and felt really good about it, but could not face the people at the church or the country club where he had been a member for almost thirty years. Many events at the club were booked prior to the revelation of his indiscretion, and as Deirdre was also a member, he would not bring me to any of them whether she attended or not. Not able to withstand the firestorm of judgments he created, he put any chance of a social life for us in his realm on the back burner, turned it on simmer and reduced me to a bittersweet syrup of "I don't think so."

Dubhlainn brought so much expansion to my heart, but reserved a conditional place within his. Within the confines of how I was able to express myself in Dubhlainn's life, Seamus was a healthy distraction from the intensity of my internal work and my issues surrounding the reflections of Dubhlainn.

Seamus, stripping down in a running phase at this particular point in his life, invited me to join him before day break to run the "Dish," a piece of property running about four miles between foothill expressway and the 280 owned by Stanford university that has a functioning radio telescope, and a couple of under ground labs. The hills steepen gradually and by the time you get to the highest point, you overlook the peninsula all the way south past the NASA hanger at Lockheed. On a clear morning you can see the buildings jutting out from the city into the San Francisco Bay.

We always met in the parking lot of a Stanford frat house shaded by giant eucalyptus. The first cool breath from the aroma of the trees was exhilarating as we stretched a bit before hitting the trail. Seamus was brilliant and loved to talk. He pondered many things like the big bang theory, the price of pickles in Poughkeepsie, the nature of the atom and other thought provoking topics mostly about himself.

The first time he dragged me out there, looking up the first hill I wondered how the hell I could do it. He assured me it would get easier and that I had to get control of two things, my attitude, and my air, because it burned like a mother for a while as my lungs opened up and he didn't want to hear any complaining.

Seamus moved with lighter strides, being taller than the height of a newborn giraffe, his naturally larger steps equaling two and one half of mine. Keeping up was challenging as he trotted and I jogged to stay up to speed. My steps were initially heavy and my energy pulled into the ground the first week I ran with him. He was my centurion, stretching me physically way beyond my feminine parameters. Seamus kept me in tow with his enormous energy, interesting perceptions and stories of his many hilarious adventures.

Home from running by 7AM, with Dubhlainn and Anastasia midway thru tea and toast, I would shower and drive her to school. Dubhlainn and Anastasia got along fabulously and he never had a problem with the morning routine if I wasn't around. He addressed Anastasia as "her ladyship," and impressed upon her even more than I the importance of good social graces. Dubhlainn and I were very good at the mundane things in life, the routine day to day accomplishing much in this way. He was a rock for me and I was whole-heartedly wanting to be engaged in his life, but he kept me out of his social loop for well over a year. Even though my Spirit was keeping me out of it for reasons at that time were beyond my grasp, I was pissed off that he still had two different lives and I was trying to feel right about my loyalty divided into fourths.

Dubhlainn did everything but shake Seamus' hand in gratitude for keeping me occupied while he tried to come to terms with his own dealings. He was happy we got on so well and enjoyed things together that Dubhlainn and I could not. Seamus and I shared the love of anchovies, vegetables, dirt and sitting in fig trees stuffing our faces. We also laughed while dropping by friends' houses in the redwoods unannounced for tea and the chance to hold a baby hedgehog.

In all of my fun with Seamus, the thought of the golf club began losing interest for me, and admitting how boring it would actually be I abandoned all desire to share it with Dubhlainn.

I continued to meet Seamus at 5:30 a.m. quickly building my strength to master that three and one half mile loop. I loved running up in those beautiful hills dotted with oak trees some long into their hundredth year. We ran in the rain, fog and sunshine. He was no sissy and you could not be a sissy and run anywhere with him. The dish was home to many wild creatures and we saw them nearly every time we were there. All the nocturnals would be heading home about the time we pounded dirt up the trail. Various types of owls flew low above our heads on the way back to their trees and burrows, while in the early fall, large soft hairy tarantulas moved gracefully into the grass concluding a long night's hunt.

Hawks and Golden Eagles soared above us, with the sound of the meadow larks piercing the dispersing fog like the first rays of the morning sun. Coyotes were common place and the discovery of a whole deer's leg stripped of flesh to the knee joint told me there was something bigger than that roaming the hills, but I never thought about it and never once laid eyes on a mountain lion.

We caffeinated at the local Peet's or Tressider Hall bringing an end to our wake-up time that got us ready for the rest of our day. When the dish ceased to be a challenge, we converged before dawn at the trail head of Wunderlich at the Folger estate equestrian stable. The loop we ran was five miles through the redwoods up switchbacks and hills, both up and down with a small flat stretch through a meadow. The "forest dirt was much softer and the energetic embrace of the colossal redwood trees added several dimensions to my experience. We ran that trail faithfully and got so good at it, Seamus started setting his watch and carving our best times on the post at the bottom of the hill. Our best time ever was forty-nine minutes ten seconds. The trail grounded me more, cleared my head and helped with the constant integration of my internal world which made for greater stability, and a stronger mind and body.

Seamus kept raising my physical bar and we hiked the Pinnacles an entire day without a map or a trail guide. He hiked me all through the hills in the blazing heat while he identified all the various plants. We rolled around in the dirt and crawled over boulders. In Bear Gulch cave we decided to go up and out the top the hard way through an extremely narrow passage to the sunshine we knew was some where on the other side. It was dark, we had no flashlight and water poured down on us as we made our way up one behind the other and I emerged a better man than I had entered.

Differing in opinions and notions on most subjects, Seamus called me crazy for entertaining the thought that our souls were not from this world, and that I felt mine was not from the earth at all, but rather the stars. He taught me many things and the most important was "to thine own self be true." It was a feeling reminiscent of years past, but with a different meaning than before. He followed his spirit without hesitation, not bound by marriage vows or other man-made rules that keep a soul suppressed. The word "sublimation" made its way into my vocabulary through Seamus and he awakened me to the truth that sexual energy and creative energy are the same thing. As much as I hate to admit it, "tension is good" as John D. Spooner puts it; creativity fuels the fire and feeds our souls. Seamus was loyal to himself above all others and told me not to forget to take the plate after I finished eating the cake. He created his world from the dust and traveled this one several times. His undying loyalty to the depths of his innermost joy taught me the value of doing the same. There was something good I felt about this, yet in my subconscious, the word "selfish" was still synonymous with guilt and betrayal.

The time had come for me to pull my life in one solid direction, and I consulted my heart. I loved Dubhlainn and decided to reel myself in and focus on us and to bring it all together. Cutting off my hair, I focused on my spiritual practice, and my home. Giving notice to Seamus, knowing it was the right thing to do, I spent my early mornings running the dish by myself, creating a brochure and finding another part- time job.

Dubhlainn, having been in the seminary for three years, knew the discipline required for prayer and contemplation. He understood my need for solitude and silence in ways few can understand unless they have devoted their lives in some way to the path of the priest. Anastasia and he had a great time out playing when I required quiet alone time at home. They would take the cars to the car wash down the road, enjoying complimentary refreshments while the car made its way for twenty minutes thru the various cleaning phases. They filled their red and white striped paper bags with popcorn and sipped cold lemonade, sitting under an umbrellaed table near the palm trees. They often went shopping afterward to buy me a couple hours of much appreciated solitude.

Dubhlainn often spoke of how I was always in my own world, but that was partly because I did not want to be completely rooted in his. He sang a few songs around the house, but the line "welcome to my world" was the one that stood out, and the one I walked away from every time. He admired my spirit and he loved to play in my fire, it fueled him, gave him energy and became a source for him rather than the ignition that sparked his own. Everything began to flow so much better; and he did wonderfully given the consciousness of the generation from which he was born. My inner work was non-stop and we both benefited so much from my love's integration, yet he somewhat resented me for having the strength to embrace the demons he did not have the courage face.

Gary reminded me that no matter how I felt, it was already there and Dubhlainn was merely a refection. He constantly turned me inward to find the energy where it originated and reminded me to do the integration work. The trickiest thing was not blaming Dubhlainn and remembering not to project my unintegrated perception.

The brain drain of my thoughtless "morning pages" helped purge my negative thoughts about the subject, and Gary always encouraged me to take the higher road and not give up.

The division between me, myself and I got bigger in reflection at times. The results I witnessed by doing the work to love myself kindled my desire to experience wholeness, not just know it in my mind. Indeed I began seeing the characters in life as an opportunity for personal growth and how everything DID begin and end with me and how I had the power to change any situation through the process of loving myself more. Gathering my strength and confidence I continued trusting that more would be revealed.

Immersing myself in gourmet cooking catering to Dubhlainn's more sophisticated European palate, Draeger's market became part of my weekly ritual and *Bon Appetit* magazine my favorite muse. Over the top cream and butter, savory and sweet crusts, Napoleons, salmon and rich sauces, pastas and Wellingtons all paired with perfect wines became a regularity I truly enjoyed.

In our indulgences I gained around twenty pounds, and my health started to show signs of resistance. I began enjoying wine again though it was never good for me to drink, especially in excess and he knew that. He never sought to control what was not good for me, only the things that were. When I did drink too much, at the bottom of every glass I found a young girl trying to find a way out. Bladder infections manifested again and it was an inner battle on all fronts.

Familiarizing myself more with the subtleties of transmuting emotions within my auric field, every conceivable level of anger competed for center stage. Fear and guilt arose initially, wanting to protect me from the magnitude of my inner child's rage. By loving her enough to move through the fear, she felt safe enough to unleash holy hell, and she did.

Those who believe wholeness comes solely by way of mind will know only half of the truth.

- Siobhan Nicolaou, The Sword of Truth

Each time I went deep inside the emotional body, my child needed to express some level of anger and in my experiences I came to define them all through my feelings. Becoming expert in taking myself through the process, I felt confident and victorious, and made a list of all I could remember from childhood. Sitting for hours, I located where within I was holding the energy, and transmuted layer after layer. The suppressed child finally trusted my loving attention and in my unedited inner expression of her true feelings, I began experiencing liberation from the bondage.

Reflections of perverse darkness along with beauty, abundance and love revealed the content of my inner world. Gary patiently encouraged me to continue with the process and have faith that one day I would become "one" instead of one or the other.

Bladder infections were constant for a while rotating four different doctors and an emergency clinic to get them to give me prescriptions to kill the symptoms. My primary care physician was so freaked out he wanted to test to see if I had cancer because he could not explain the problem. When I assured him it was emotionally based and the inner expression of anger at its most outrageous levels, he scratched his head more than twice and wrote me my prescriptions. My mother told me it was all the coffee I consumed, I told her that was funny, because every time I went inside to heal my rage, I found her, not a coffee bean!

It was not until I transmuted the energy within me enough that the bladder infections finally stopped. Over this two year period it was my new challenge to dive repeatedly into my shadowy self and transmute the child back into the light, and not focus on the vibration of the remaining shadow when she came up for air outside of session. Morning sessions were filled with inner work, and the depths of the pain was so great at times it took my breath away. I retreated often into my garden where everything reflected the colorful life force beginning to vibrate more within me. In states of a deep surrender, my heart broke open and poured with gratitude, experiencing the agony and the ecstasy as I moved more completely through the transformation of my pain.

The energy preceding the birth of Silicon Valley was building and stimulating our senses. The electrical energy of money and innovation was buzzing everywhere and new levels of stress were reaching not only the adults but the children. School, like everything else, was changing. My joy and my daughter's joy were synonymous and something I was unwilling to sacrifice for any amount of "shoulds" or "have to's" to keep up with the status quo.

A highly regarded public school within walking distance from our home was a great start for Anastasia through second grade. Upon entering third grade, we were met with a class size that became so large there were four third grade classes, a computer for each child and three hours of nightly homework. This was as much about competition over money as it was grooming the child mind for the future workforce of drones. As education became big business, it was their way of generating the best test scores ensuring they gained in dollars and reputation.

Art was no longer part of the equation and her teacher's personality matched her drab brown suits and shoes. The principal, unwilling to work with us on transferring her to another teacher's class, got her pulled out mid year after finding a Waldorf School in Los Altos Hills. Rudolph Steiner's philosophy of education worked for Anastasia having been raised holistically by me. Nurturing her body, mind, and soul, art was back in her curriculum and she learned to knit, crochet, dance and play the violin. I always encouraged theatre, classical music, dance and opera familiarizing her with it through Classic Kids tapes of the great composers. We listened to them for hours when Anastasia was a toddler as she painted, drew pictures and ran around with glue sticks and blunt scissors.

Private school yielded more perks than I realized and we traveled to Europe that spring for a month to meet Dubhlainn's family in England and Ireland. We gathered information for homework assignments and added more dimensions to Anastasia's well rounded education, and I began dreaming of Ireland days before our trip.

April 2005 Dreamtime

I dreamt Dubhlainn and I had a three story house and out in the side yard there was a burial mound. We dug it up and first found some old dishes blue and white, some with crosses, big crosses. One dish was square shaped white porcelain with gold trim and writing. It came from a specific county in Ireland and had a rhyme written on it referring to a man who committed a crime and was never proven guilty. It was a commemorative plate of the event. It felt like the whole town knew he was guilty. The trial had been long and everyone who believed him had this dish. There were layers of tapestries and old albums, and bags of old coins. The deeper we dug, the more current the items became. I looked up in a second story window and a skinny young black cat came from the top of the blind knocking it off the bracket causing him to slide down to the sill and then run away. One tapestry had a white cross and lilies . . . I woke up seeing it was 7:08 AM

The first stop on the trip was meeting Dubhlainn's twin brother who lived in England, and we stayed a few days with him. Declan was a doctor in a town outside of London and had a huge house with stunning foliage and an enclosed out-door swimming pool. His English garden was enchanting, and his foxgloves so tall and magnificent I stood in front of them to feel their presence and inhaled the flora of England. Welcomed warmly, we sat around the coal fireplace in the parlor sipping sherry before his children and grandchildren showed up for dinner. Declan's house teamed with the life of his grown children who lived close by and the fruits of their labor as parents was acknowledged by the smiles on their faces. Too busy with the schedule of the house and with no real private space, meditation for any length of time was almost impossible. Declan looking so much like Dubhlainn was a little unsettling, knowing there were two of them.

Venturing into London, we stopped over at the cousins, shopped at Harrod's and enjoyed a few sips of a cold pint with our fish and chips at lunch. Over lunch his cousin asked me to meet a friend of hers who wanted a reading and some help with her energy. I left them at the restaurant and made my way to the address. Walking up the stairs in London to the very old flat, the energy was as thick and layered as the paint on the railing leading up to the door.

Compassion swept over me as she opened the door and invited me in. Worn way before her years, her sweet soul, though slight, was still apparent through the energy now consuming her frail form. Spirit moved me to sit her down and use my hands to bring light in then through her chakras and down into the top of her head. Grounded in the light, I moved the energy that looked like the sludge of a compacted drain pipe up and out, slowly at first. As the energy began to move so did the frame of her delicate being as she writhed and retched. Tears streamed down my face as I felt her torture, and I remained concentrated on the movement of the light. She stayed with it during the thirty minutes it took her to let it go, and when she did, it slid out as a small peculiar form coated in slime. Finding it interesting and ignoring it all at the same time, I cleansed her body with light inside and out and recommended she meditate daily. Her face, eyes and energy were calm and holding the light. I hugged her and wished her well. I heard months later she was able to quit smoking and had made other positive life changes.

Converging later at the cousin's flat, we showered and imbibed before having dinner out and seeing Riverdance at the Apollo theatre. Sitting four rows from the front was an intense and moving experience. Practically eye level with the stage, the sound of the dancer's feet moving at what seemed as fast as a hummingbirds wings per second, pounded through my chest shooting me instantly into the vein of my soul. The feeling of oneness in the dance brought me to an even greater longing to experience life in only this way, and with a deep breath and tear-filled eyes I reconfirmed my desire for wholeness.

Waving goodbye to the women, we tossed our bags into the Mercedes and drove out with Declan to his cottage in Wales nestled above the Irish sea on a hillside in the town of Harlech. Magic is the word that best describes this enchanting country with its old churches, castles and bluebells.

2005 Dreamtime

I was swimming with the dolphins that I knew were out in the Irish Sea. In the second dream I felt I needed to call to find out how Seamus was. He had been on my mind a lot. In real time, he was in Greece and I kept hearing in my dream "It's only three hours away" and I felt as though I should drop everything and get on the next plane.

It seemed as though Welsh was the only language spoken when we dined out, but we were happy with what we received, not being exactly sure what we ordered. Visiting Harlech castle was an adventure. I shivered and was unusually cold in a few places and my legs felt extremely heavy as we walked over the top of the old dungeon. The drive north to Portmeirion was lush and the village was wholly of Italian design. Sharing a love of the passion flower with Seamus, I bought him a quiche dish from the botanical collection and took in the beauty of the abundant gardens.

We combined laughter and hugs in our departure of mixed emotion that left us boarding the ferry at Holyhead. The best part of crossing the Irish Sea was the green of the water, looking like marble the way the white ribbons of sea foam swirled through its opaque surface.The passage was smooth, the boat was tolerable, but I found the passengers obnoxious.

Dubhlainn's sister Ailish picked us up from the ferry terminal; then we joined some solicitor friends in Dublin, dining on Dover sole and French wine. Ailish was older, and her eyes showed absolutely no signs of light. She was pretentious, quietly disapproving, and softly spoke with Anastasia to get a better sense of me. Ailish had the facial features of the old wicked witch that offered the apple to Snow White, my favorite childhood movie. Her accent was of Irish aristocracy not that of the village people, and the family took great pride in their esteemed Irish roots. Her energy was thick and stuffy and she spent most of her days smoking, golfing and having tea.

After our lengthy lunch we drove Ailish to her home in Black Rock, staying briefly for tea and cake then drove out to the midlands. The roads were narrow and lined for miles with hedges of fuchsia, visible through the gray mist of the fog dotted with bright pops of purple and red. The sound of the wind shield wipers begged to calm me as I dealt with the uneasiness of driving on the left side of the road and not being in control of anything.

We drove into his home town, stopping on the way at the old mental hospital where Dubhlainn had been raised. Dubhlainn's father was a doctor, the Chief Medical Resident of the hospital in the 1930's and 40's. The good doctor was ahead of his time when it came to his patients and he wrote papers studying the link between diet and epilepsy, and maintained a one to two ratio of caretakers and patients. His theories and findings were published in a medical journal and way ahead of the times. His genuine care for his patients well being earned him that papal award making him a saint in the community and opened many doors for his family.

Dubhlainn drove us around the gothic castle pointing out his old residence in the middle third, with male patients housed on the right third and the female on the left. The structure is nearly three fourths of a mile long, all connected and this incredible mass of solid limestone seemed to go on forever. It was well built with beautifully crafted glass work in sections. There were a couple of large mysterious out buildings and a free standing chapel. I imagined brightly colored flowers overflowing from sturdy wire and moss baskets, suspended by black iron hangers against the stone walls as we drove around. It must have looked fantastic brand new with manicured grounds in the late spring of 1886.

A variety of feelings and emotions coursed though my awareness as we encircled the property and I exhaled deeply exiting onto the highway. Discovering where he grew up and how he was raised by staff made his mannerisms, manners and lack thereof at times make sense to me.

Arriving at his other sister Aifric's home, the family greeting was warm and welcoming. She had a huge house with five bedrooms and one bathroom. The bath and shower were separate from the toilet and it was so much more efficient that way I thought. There was a wood stove in the kitchen with a huge boiler that kept the kitchen cozy and searing hot tea kettles with ready boiling water. Aifric's husband had his routine each day, meeting with Anastasia as she played in the kitchen early each morning with the sort of strange and unfriendly family canine, Plato. They shared thoughts and laughs over scrambled eggs and toast with jam, melting a spot in the old man's heart he admitted his own children had never touched, and love blossomed on the old branches of the graying family tree. At half nine, the house keeper showed up and promptly prepared a silver tray with toast and tea with the morning paper, walking it carefully up the stairs to Aifric's"s room. The rest of us got up at our leisure and were served anything we wanted on old family china in the dining room around the long table.

In my Michelin guide, I learned that the largest ancient Druid sanctuary in Ireland was about eight miles from where we were, over a couple of fences down a small stretch of a road lined with stinging nettles and through a pasture and up a hill. The sign on the fence read "lands preserved and poisoned, beware of suckler cows" and I laughed wondering what the hell that was supposed to mean. Squeezing thru the fence and walking across the pasture up to the top of the hill, intuition guided me to the capstone that marked the place where once the five provinces met. Obtaining a 360 degree view of what I otherwise believed to be a completely flat country, I was flabbergasted. The countryside was dappled with small hills indicative of the burial mounds of ancient kings, and by the look and feel of where I was standing, no one had been around there for a long time. There were no signs of any pagan celebrations or destruction, it was the mid-nineties and still pristine.

Sitting on the ground, I tuned into the energy, which felt mostly quiet. Grounding golden roots of light into the earth, the energy changed and I became aware of Druid energy all around me. Then a different vibration, that of the Christians approached from the left. As the energy moved closer, I felt the Druid's resistance become stronger. There was no real animosity in this particular place I felt between the two, but the fear and righteousness generated from each side created the division among them. Sitting observing them holding fast to their individual set of beliefs, I realized their unwillingness to integrate each other's wisdom is what kept them from becoming whole. I continued to ground the golden light into the earth, activating the grid, waiting for the energy to integrate before coming out of meditation. Standing at the obvious high point, I took one last look around and ventured off thru the poisoned land of suckler cows, wire fences and stinging nettles to get back to the car.

Driving west to Galway to make some new memories on the coast, I asked Dubhlainn to stop at a pub along the side of the road in the middle of nowhere so I could use the restroom. Walking into the old building with a thatched roof, I ducked my head to enter. Looking around

151

to find a door with a clue, I noticed that the low ceilings worked fine for all the folks inside.

Moving like a giant among them, feeling squished and suffocated by the smoke and the lack of sufficient ventilation, I was planning to make this quick. Standing out amidst the patrons who spoke only Gaelic, I kept to myself and made my way to the back guided by the silent direction of many probing eyes. The toilets were rather primitive and small, and I was happy I had a hanky. Feeling like I stepped into a time machine that took me back to a time few modern people remember and even fewer know still exists, I took a deep breath and prepared for my exit. Not sure what I would meet on the other side of the door now that in my mind they had me cornered on their turf, I walked out of the restroom smiling. I nodded politely passing the faces representing many generations of the local people, still steeped within the roots of their amazing culture.

The coastline was beautiful and the chowder a bit too salty but a nice respite before our drive back to the east coast where we met Ailish at her summer house for a couple of days of golf. Anastasia and I laid low around the house and tried to relax, preparing for what we knew would be the end of our vacation.

I was not feeling like myself. My aura was flooded with energy of all kinds and I couldn't begin to sort out the black and white ribbons of discord roiling inside of me. Between the cold dark churches, some older than the six-hundred year old familial homes, the pagan sites, the mental hospital property and all the thick secrets our souls shared, overwhelmed seems a mild description. Interwoven with remnants of my soul throughout the country, my aura was a sticky black mess and it was time for me to go. My eyes appeared blacker than black, yet retained their sparkle. Absolutely sick to my stomach I was relieved to be leaving, and needing down time to detox and integrate, so we jetted off to Paris to decompress before going home.

Our flight was short, uneventful and sunny. Paris was beautiful and feminine and so unlike my masculine Rome. The first night we went out to eat, then I went back to our room and spent some alone time projectile vomiting. No one else was sick and I found relief in the process and after a good night's sleep convinced it had more to do with the energy than anything else.

Spring in Paris is lovely, we walked around the city sounding ooos and ahhhs, admiring the flowers, the red cafe umbrellas and baguettes with meat and cheese. The line at the Louvre was about an hour and a half deep and, not prepared to wait that long with or without a five year old, we ate sorbet on cones at the Arc d' Triomphe. We walked the bridges, took pictures at the fountains and strolled through the streets of all things Paris. Notre Dame cathedral was interesting, and first inside I saw a monk sitting on the bench whose robe seemed worn; when I did a double-take, the bench was empty. The organ was remarkable, but nothing compared to scenes on the walls of entire rooms created in the art of marqueterie. Touching such intricate beauty crafted in such detail by the precise hands and hearts of these devoted artists left me charged with a feeling of the men whose silent connection to the true creator was deep and unwavering. Inspired to remember why I wanted to always feel aligned, I found my spiritual aspirations recharged and carried me beyond our flight home the next day into the next phase of awakening.

Life in Los Altos settled back into its routine. Anastasia was ecstatic about life and I continued to work at a neighborhood cafe while seeing some clients in my home and juggling the irritations I occasionally felt with Dubhlainn regarding the chores.

Wanting to devote time to my spiritual work and put myself first for once, I allowed myself creative expression before tending to the mundane tasks, and all fell into place. Gary reminded me that the more I focused on my creative pursuits bringing my masculine energy of action to serve my feminine creative self, the more everything would have to shift. It wasn't long before I witnessed again the outward reflection of my new inner relationship as Dubhlainn began dedicating himself to the dishes after I cooked. He continued to lighten my load dramatically and we reached a place of harmony and flow.

An interest in cleansing at deeper physical levels came into my awareness, and quite naturally many resources flowed to me. I put myself under the wing of the "Arise and Shine" method of cleansing and within one month released more garbage from my organs, skin and bowels than I care to describe further. Unable to function mentally or physically at the capacity my family required when I was home, I stayed the master phase week in southern California spaced out on chomper, liquids and coffee enemas. Soaking up the luxury of a San Diego hillside mansion with a negative edge pool surrounded by lush gardens. I didn't have to talk or cook for anybody and returning home things felt much lighter falling back into routine.

Dubhlainn attended church every Sunday at St Nicholas, and for a while I went as well in an attempt to support his chosen path. The priest there was so bent on renouncing Satan that each Sunday he had the congregation recite what is normally reserved for the godparents in the rite of baptism. As the priest thundered "Do you reject Satan and all his works?" my heart felt heavy, tears came to my eyes and I could not abide knowing that I did not condone, but that somehow love, not rejection was the key. Not willing to bow to this notion or follow the priests lead in collectively resounding "Lord I am not worthy to receive you," I left Dubhlainn to his Sunday morning ritual.

After honoring myself by no longer attending church, dreamtime gave me something else to think about.

2005 Dreamtime

I dreamed about "the church within the church" as I heard it in my dream. A priest who was a priest by day came to a heavy wooden door that I was asked to open. He went through the door and down a dark staircase. At the bottom of the stairs was a skeleton crumpled on its side. As he made his way down, I saw other skeletons, even one hanging in shackles. To the left of the staircase, farther in the room, was an altar with a body lying there starving and helplessly bound to it. I watched him remove his white vestment and put on a black hooded robe. As I approached him, he turned to look at me and his face was skeletal; he had been molesting the boy on the altar.

The more golden light I brought to the murky depths of my emotional body, the more the faces of my dark inner past surfaced for resolution. Studying this energy and its interplay by practicing techniques of integration I observed the results and my work evolved. As I experienced awakening after awakening, I became more aligned with my soul; my inner work became my joyful preoccupation. Now experiencing what I had heard from Gary as truth for myself, I began to feel the difference between embodying truth and just knowing it to be true.

My outer world began to reflect more of my highest self, but my subconscious reflected the parts of my light still hiding within my emotional and physical body as dreams came in flurries to bring my attention to them. I wrote them down and then paid them no heed . . . I did not see how they were pertinent to my outer world, and chose to focus only on that which was light not yet completely able to see them as one in the same. What I accomplished was sort of the reverse of my earlier life experience. My life reflected more of my inner light, but the darkness had a life in my dreams more than my reality, but still had a vibration of its own that would not take no for an answer.

May 22, 1995 Dreamtime

Marius came over to my old house on Acorn Ave in a brand new beautiful new car with all kinds of antique clothes for an antique shoppe, but they fit me. He also had a bunch of papers and bottles for recycling etc. I asked him if the car was his and he said no. I asked if I could drive it. He had a girl with him about nineteen years old. I moved the car but the brakes did not work well, and I had to push really hard. I remembered in the dream what it was always like when he came over and how we never had to speak to each other to know what to do or how to act.

May 28, 1995 Dreamtime

Marius moved into a new house. It was spacious with lots of room, light carpets and pastel colored paintings. It was nice and gave me the feeling he was peaceful there.

May 30, 1995 Dreamtime

Dreamed again about Marius and went to his spacious home. I walked into his bedroom and found two men sleeping in his bed fully clothed. I ordered them out and told them if Marius had found them there they would have been killed. In his garage, I found a fat woman taking food and other things from his shelves. She was clean, well-kept, and she didn't seem to be hungry. She was just taking things to take them. I got her to leave as well. I found my diamond ring.

My longer meditations brought night sweats and meditations of greater intensity. My practice of remaining grounded out of session was now my focus all day every day. One afternoon grounded in meditation, my head bent slightly forward, my energy grounded deep in to the earth, Archangel Michael appeared showing me his sword of blue-white light. As I gazed upon it, he spoke to me telling me, No longer shall you use the sword to fight in the name of God, you shall become the sword itself. Do not march powerfully with the light of God, walk fearlessly within it. As I bowed my head to receive this subtle transmission, he thrust the sword down my spine from the back of my neck and drove it to the base of my spine, where it created an intense electrical blue-white current that ripped intensely through my aura.

"You must be willing to be called crazy."

- Archangel Michael

Meditating until the energy calmed down, I spent the rest of my afternoon quietly lying on a blanket under the branches of our waxed leaf privet, watching the hummingbirds come and go from their sweet little nest while my body integrated the new pattern of energy before school ended and evening activities demanded my attention. I parted with an antique Spanish broadsword I had kept on my mantle for years, bestowing it upon a young woman who was in search of this level of strength.

I am not afraid of death, I am more afraid of living a boring limited life.

- Siobhan Nicolaou, The Sword of Truth

Life slowed down physically as I pulled more of my focus inward and running on a trail anywhere wasn't going to happen. I joined the Los Altos Spa to soak in the gorgeous amenities, get a good sauna and hoped that would help me lose the weight I was becoming increasingly uncomfortable with. Slowed to the point of squishy, my vitality was siphoned away in the new, slower rhythm of living. Abundance and plenty over- flowed from everywhere. Living a life completely taken care of by what I still perceived as coming solely through my husband felt like giving my power away because the sacrifice of my independence felt so huge.

Gary's only solution to my inquiries was to continue with my inner work and find the reflection in my feelings and transform them. Dubhlainn systematically replaced everything I owned except the art work and kitchen tools, and I felt the draw Dubhlainn continually took from my energy in exchange for these comforts. When alone, I was preparing to take myself into the world with my ability to read auras, commune with the angels and help people go further with my expanded portfolio of skills.

"Knowing your own darkness is the best method for dealing with the darkness of other people."

- Dr. Carl G. Jung

Inside I was afraid I was not good enough and unsure of myself, but it was time. I looked up bookstores that featured psychic readers and put some material together. I checked out two on the peninsula, one a novelty sort of place and the other a well established metaphysical bookstore that had recently moved from its small space in Menlo Park. Both of these establishments were within a half mile of each other, so I figured I would check out the smaller one first.

Walking into the store with shelves lined with all sorts of wax figurines and crystal balls, I surmised they catered to a different kind of spiritual clientele. Walking further toward the back of the store, I noticed in my peripheral vision the shadow of a woman darting around the shelves from different angles, watching me as I continued to walk closer to the rear looking for someone to speak with.

Finally, popping out of the shadows, she made herself apparent, with long curly hair partially covered and tied back by a long purple scarf matching the classic velvet gypsy skirt, white peasant top with billowy sleeves and silver hoop earrings. Almost laughing aloud, I wondered if her clothes were on purpose, as she asked if I was interested in a reading. Thinking she was not very intuitive to ask me that, I said "No, I think all my questions have been answered," and I turned around and walked to the exit.

Feeling a bit guilty in my quick judgment of her, I got in my car pointing it in the direction of home, telling myself I would call it a day and go to the store I really wanted to work in at another time. Turning right onto the El Camino as I stopped at the first light, a stern audible voice from the left told me to "turn around." Immediately I got into the left turn lane, making a U-turn knowing the instruction meant to go to the other bookstore NOW, and I immediately complied.

East West was the bookstore of bookstores and I liked the energy very much. The people who ran the store in all capacities were bright, skilled and gifted souls of love and service. It was easy to communicate my desire to offer my services as someone who gave Angel Readings, and I set up a time for the second interview later that week.

The store manager interviewed me by asking me for a reading. She asked me questions about the resistance from the local community and civil servants they received being a fairly new establishment on the street in regard to codes and obtaining permits and other requirements that seemed difficult. The image I saw was huge mass of white light making its way across the sky from Menlo Park to Mountain View, where the energy was much more dense, thereby creating some difficulty with communication, paperwork and alignment as the opposing currents attempted to harmonize.

I explained that taking such light-infused intention from its location of twenty-seven years, blowing it up five times the size and setting it down in the middle of the Castro Street was creating the electrical storm and that it would soon settle down when the energy adjusted.

Castro Street at that time was barely an up-and-coming strip of shops that included a Chinese supermarket piled high with mounds of iced fresh fish with a smell that lingered on the sidewalk for a block and a half. The Chinese apothecary on the corner was stocked ceiling to floor with everything from dried seahorses and ginseng root to bat wings and shark fins for cures. There were a few really good Chinese restaurants and other small businesses that were not used to seeing such bright faces and soft spoken hearts overflowing with such bright light.

Red flags surely went up when the neighborhood business people noticed every body representing the book store was happy, wearing lightweight mostly cotton fabrics and Birkenstocks, sometimes with socks. To many people that screams "cult," and I am sure there were folks relieved when the first summer passed without seeing a Kool aid stand out on the sidewalk!

I was hired, handed them a bio and a photo and was posted in their magazine with the other readers. We all did different work; some had been there for years and I humbly and gratefully showed up each week. On my first day, my one appointment was a fellow reader who also had a masters in psychology. It was an honor reading an aura so connected to his entourage that introduced itself in a way that shared so completely. His sweetness poured into the room as I drew forth information from his auric field and shared with him from the clarity of my soul. The conclusion of our hour session met with a hug and connected our hearts with a subtle fondness and I rarely saw him again.

My second week showed me something different. A man came in for a reading very closed, without an ice-breaking question. Immediately, images of hundreds of snakes surrounded him as if he purposefully flooded the room with them. He was smug and challenging at first; then I felt the fear in his need to project this energy to keep others, especially women, at a distance and pointed out the lack of relationship in his life, his problems with women and the root of his behavior. He was very bright, having fine-tuned his skills with words when dealing with the average mind, as was evident in the words that rolled off what appeared to be his forked-like tongue. Unveiling his unique career, I brought light to a framework he could use in a spiritual way to discover its higher meaning. I explained the profundity of how it could give him much assistance deciphering and interpreting his past while using the same formulae to bring about his own healing.

I offered my assistance if he chose to pursue this avenue further and he left as closed as he arrived. The following week, I received a card from him with the image of a dark angel on the front saying how he felt he got nothing from our time in session, and how it did not bode well for someone like me who chose to be a reader. Not taking it personally, seeing him instead as a reflection of my greatest saboteur, I knew he represented the part of me always seeking to shut my power down. He showed me my doubts and fears of coming into my own power and the other parts that had already surfaced along my timeline.

Anchoring a beacon of golden light, claiming the little room with gratitude for the privilege to serve among the energy of the Masters, my appointment book filled up. Many people were interested in taking my workshops and attending talks I gave on various metaphysical topics. I gave up my part-time job and focused on my vocation. Fridays always filled, sometimes keeping me reading for people back-to-back for seven hours, taking only a short break. Thursday afternoons I taught progressive classes requiring thirteen weeks from start to finish. When the bookstore was not able to accommodate my requests for classroom space, a client named Barbara handed me a key and offered her large, lovely home for my use for additional workshops and a weekly meditation gathering.

One can only help others to the extent they have helped themselves; the same holds true in matters of love.

- Siobhan Nicolaou, The Sword of Truth

My workshops birthed from the passion of my soul, encompassing everything from the transmutation of energy in the aura to mediumship and grief counseling, kept me happily busy. Energy being my forté, I fell in love with my soul's work. Opening people to their potential, watching them transform and thrive is the best work there is.

One-on-one sessions were equally fulfilling when someone had an opening to a greater level of awareness and healing when their hearts broke open to feel true love's embrace inside themselves for the very first time. Clearing energies in homes and on properties and mediating both sides to peace is a favorite part of my service. Grace, reverence and love filled my days and life continued to produce the fruits of my giving. For the first time in my life, I was living my purpose and felt how life was truly intended to be.

Creativity begets creativity, and I branched out to include my love for painting. The muse inspired me to paint my daughter's bare wooden desk sky blue, depicting Native American images. From the beautiful Sacred Path Cards, I painted "dreamtime," "peyote ceremony," "vision quest," and "thunder beings." Painting a purple mountain landscape, a prickly cactus in bloom, a copper-colored rattlesnake and colorful detailed intricate patterns brought this desk to life. The finishing touches were the ceramic knobs in the shape of red chili peppers, crescent moons and stars. My smile and soul beamed with bright acrylic paint and a vision of my future.

Dubhlainn always said he supported my work and at the same time he had a hard time with my drive for independence. I always felt uneasiness behind his gentle Irish smiles and his mild mannered swag. Dubhlainn's fear caused him to hold on way too tight and when I figured that out, I helped him let go. We worked through enough for him to hear that he needed space too and it worked well for us to do our own thing. He went on golf trips and took three weeks to visit his buddy in Australia, enjoying whatever men do when out sailing in and out of the Royal Perth Yacht Club. He called me to let me know he was having fun, and I laughed knowing he was in his own brand of heaven.

> *There is no love that is given or received when extended from the wounded self.*
>
> *- Siobhan Nicolaou, The Sword of Truth*

When Dubhlainn felt it was time to reel me in, we traveled together - which was always a compromise - mostly to visit family. We all went to Canada one year for the most surreal Christmas ever. Staying in a storybook house in a storybook neighborhood steeped in tradition and denial, I felt I could suffocate in the density of it's stratus. Everybody lived the same routine and nothing had changed for generations. The same time, the same breakfast flakes, the same tea, the same newspaper, the same hair, the same style, the same greetings and mannerisms. It reminded me of The Truman Show, but no one here was ever going to leave the movie.

My stomach cramped in the stuffiness, the air barely stirred, and I had to get outside to breathe. Meditation was sporadic for the week and I felt mostly restless. God was recognized in their life by the photographs dotted around the house of an uncle who was a Cistercian Abbot, who was called upon to bless our food at evening's supper. Sundays, everyone drove to church to connect with the God they believed to be outside of themselves, while Anastasia and I stayed behind basking in the joy of our solitude and the warmth of our inner light.

The smell of mulled wine infused with subtle wisps of pine from the enormous Christmas tree permeated the great room of the beautiful Toronto mansion, and the champagne sparkled like the eyes of all the guests that came by to spread cheer and nibble on fine cheeses. Through the kitchen window, I saw my first red cardinal sitting on the perch of a birdhouse in the low branches of a snow-covered pine. I knew right then I was in a Hallmark Christmas card. It was beautiful.

The family table was adorned with handcrafted Irish lace table cloths and impeccably pressed linens supporting eight silver utensils representing each course. The only thing more perfect than the hand- crafted glassware and the handmade patchwork quilts draped over the expertly carved wooden racks in each room was the roast beef with mustard, mashed potatoes and English peas. The plum pudding was ignited at table, and an enchanting Christmas cake with a marzipan village with a snow man was carried in on a silver tray. Sprinkling the scene with confectioners sugar at table made the magic of the Christmas scene come alive.

Wanting to get home where life moved with the breath, instead of within a tedious construct, the trip once again inspired my purpose and ignited the fuse toward discovering greater truth in my own life.

My desire for growth guided me to organize a tour and lead a group to ancient England from Tintagel to Glastonbury, from the birth to the resting place of the legendary King Arthur. Each location offered its own energetic experience and discovery. Sara helped with the logistics of the tour, living in Windsor at the time of my trip. Arriving a couple days early and staying a few days late to venture on our own, we walked the Thames to feed the swans and visited the tombs in St George's Chapel. Putting the top down of her Saab convertible, we took a jaunt to Bath, where the energy of our ancestors still remains so powerfully that I felt as if I had left Britain for a day and returned to the Roman countryside.

Reading nothing about the details about where we were going other than enough to make reservations for our lodging and choose a couple of specific adventures, the slate was open to the moment. In Cornwall, I planned to go to Tintagel castle and climb around in Merlin's cave with a walk across the Bodmin Moor and, like always, I had no idea what to expect.

Holding the space for groups does present its challenges dealing with situations that arise from the veils of everybody's assorted baggage and I remained compassionately detached. Blessed with outstanding weather our entire trip and sunshine our three days in Cornwall, I laughed over hearing a complaint through a door from one of our troupe about not receiving a full English breakfast she expected would be available each morning. She obviously had no idea how bad the weather could be, and neglected to read the part of the brochure referring to a continental breakfast being included in her stay at the Inn. Giving thanks for the tea, crumpets and assorted dry cereals that adorned our table, I thought of it as an opportunity for a little weight loss and took advantage of the sunshine and the putting green at our disposal.

Walking across the grass-covered hills by the castle showed me an astral imprint of a skirmish still being fought and beings described as "piskies" darted around in glimpses mostly around the bushes. Merlin's cave was marked with the energy of pagan incantations, but the varying colors of green and blue that made up the rocks, seaweed, and water coming together to create this space spoke of a different kind of magic.

Bombarded with leaflets from the B&B foyer of other places the group was excited to explore, I explained we would stay on track with the plans outlined in the trip and see what happened from there.

I was drawn to a small flier in the pile that described St. Nectan's Glen. It felt right and did not look to be that far. The map directed by way of a short squiggly line through pastures and the woods where X marked the spot. Sara and I decided to go first to test its viability. Over fences and through mushy cow pastures, we laughed as we made our way down the hill toward the trees of the glen.

Stopped for a moment by a severe allergic reaction to something we were never able to identify, I stood and called for Sara. Standing perfectly still, I observed the horror in her eyes as my face became distorted and my throat began to swell shut. My face morphed into the likeness of an alien from the Deep Space Nine cast, and she asked if I was okay. Grounding my energy to determine if I was going to need medical attention, I felt the swelling begin to subside. Judging I was going to live, we regrouped and walked into the glen. Lush ferns and grasses blanketed the woodland floor and we found a trail mostly concealed by leaves and foliage vaguely marking the way.

The rushing movement of the water was softened by the moss-covered rocks lining the bed of the stream, and the birds chirped happily, bouncing among the branches in the canopy of the tall shady trees. Following the narrow foot path over a bridge and up the hill, we walked to the cell of St. Nectan. The energy changed, with the force of the waterfall apparent as we turned the corner. Down the path we climbed, standing at the edge of the still water's pool in awe of the beauty of the embankment encircling the 60ft waterfall.

On bended knee, I cupped the water with both hands and brought it up to my swollen face, pressing the water to my skin. Hands over my eyes, a feeling of profound humility poured through me as my heart cracked open, my shoulders let go and I wept into my palms. In my mind's eye, I saw myself standing there in armor as my breastplate and pauldron fell into the water. This vision moved me to my core and I opened my eyes to see thousands of angels hovering along the waterfall's ridge. The minutes that followed kept me in the silence of my heart. I knew I wanted to bring the girls back to experience the beauty of this transformative energy.

The next day we went on our pre-determined journey across the Bodmin Moor which proved to be an exercise in trust. I refused to look at the maps or to think about the course ahead. I tuned out the chatter of their minds and mouths, thanked our driver who dropped us at the trail head and told them to follow me. Leading the group I encouraged them to stay inward and step where I stepped to ensure their safety.

One and a half hours later and halfway across the moor, fear took hold of Barbara who began to feel a bit out of control. She began singing show tunes, breaking the energy of our collective intuitive chain. I stayed grounded, letting her have her experience and continued to lead. As she disconnected more from her inner being, the energy shifted completely to her mind and her resistance took her in its own direction.

Stepping to the right with both feet, Barbara sunk immediately to her knees which thrust her forward with enough force that her hands went forward and up to her elbows into the mire as well. No one said a word, not knowing quite how to respond and not sure what would happen next. Barbara got grounded and decided she needed to free herself-one arm, then one leg at a time-without our help, and miraculously both shoes remained on her feet. She fell back, creating some distance between herself and the others as the moor mud dried to various colors on her clothing, arms and legs.

Our walk took three hours and to heights of 1400ft climbing Brown Willy, the highest point in Cornwall, then down to the Jamaica Inn. The Jamaica Inn is a three hundred year old pub where we refreshed ourselves with a pint and lunch. We had the blessing of meeting a couple who had stopped there on the way home from the doctor with their very young son who had just received one of several treatments on his kidneys. The child showed an interest for me to hold him and he drifted almost to sleep in my arms as I sat with my hands pouring energy and light into the longing of his weakened little form.

Gazing out the window of the pub, we noticed a sign indicating one and one half miles to Dozmary Pool. Not being part of the plan, we were overjoyed at the synchronicity and asked the driver to take us by there before driving back to the B&B. The pool was a lake about one mile in circumference and glassy still due to its consistently shallow depth across; the energy at the pool was indeed very feminine and peaceful as described in the Arthurian legend as the resting place of the sword Excalibur, broken by the ego of King Arthur and repaired by the awakening of his heart discovering its power and true purpose.

Glastonbury had an energy all its own and was markedly different from the innocence of Cornwall. The Abbey is an ancient site that goes back to the bronze age, (and the roots of Joseph of Arimathea) predating the Benedictines. Joseph was rooted in the consciousness of Yeshua, and the one who is said to to have grown the sacred thorn tree from the staff he stuck in the ground on Wearyall Hill. The thorn tree blooms in the dead of English winter and once more in the spring. It is said that Joseph brought the Holy Grail with him to Britain, and with it a different consciousness than that which preceded him.

Tuning into the energy where I stood, I felt the grounds consecrated in three different ways and each with its own form of thought. In my mind I saw three grids overlapping with one line running straight through. Each of the three rigid structures of thought were visible in white light except the straight line, which was gold. The white grids felt fixed with the ethereal symbols that constructed them, but the single gold line felt soft, strong, fiery and malleable. Resonating with the golden light, I imprinted the visual in my mind with the accompanying feeling.

Entering the chapel of St. Patrick, I was met with huge resistance from an unseen force. A wall of energy as close as my nose tried to block my passage and intimidate me to leave. Without any thoughts or feelings of opposition, I continued to walk in the golden light and sit down on one of the little chairs. I closed my eyes and opened my heart, meditating silently. Consciously focused on the golden vibration of love, I grounded it through my body and down into the earth. As I activated the golden grid within the earth, the energy began to harmonize. The wall of energy eventually subsided, moved up and settled to the left of the altar.

Climbing the ancient hill to St. Michael's Tor, I was aware of many artifacts within the mound itself at the top the stunning view which filled my eyes in all directions. On the gentle breeze the words "secrets, still and silent secrets" drifted through my empty mind. Sacred geometry and intention create the ley lines, making the Tor the sacred heart of England, connecting it to all spiritual sites both pagan and Christian. St Michael's Tor is the metaphorical cup that runneth over, the energy of the blood of a new and everlasting life. It is the grail itself holding the message "You and the Father are one."

Our journey to England was profound in many ways. Much of it would not make complete sense to me for another twelve years - like most of my experiences - but the trip catapulted me into a huge expansion. My desire to shed more armor began stretching the parameters that had cradled me so comfortably for nearly six years and it wasn't long before the seams would begin to show signs of pressure.

The blackest of my veils lightened up with the love I discovered at the core within each of them, and though some thick, opaque and even- tar like in places, my awareness in the truth of love made them softer. The black turned to dark gray, revealing the face of shamanism and soon different layers of the same issues concerning manipulation and control started to rise up from within.

"Liebe versüßt jede Qual jedes Geschöpf bietet sich ihr ." (Love sweetens every torment; every creature offers itself to her.)

- Pamina, The Magic Flute, W. A. Mozart

Dubhlainn was making plans to retire from the firm and we talked about moving out of the insanity and excessive indulgence that had become Silicon Valley. Deciding at that point to get married, we had a small and elegant ceremony in Carmel. Though I loved Dubhlainn, I felt unworthy of receiving all he gave me, partly because I could feel expectation instead of love in every gift he offered. It was a old pattern between us trying to find its way to love, and we did a great job given who we were at the time.

Looking for a larger place so I could work more from home, the vibration of elegant rustic simplicity I was emitting so strongly, drew my artist soul to a new and exciting land. Dubhlainn, Anastasia and I flew to Albuquerque, driving an hour up to the high desert that holds the energy of the planet called Santa Fe.

Unplugged that weekend from the intense airwaves of the newly hardwired Bay Area, my being was enfolded in the silence of the stars and I felt like I had come home. Without doubt or any logical basis, I knew it was our next home. We looked through real estate magazines and set the ball in motion to look at a few places. Our relationship never being based on communication or total honesty, Dubhlainn kept his true feelings in check and followed my heart instead of his own, and handed me the reigns.

I spoke with Gary about the idea of getting a home where I could hold retreats and create a B&B, the words themselves seemed to move me closer. Gary and I spent a huge amount of time and resources together and our lives were enmeshed like family more than professionally. Not believing Gary was supportive, my feelings were hurt not having his approval which I had always sought. Having put him above myself like I was trained to do with all male spiritual authority figures brought me to immense feelings of rage. As veils began falling away, the anger I had about all I had observed and glossed over in my need to be loved and approved of by him came spewing out as I sought to integrate another level of my false self.

Struggling to regain my own power, I began behaving in the only way I knew to break that pattern. Inadequacy and unworthiness that blanketed me since birth were again a focus of mine to transmute. I shadow-boxed painfully through this transformation, finding the love reborn again and again within the shadow of self.

> *"Remain unaffected by the one that paces, curses and blames; know it to be the revolt of his self against his uncontrolled mind."*
>
> *- Sathya Sai Baba*

Determined to free myself from the weight of my pettiness and insecurity, I reached down deeper while continually transmuting the energy of our past. Searching deep into my timeline for old patterns between us, I saw us as brothers who were fierce rivals and *schwartz* comparing competitors. He once betrayed me having sold me out to our enemy to have me imprisoned for the rest of my life. I also surfaced as a man who followed a guru in India and saw myself old, disempowered and starving. Disgruntled from following what turned out to be false promises, I gave everything to him at my own expense, and lay wallowing in the hopeless mud of bitterness. My inner rage fueled the fire of transmutation through this life and began changing my path, and I watched as my personal and professional relationship with Gary took a major turn. My old pattern of "guru" and "disciple" changed color like the leaves of my Aspen trees that fell to the earth and quickly became the mulch that bore the promise of more fertile ground.

On the other side of the fire and forgiveness came an awareness that explained my abhorrence of Indian food and the whole guru notion. Another lesson in what it meant to give my power away to another, it drove me further inward deeper to find my own voice.

Before long the house was entirely packed, with much of the new hand-carved antique teak pieces I bought from the Los Altos Consignment Center wrapped and organized on our massive back porch. We traveled back and forth to the land of Fe finalizing the paperwork on our new property. It was a five-acre piece adjoining the Santa Fe national forest with about seven-thousand more square feet of living space than I was used to. Apple trees, terraced gardens and chicken coop in the middle of nowhere about ten miles north of town.

The favorite feature of my pueblo home was that the floors were a tight brick design on sand and soil. I gravitated to the remaining part of the old Valencia familial homestead which was the kitchen, dining room and breakfast room. We had *vigas,* a n d *saltillo* tile throughout the studio and mud room and bought some of the furniture in the house as part of the deal. I found myself leaning toward an Italian rustic and leather style rather than the floral prints of our fluffy Los Altos pieces.

My vision was to create a bed and breakfast, hold classes in my studio, have it all under one roof, (as it were) streamlining life to meet everybody's needs. It promised to be a project to get the place functioning in a harmonious rhythm, and I was under the impression we would figure it out together. Dubhlainn, led me to believe we would dive into the project then balked at spending the money required to come up to certain codes. The subconscious fear in Dubhlainn too huge to articulate created his unwillingness to let go of the country club, the Mercedes and his favorite restaurants. He rented a couple of rooms for his pleasure from some old family friends in the North Bay and came out when I traveled.

Having arrived in August, we were rapidly prepared for the onset of school year. The sky was blue, the air was fresh and my Roman lineage compelled me to want to build my empire in a day. Overwhelmed by everything in the house, I focused on my essentials and awakened to the fact I had to think about everything differently living in a country home with fewer modern conveniences. My vegetable scraps were split between the chickens and the compost heap I dug out at the fence line; there were no colorful recycling bins to sort things out, and there would be wood to chop.

Knowing nothing about our new corner of the galaxy except the location of the school and the grocery store and that there would be snow, we bought a four wheel drive to manage. Anastasia adopted a kitten from the shelter and named her Lucia like my two cats that preceded her. My two and a half carat solitaire felt rather pretentious in my new world and I slipped it off and into a drawer.

Clearing and shifting the energy of the property stirred things up and brought to my awareness the spirit of a young girl who was raped and killed at the end of our dirt road next to the highway. She wanted my help and resolution, so I enlisted the help of Archangel Michael to relieve the terror and restlessness of her soul, and thanked her for calling upon me.

It seemed that every visit Dubhlainn made to the property resulted in an accident. He stepped on a rusty nail that went halfway through his foot; a wheel flew off of the trailer he was driving to the dump. He admitted he couldn't stand the poverty he saw all around us, referring to the reservations and his perception of the Pueblo Indian simplicity. Santa Fe was all too earthy for Dubhlainn, and he left me to it all as we passed like ships in the night between California and New Mexico about every five weeks so I could maintain my client base.

Opening the door for Lucia one nippy fall morning, she bristled like a porcupine and came running back through door. The hair stood up on the back of my neck, and I was alarmed. A bear had tossed the compost heap, and I looked up in time to see dirt fly from his paws as he ran off and around back. Standing there not knowing what to do, overtaken by a Green Acres moment, I thought, a bear? Okay, so that explained the unidentified piles of the light green gelatinous substance that I found underneath the apple trees. . . but would they try to knock down the doors? Do they camp? Should I cook? Where is my husband? And gee whiz, why was I always the one who got up to check out noises in the middle of the night? It was this event that I prompted me to draw the line and flat out told Dubhlainn that we were doing life together or we were not doing it at all.

Anastasia was greatly saddened by the news we were filing for divorce and wrote about her feelings in her journal. We spent time playing with our new kitten and new found friends. Holiday activities began immediately at the Waldorf school. We met some really fantastic families from the school and play-dates to make our costumes for Halloween and dinner parties filled the time left on the calendar. By the time the pumpkins arrived at the market for Thanksgiving the anger Dubhlainn felt was becoming apparent. He came out to Santa Fe out for a couple of weeks for the holiday, but felt me walking firmly in the other direction. He bought me two paintings I loved for my birthday hoping to get me to turn back around. Divorce was becoming a reality with our lack of ability to effectively do anything else, and he left Santa Fe undecided about many things, but clear that divorce be my decision, he wanted me out of his house. I stayed by the fire instead of attending the lighting of the Christmas tree on the plaza and began looking on Craigslist for places to rent closer to town.

January 2000 Dreamtime

Had a dream that Dubhlainn has been lying to me about his intentions. He is going to his daughter's house and says she bought him a ticket, but I do not believe him. He was kissing, a woman and said to me "she said it was not cheating" trying to get himself off of the hook by not taking responsibility. I was so pissed off I slapped him in the face again and again. He turned into a little boy who could barely speak, then became shy and almost retarded. As this happened I began to feel badly and told him that "one slap in the face straightened me up into speaking the truth." I began to spread some jam on small pieces of toast to give to him to see if that would snap him out of it.

On a chilly, stressful afternoon on the Paseo Sin Nombre, I answered a phone call from Dolores, a client from California who I had not spoken with for a few months. She expressed interest in working with me more regularly, and offered to host a workshop in her South Bay home on my next trip out to California. So I agreed and stopped by on my next trip out. The air in her home was rigidly still, and the large back yard where the children played was entirely covered with astro turf. Her two youngest children displayed little emotion and the oldest daughter, who was bright and capable, was trying to shine through clouds of low self esteem while attending

Catholic school and following all the rules within the many confines of her reality.

Dolores's husband was a smart, hard-wired computer guy who was able to work from home and was nice enough if you were designed a similar way. He believed in all things Disney: clocks that ran backwards and all things moving counter to the natural order of things. When I showed up in his wife's stifling life, things began to change; she opened up, started to feel more confident, began to breathe again, and he became fearful. The golden light, now anchored in their home, softened the angles and warmed the air along with the frosty edges of her not-so-sociable husband. They agreed to get their house ready to sell, and within four months she was coming out to Santa Fe to look at homes.

Chapter VIII

Stigmata

Stigmata is life as a conscious immortal, willing to be the brunt of the ignorance that pummels it, until it frees itself entirely from illusion.

- Siobhan Nicolaou, *The Sword of Truth*

Stigmata

The blue of the desert's celestial dome watched over us and never blinked even in the cold of January. We located a manageable Mediterranean style house in Eldorado to rent one fourth the size of Dubhlainn's with a perfect floor plan in Eldorado much closer to town. We loaded up the teak, my kitchen and other personal things from Dubhlainn's house and moved on in. I turned my diamonds into a huge Karastan rug and a complete set of rustic Italian leather furniture for the living room. I had a blast painting each room its own color. I found my housekeeper who I predicted by name, and focused on building my new Santa Fe style life. We had *saltillo* tile throughout the house, except the bedrooms and my office that were softened by the fibers of quality wool berber. The skylights brought so much light into the house that I laughed at myself reaching for the switch to turn "the lights" off when entering and exiting the rooms. Lucia adjusted easily, finding her place in the sun while Anastasia settled into a comfier bedroom and a more nurturing home.

The silence of morning winter was broken by the crackling of kindling catching fire in the living room kiva. My senses were subtly enlivened by the scent of the burning pinion that wafted in ribbons through the brisk morning air. Warmed by a soft pashmina shawl, I sat eyes wide open, blank staring at the flames as my mind hatched slowly to the dawn of a new day.

Coffee . . . the first real thought to enter my brain, lifted me gently from the embrace of my fine leather chair and into my kitchen to prepare a strong batch of brew. The aroma of Peet's coffee quickly filled the air. I inhaled deeply, reaching across my white unfinished marble baking table to the bowl in the center overflowing with fruit. Selecting an apple, I washed its red, yellow and greenish skin. The burst of sweet and tart that stimulated my tastebuds as I bit into its crisp juicy flesh brought me fully into my senses; my lips were drenched with the first sweet taste of my day. I wiped my chin and bid Lucia *buon giorno* as she walked over and rubbed her silky fur against my legs. Anastasia emerged from her room down the hall to give me a hug, then curled up in the chair for a moment, basking in the glow of the fire before getting ready for breakfast and school.

A mental note chimed that two cords of wood would be delivered later as I grabbed my keys and gym bag and made my way through my office to the garage, child and lunch in tow. The snow was slight this year and the plants showed signs of an early spring.

Spring arrived with frequent travel back and forth to California, and Dolores graciously hosted Anastasia at these times. Our daughters were friends and almost the same age and went to the same school. Down in Albuquerque, standing in the front of the Wyndham airport hotel where I stayed the night before my early flight, I saw a plane in my mind's eye go right into the side of the mirrored building. As always when I see things of this nature, I grounded and felt what it meant. Not feeling as though it was unsafe for me to stay, I rested quietly and safely on the fifteenth floor.

Upon my return, Sara called to announce she wished to take me with her to Puerto Rico, all expenses paid, having won a vacation for two at the Westin Rio Mar for five days for being a top sales person in her company. I accepted and made plans to go. Our trip to Puerto Rico was for five glorious days in the middle of April, and we spent our time indulging in the best the resort had to offer. Being inspired to visit Garabandal, a village in the San Sebastian region of northern Spain, I took advantage of the opportunity and rerouted my return flight through Bilbao.

Garabandal was declared a sacred place in 1961-1964 after apparitions of Archangel Michael and Mother Mary visited several young girls of the village. The girls, in a state of ecstasy, channeled messages from Mother Mary. The church and scientists studied the girls when in this state and after viewing photographs and film of the study, I wanted to feel this out for myself.

Not speaking a word of Spanish and trusting entirely in my guidance, I landed in Bilbao not knowing how to get to Garabandal or where I would be staying. The airport was cold, spacious and steel with hard floors that amplified the stomping of the soldiers' heels as they marched in unison through the lobby with matching machine guns strapped to their shoulders. Exhausted from the route I had to take to get to Spain, my brain tried to coordinate with my fingers in order to locate my passport somewhere in my handbag.

Fumbling through my bag, approaching the serious faces of the *polizia* standing at the podium, I produced my passport wallet for the *guardia* with a smile. The energy was stern and unwelcoming and I began to lose my breath in a sudden fear. They said something to each other while stamping my passport, handed it back to me and I made a beeline for the loo. I sat on the toilet seat behind the closed door of the stall and forced myself to breathe, drawing myself inward and closing my mind out completely. Quiet and ease enveloped me again as I found my center and listened for my next move. Brushing my teeth and washing my face, I felt ready to embrace the journey.

Walking slowly down the wide hall, I rounded the corner to a series of desks where I could exchange currency. Around the next corner was an information booth and I asked how to get to Garabandal. I was handed a map and instructed in Basque to take a cab to the bus station, get on a bus to Cabezon where I could get a cab to take me the rest of the way. Holding myself inward to hear the voice of my intuition, where all other languages are magically translated, I gave thanks for my ability to understand and for each direction guiding my steps. Walking forward in my gratitude, faith and feelings of abundance, I bought an ornate box of handmade chocolates and walked out to the cab stand.

Finding my way around the massive bus terminal, I bought my ticket to Cabezon. The busses were European, modern, impeccably clean, and the male driver took enormous pride in keeping it that way. Having no idea what was going on, halfway through our two hour drive, the bus made an unexpected stop at an outdoor plaza with food stands, bathrooms and kiosks. Everybody piled out, and I walked around in silence, stretching and listening for a clue. After about fifteen minutes had passed, everybody piled back in and we drove farther into the country. Green hills with houses and walls built of stone were all that were apparent for miles as the bus pulled over to a bench on the side of the road. The driver indicated this was my stop, pointing to the little wooden sign nailed to the wooden awning above the bench that said, "Cabezon." I stepped from the bus, the only one to get off at this stop, and sat down on the bench in the middle of the countryside with my small carry-on and box of chocolates. Looking around at nothing but hills, I was freezing solidly to the bench and asked what to do next. "get up and walk" were the words of encouragement, and I left the bench walking across the road upward to the top of the knoll. As my head rose above the crest, I found myself looking at a a semi-circle of cab drivers waiting for passengers in a small town center. I chose my cab, and shared some chocolates with my driver. We laughed as we tried to communicate, though he knew Garabandal, and we drove up through the Pena Sangra mountains for another forty-five minutes all the way to the top.

I shivered, feeling the dramatically cooler temperature of the elevation walking up to the Inn from the road. Surprised to see a group of American folk sitting on a bench out front, I introduced myself and asked about lodging. A man named Michael, wearing a massive crucifix on a sturdy chain, informed me that it was Easter week and all the inns were full with devoted Catholics. The three women he was with asked how I got there, surprised and amazed I would travel so far by myself without a group or a plan. Michael made a mumbled reference to a dark haired woman and "Satan," and I walked away cutting his thread with a "thank you." After I wandered another five minutes into the village, Michael rushed up I suppose feeling his Christian obligation to assist me, and brought me to the small village grocery. He spoke to Rosario, who offered me a room in her house upstairs above the store, and I gratefully accepted. She had me wait in her immaculately clean kitchen while she made the bed and showed me how to lock and unlock the door, demonstrating the importance of doing it correctly.

Nodding my head with a smile of reassurance, I took the key and entered the delightful room still unclear about how much I agreed to compensate her. Lifting my suitcase onto the bed and offering my gratitude to the angels, I looked around for a heater. Without any indication of a heat source, I did the next logical thing to get warm.

Slowly turning the knob in the shower, ecstatic to discover the water ran hot to scalding, I stood heavy and still, soaking in the heat to the cells of my bones. My mind responded to the warmth and relaxation by going peacefully blank. The words "Easter week" emerged from the depths of my mind while sudsing and rinsing my hair, then reaching for my bar of herbal soap and wash cloth. "How could that be, Easter and Orthodox Easter on the same day" ? My thoughts on the matter brought me around to semi- consciousness and a smile emerged on my face as I dried off, recalling Father Dogias at Easter mass some years prior in Sacramento cracking a joke wondering who the Catholics had buried the week before.

Immediately towel drying my hair and twisting it up with a clip, I felt a moment of regret remembering I brought no hair dryer. Quickly putting on multiple layers of cotton, silk and wool, I jumped into bed to retain my heat. Nestling into the sheets and blankets, placing a dry towel on my pillow, I prayed my long hair would dry in the cold air over night. Too tired to give it another thought, I turned off the switch and passed out with the light.

At sunrise, I woke curiously to the sound of bawling cattle. Darting to the window to open the shutters, I realized my room was at the side of the house with neighbors directly across the narrow alley and a view of a path up the hill beyond them. I laughed out loud watching the cows running through the tight passage of the cobblestone lane, pushing and squeezing their way to the next pasture for grazing.

Finding my hair still damp and cold, I brushed it through, twisted it up again and scouted the village for coffee. There was a bar that served coffee that was ridiculously delicious. Receiving it as another blessing, I smiled and bellied up. The coffee, hot and nurturing, set the tune happily for my day. I inquired as to a cafe or restaurant. There were three meals a day served at the inn at specific times, and after walking by and seeing the weight of the offerings, I opted for cake and yoghurt from the grocery. Asking the Americans where to find fruit, I was told a truck came once a week on Thursday loaded with goods for the locals. I looked forward to 10 a.m. the next day to stock up for my last days in the village.

The path to the pines at the top of the hill is lined with the Via Crucis, and many American Catholics stopped to kneel down at each one and sorrowfully pray. Consequently, it took them hours to get to the top and I tried to understand the mind set of these people. I respectfully hiked on by, appreciating the beauty of the land, and meditated in the misty mountain air at the foot of the pines. The air was refreshing and beautiful and the vibration of white light purity filled my lungs with every deep breath and seemed to elongate my spine. Finding it difficult to ground my energy here, I let it go and let the peace I felt infuse me.

Roman forts built of stone could be seen on the distant hilltops as old as the church in the village which was established in 1600. I picked the colorful wild flowers dotted the green hills to press in my book, and each morning I gathered a small bouquet to place in the church. The church was stone with French architecture, beautiful and quiet. I stopped in purposefully when mass was not being said and was void of other people. Placing the flowers at the foot of Our Lady, I took my seat about midway from the isle on a pew to the left. It was easy to ground my energy there, so I followed my normal meditation process and steeped in the love I could feel in and around me.

About fifteen minutes into my meditation, the door of the church opened. Holding my energy peacefully inward, I did not open my eyes or break my flow. I heard people file into the pews behind and in front of me, and one woman in the front led the other women in the rosary. Sitting in my meditation, I listened to them pray. Tears welled in my eyes feeling the vibration of their love and devotion to the Divine Feminine and it opened my heart incredibly. Halfway through their prayers, I opened my eyes to see a large golden ball of light form in the center isle toward the altar. It faded away as feelings of unworthiness over shadowed the beauty of what was happening right before my eyes.When they were finished, the women left in a quiet and orderly fashion. I remained meditating, with tears drying to the sides of my cheeks after being moved by this experience so deeply.

Walking from the pines the next morning, I saw the old white truck with a rounded canopy of canvas pull up and unload its contents onto several long tables. The mostly older women emerged from their homes wearing their wooden clogs and crocheted shawls, carrying sturdy hand woven baskets. Standing back, I made room for them to pass and observed how it was done.

Although our souls bonded in the rosary experience the previous day, being an outsider I felt it good manners to be in the back of the line while the locals picked over the goods first. Traveling through Europe many times I have felt embarrassed to be American by how Americans behave, and all the way up in the Cantabrian Mountains was no exception. Our contentment was loudly interrupted by an American woman pushing her way ahead of the others to reach in front of them and shove fruit into her bag. I watched her try to negotiate the price in a one-sided argument with the vendor, and abruptly leave. Giving up a prayer that she awaken to inner peace, I bought my fruit and wove the stem of a bright pink wildflower into the black crocheted shawl of the woman standing next to me who smiled and walked home a little brighter than she had arrived.

The American Catholics were not without their processions for holy week, and I heard them from my room making their way down the hill marching with huge wooden crosses clutched securely in their hands. Heavy crosses dangled from the necks of those in the lead, swaying from left to right. Finding this amusing, I rushed to my bedroom door to go outside only to find myself locked in my room. My thoughts went from "Could this be what Rosario was trying to show me? I've had no trouble with it before now, and how the hell am I gonna get out of here?" With nothing to do but wait, I sat at my open window for a familiar face to walk by. After some time, Michael passed by, I gave him a holler and tossed him my key, and he came to unlock me from my room. I thought the timing of that was interesting, and I never had any trouble with the lock after that.

My last day I spent in meditation and silence, paying one last visit to the bar for coffee and to say good-bye to the man who always graciously served me. The Ladies of Michael were there and hugged me goodbye. Kathleen handed me a red plastic rosary with a charm attached to a small piece of a page of the book Mother Mary kissed in a visitation to the girls. She told me to take it for protection and I thanked her for her thoughtful gesture. I packed and got ready for my early departure to Bilbao, having no idea where the cab would be coming from to take me there. By the time I reached the end of the road, a cabbie was driving someone in, and I pulled him over.

The driver agreed to take me all the way to Bilbao and we drove through the mountains sharing my last few chocolates. Feeling safe in the Basque country, I had no worry or suspicion when the driver stopped at a roadside cafe for a coffee per his insistence. We walked in, he went to the back, and I ordered a couple of *esnea lurrunetan batera kafea* (coffee with steamed milk). We sat at the bar quietly sipping our coffee. When we were finished, he lifted his square chin slightly toward me, winked and subtly motioned his head to the door.

We drove to the Ritz where I luxuriated in a two-hour shower with lots of scented soap. A soft robe and a hair dryer were topped only by the feel of a lined wool skirt, a silk top and well made Italian pumps that got me grounded again. Strolling the city of Bilbao, I popped into a couple of shops before dinner. Reminiscent of Roma in the early eighties before they cleaned the soot from the statues, I fell in love with the nostalgia of another European city. Indulging in a warm meal of beautifully prepared fish and a glass of wine, I was unwound to bliss bringing me to immense gratitude for the whole fabulous experience. At day break we drove out of the city past the Guggenheim Museum that sits along the banks of the Nervion River flowing with my thoughts to the Cantabrian sea. The sea and the land passed underneath me, anchoring me again in everyday life, the closer I got to the colorful land of Fe.

Dolores and family decided to move out to Santa Fe, and I supported her emotionally and intuitively in making the transition. She left the Bay Area after her early retirement from the corporate world, bought a home close to mine, and continued with her personal development. Our lives intertwined and we proved to be constant companions for each other in many ways and life continued to expand. The new routine felt solid and organized, with each morning a little brighter and each day feeling settled and more optimistic. Everything was functional and supportive and I was expanding my circle of friends.

Spring bloomed as did the news of the dot com crash in Silicon Valley which filled the airwaves shortly thereafter and my thoughts of offering more European tours shrank to the inspiration of hosting week long retreats in Sacred Santa Fe. My local workshops had great turnouts and I took everyone to sacred sites I too wanted to discover.

My first summer in Santa Fe was full of having fun taking my clients to climb the cliff dwellings of the ancient Anasazi, to the Loretto Chapel, the St. Francis Cathedral, and the El Santuario de Chimayo to gather some sacred soil from the hole in the chapel floor.

In the fall of 2000, I focused on establishing a flow within my home. Things were uneventful and peaceful for months. Dreamtime went flat but my enthusiasm brought us through the Santa Fe holiday experience with sparkling ribbons and gifts of unending friendships and joy. We slid into 2001 with a sense of ease having had a rest from all the movement the previous year, and I decided it was time to step up from a licentiate minister to an ordained priest.

Early in the spring, a client named Katerina organized a group of Tibetan monks for their tour in California and New Mexico, stayed with us several times in Santa Fe. While visiting, she introduced me to Indian food and a wonderful beverage called chai. I was really happy to notice how my resistance to Indian cuisine was no longer there and how we found an amazing place right downtown.

While I was visiting Katerina in Palo Alto, she took me to a woman's house who was in her eighties and looked about sixty. She had been the personal assistant of Sathya Sai Baba for sixteen years in her younger years. Her house was simple, warm and peaceful. A huge shallow round brass bowl sat in the center of her living room table filled with and abundance of brightly colored flowers afloat on the water's surface. We sat on the couch making ourselves at home, and Doris emerged in minutes with a tray of cookies and tea. Her shelves were lined with books and potted plants, and she invited me to walk around and have a look at her things.

On the back wall in a glass case hung an orange robe that had belonged to Sathya Sai Baba, and an 8 1/2 x 11 portrait of his face hung above the case. The robe was much smaller than I ever would have imagined, and I walked up to the case convinced I wouldn't feel a darned thing. Feeling a huge pressure immediately in my chest, I stepped back. As sure as I could feel it was as sure I was going to deny it, and I sat back down on the couch not saying a word. We looked through her personal photo album of her time in India, and when we left, she gave us two big hugs and two bags of a scented ash called *vibuthi*. Feeling blessed both coming and going from the sweetness of her dwelling, I waited until we left to ask Katerina what *vibuthi* was all about. She explained *vibuthi* is sacred ash that manifests through the hands of Sathya Sai Baba and can be used many ways, but most put it as a dot on their forehead.

A few weeks later, Katerina visited Santa Fe again and we took a trip to the VLA (Very Large Array), a radio astronomy observatory comprised of twenty-seven radio telescope dishes outside of Socorro. The array is used to make observations of black holes and proto-planetary disks around young stars and is quite an amazing spectacle. Passing through a very small nearby town called Magdalena she bought me an antique silver Jerusalem cross with a huge aquamarine in the center for my upcoming ordination.

Summer was almost upon us as was the demand for change. An eruption of dark dreams concerning Marius exploded into my awareness interrupted only by one colorful dream involving an adventure with Madonna and the battle of my divided consciousness marched on.

May 22, 2001 Dreamtime

Marius and I went to Las Vegas where he met up with a girl he knew. He went to sit with one of the guys to watch a boxing match. I finally had it and told him I wouldn't do this anymore, that I deserve to be respected, loved and appreciated. I packed my dresses, calling for a bellman. The maid came in to clean up. I told him it took me years to realize many things about our time together, and I went to another hotel and then out to the opera. Marius ignored me the whole time. I asked him how he would feel if it were done to him and he would not answer me, as always.

May 24, 2001 Dreamtime

Madonna and I spent hours in her bed sharing to the depths of our souls. I attended a creative university in Portland Oregon where there were wonderful fabrics from the 1960's and 1970's, chartreuse and apple green shades, paisley and other happy designs. The people were fun and lively. I felt this to be a powerful metaphor for the growing creative connection building within me.

May 26, 2001 Dreamtime

Five henchmen came by my house and let me know they knew I still had photos they wanted. I was busy trying to coordinate time with my computer guy, when they interrupted. So I changed my evening plans to deal with this. They said wanted the photos and were not leaving without them. I handed them over; we chatted for a bit, as I closed the front door behind them. I was not scared.

June 06, 2001 Journal Entry/ Real time

I burned the remaining photos of my weddings, marriage certificates, my little black dress and threw away various gifts I was still hanging onto.

June 07, 2001 Dreamtime

I met an Italian family that had a boat that could not float because there was no water, so we got the fire department to flood the canal so we could leave. I met up with Marius; he was in need of money. He was stripping down. I had only a couple things-a green crocheted skirt and silk Chinese dress- but I got them for him to sell. I told him how much I profited the last time I sold some boxes of my old stuff. We got in the boat and the water was muddy. We came to a fork and I suggested we go left; he steered the boat right, but we ended up back on the left, then merged with one river. Stopping at a metaphysical book store to get a rare herb I needed, the woman told me I had fallen victim to something. I looked right at her and said "I don't believe I have fallen victim to anything." Sitting in front of the cards and crystals, the woman pulled some cards for Marius. The first card showed a picture of the bright sun with rays; the second card showed a rain cloud, and the third card was as a circle with one half black and one half white. Marius felt uncomfortable, got up and continued to look around. The woman stopped him and spoke to Marius' heart as if he were a very small child. He had no use of his adult mind; it was not able to respond or comprehend, he was starry-eyed. She put down some artwork on a piece of paper with a young girl's face on it and a half circle of pink/red over the bottom half of the picture and told him to sit with it.

Marius turned into a little boy and fell deeply into the picture. His sparkling gray / blue eyes were outstanding against his reddish white cheeks, and I recalled a picture his mother had of him taken when he was a young boy.

June 08, 2001 Journal Entry /Real Time

My morning inner sessions, took me through the myriad of feelings I had departing with some of the last physical pieces from men I loved. It took willingness and focus and keeping my eye on the gratitude I felt afterward knowing I was reclaiming deeper levels of the darkness still enmeshed in my being.

I was eagerly anticipating my ordination planned for the end of June when focused on fun outside of my morning sessions. Dubhlainn came out for the service and celebration, relieved I had set up life and got things settled. He loved the home I created throughout the previous year with rich and warm Ralph Lauren colors and leather. I resented his desire to want to try our marriage again after all the work I had done to get things in order without his help. He toyed with the idea of moving back, selling real estate, and I sat on the fence.

Katerina came out for my ordination soon after a trip to India, and I spoke to her about the monks she adored and how little it took to keep oneself attuned to God while concealed from society on a mountain top in a monastery. My spirit's expression through the lens of my sometimes irreverent truth couldn't help saying it took nothing to be at peace with no reflections. Channeling my inner "Joannie," I remarked how ridiculous it is that people without discernment, fall at the feet of anyone who declares their devotion to God, shaves their head, and wraps themselves in an orange robe. She tolerated my irreverent, humorous rants but did not laugh with me at times. Katerina was a devotee of Sathya Sai Baba, and more attuned to the mind than realization through the integration of opposites.

When staying at her house, we met after morning coffee in her bedroom to meditate, and settled on different sides of her big bed. Surrendering deeply into the meditation, I felt a surge of energy rush from the base of my spine to my heart chakra, bursting it wide open. Tears overwhelmed me, and my heart opened to the face of Sathya Sai Baba who was there smiling at me. My heart smiled back as an acknowledgement of his presence and I felt the vibration of divine laughter that accompanied him. He came to me to show me my heart, his love, and my next level of mastery. My connection with him added different dimensions to my spiritual experience, as he began to show up everywhere in my reality, pulling up every carpet, and shining light in the unkempt corners of my soul. Katerina looked at me with the smile of knowing, and I returned the gesture with a smile, knowing no words were necessary.

Back in Santa Fe, I was becoming even more familiar with our new surroundings, and discovered that an ice chest, bottle of water and picnic blanket were as important to cart around as a spare tire. We enjoyed spontaneous outings at our favorite swimming hole and climbing to the caves of the ancient Anasazi. Mediating between worlds to harmonize the energy still at war between Native Americans and the "white man" on my client's properties and homes in Taos and Los Alamos, was quite a historical revelation. I was deeply honored to help the spirits come to a place of peace within the light of love from both sides of the conflict.

As summer waned, I treated myself and a dear friend to front row seats at the Santa Fe opera. Our journey out for the evening brought me to a very popular restaurant off the Paseo de Peralta. My girlfriend Daniela came out from Scottsdale for the event and on the way we stopped for a glass of wine and a light meal.

I chose a seat at the end of the bar against the wall, and Daniela sat between me and one of the most physically beautiful men I had ever seen. We all said hello and he introduced himself as "Gabriel." His hair was more salt than pepper, and his face and body were youthful and toned, as if carved by angels. He had wide shoulders countered by a narrow waist and hip line; his skin was tanned, hydrated, unwrinkled and smooth. His arms, hands and chest were hairless and he was wearing a perfectly pressed light blue linen summer shirt. He wore an expensive gold watch inlaid with mother of pearl that was unique and would have looked odd on any other man.

See beneath projections of love and you cannot be fooled by the fear residing within it. For it is not the actions from which one professes love, but from the source from which one extends it.

- Siobhan Nicolaou, The Sword of Truth

Looking past Daniela at each other, the masculine heat that beamed through his brown magnetic eyes locked onto my energy field and I got a bit dizzy. He smiled, my breath quickened, my lips fell apart in submission, and my body felt a pull that almost moved me completely from my chair. The energy was so powerful I was positive there was little that would keep us apart. Gabriel handed me his card and said to meet him here later that week after work for cocktails. Thanking him for the card, I went to the loo

197

to pull myself together from the high of the energy and to get grounded. All Daniela could say was "hubba hubba," and commented on the intensity of the current as she sat between the two of us during this experience.

My week passed with hardly a thought, still reeling from the exquisite performance of the soprano in Lucia di Lammermoor, until I showed up at the cafe. Gabriel introduced me to his female associate sitting on the couch adjoining his, and it wasn't long before she felt like the third wheel and excused herself. We sat smiling transfixed on each other's faces, and finished our wine. We were both members of the same tennis club, so we agreed to meet there a few days later, and took his car to lunch. More than charming, he was enchanting, soft spoken, with perfectly veneered teeth that gleamed against his blended bronze Apache and Spanish skin. He was educated and well read; we had a good conversation, a light lunch and a time limit.

Walking toward his vehicle, he unlocked the door as we crossed the circular stone paved entrance. He reached in front of me to open my door and before I could take a step up into the car, an unseen force turned me physically in his direction as if to kiss him. Stopping myself and turning quickly away, I asked him what the hell had just happened, noting how strange it was. Gabriel just smiled. I got in the car and he drove me back to the club.

Schedules with work and children kept our thoughts off of each other until the bus-i-ness of our airwaves went flat as the school year drew near. I received a phone call from him at around 11p.m. asking how I was doing, and if I wanted to come by for a glass of wine to catch up. Not sure how I felt, I suggested we leave things as they were and declined his invitation. About a week passed, and he called again around 11 PM, putting the same invitation on the table. Anastasia was hours into dreamtime, and I asked a long time friend staying with us if she would mind holding down the fort. Obtaining directions and a gate code, I drove out under the starry skies of a beautiful Santa Fe night. Gabriel lived on an estate in a beautiful house he rented from a friend who was helping him through the end of a bitter divorce. A real estate mogul for decades, he lived well and had elegant taste.

I walked with reservation into his courtyard up to the front door, which he left ajar, I took a breath and stepped in. Gabriel motioned me to take a seat on his couch, as he walked over with a warm hello, a bottle of red wine and two etched crystal and gold rimmed wine glasses. We sat sipping wine, munching on toasted pinyon, and laughed while becoming acquainted. Suddenly, all sound dissipated from the tips of our tongues as our words faded to ether. Gabriel reached his hand slowly to my face without saying a word and gently turned my chin toward his. His eyes penetrated mine and with an uninterrupted gaze he brought our lips together. My eyes lids slowly closed, and our energies combined in the heat of our kiss causing a alchemical reaction to occur. A new substance formed, possessing the most intriguing properties of the constituent energies that would hit the stage almost immediately. Our energy ignited, and after that evening we engaged in a physical relationship of convenience and discretion. Anastasia did not know he existed and I kept it that way. I was happy to have a lover to complete the one area in my life that was otherwise void, but Gabriel's energy set the fires of destruction that melted me almost completely to the core.

My physical contact with Gabriel brought to light clever dynamics of a pattern within the same old energy that would begin to take more of an animated form. From the pitch black invisible underworld, to the dark gray lower astral visible world of form. . . my demons were now demanding more of my love and integration. The devil raised the stakes, I pushed in my chips, called his hand, and my shadow play dramatically emerged.

Inhaling the morning air of September 11th while driving Anastasia to school, my mind was calm and in the mode of the morning routine. After drop off, I drove to Whole Foods, contemplating ingredients for dinner. Backing out of my parking space to leave, I hit a car passing behind me and did some damage to the front panel of a crappy Ford Taurus. Driving out of the parking lot after exchanging information, I felt strange, really altered and wondered how I did not see this guy even though I had looked behind twice while pulling out. Mentally tossing my woes to the desk of my insurance company, I turned on NPR and set the course for Eldorado. Before I could get to the highway, news came over the radio that two planes had just gone through the twin towers in New York City. A huge wave of the collective fear rippled through my body, and in that moment the accident made sense as did so many other things. My heart dropped to my fear, and uncertain about many things, I now included everything in my uncertainty.

Gabriel and I saw each other more frequently, always at his place and after my Anastasia was long asleep. With every dominant infusion of his energy, I began to split like the energy of Santa Fe itself. My multidimensional experience was made up of the stark contrast of Christianity with the lowest levels of shamanism unintegrated therein. Both sides warring in opposition and separate teachings within themselves, I experienced the beauty and the beast of it all.

Gabriel was a man of deep-seated pain masked by many faces that revealed themselves to me in glimpses, until we spent enough time together for me to see more clearly behind the curtain. Raised Catholic with a native soul, he was baptized born-again Christian when he was married for the second time. Gabriel crafted an outward image he cast like a spell that deluded all he enfolded. I never asked him when, where or what he did and only once picked up the phone to call him. Our coupling reached so deeply inside each other that no words were possible and Gabriel's energy coursed through me like an addiction that I could not get out of my veins.

The patterns of energy that became more active within me through Gabriel, I believed I had overcome years previously. I was astounded at the tirelessness of its grip and the depth with which the darkness could even hold me, and my inner work which now I could no longer ignore became once again an active part of my daily routine. I ignored one for the other, which led to the understanding how the word ignor-ance was the state of ignoring. Unworthiness and doubt crept in as my fear began to identify with the changes in outer reality and I held onto everything while trying to let go.

November 13, 2001 Journal Entry/ Real Time

Meditating and transmuting a layer of unworthiness around my father. The face of my young father appeared, glaring and daring. Out of the shadows of the a choir loft emerged about 20 bishops from the Vatican in their ornate vestments. I was screaming at them, sending back the unworthiness they put upon me so long ago, and saw my hands and wrists bleeding from stigmata as a nun. Dolores was a fellow sister and confidant then as she was in real time with me. I finished my inner session by hearing the hammer hitting nails and seeing spikes driven thru my wrists, feeling the sensations very powerfully inside of me. I finished my inner session hearing the hammer hitting nails and feeling the sensations very powerfully inside of me. Sathya

Sai Baba, Padre Pio, Mother Mary, Archangel Michael and Yeshua all stood around me, each with a different message for me to heed.

November 14, 2001 Journal Entry /Real Time

This morning my meditation was deep and intense. Dolores came in and sat down to meditate at the same time I heard and felt the hammer hitting the nails again. She got up immediately and ran into the bathroom to vomit. My feet felt open since then too. My heart opened up exposing roses and a dove that flew thru my entire form.

November 19, 2001 Journal Entry / Real Time

My legs did not function properly for days after what I would call the initiation; my wrists hurt to the shoulders and I was unable to carry anything or walk with ease.

November 27, 2001 Journal Entry / Realtime

For my birthday I was given a Mick Jagger CD as a gift: "Goddess in the Doorway." It was released six days after the stigmata initiation, which I found ironic especially listening to the lyrics of the title track. This solo album exposed the first "spiritual side" of Mick I had ever seen.

November 30, 2001 Dreamtime

Last night I was looking at the palms of my hands that were inlaid with diamonds and Sathya Sai Baba was there all night it seemed. Seeing a snake moving in and through some dried cat food, I reached in to pull it out and it came out, turned into a cobra and bit me on the crown chakra. Also dreamed a minion was in my home; his black jacket was over the back of the chair.

There were white chairs in three rows for a gathering of some sort. He was quietly reading books and looking thru a huge pornographic coloring book. I noticed but said nothing. No one really paid any attention to him we all just let him be. After the kids went to bed he pulled out some cocaine and a tray, vial and screen. He was extremely organized, clean and neat about everything. I walked up and thanked him for waiting for the kids to go to bed to indulge and to also let him know I was not really happy that he was even there.

woke up to Sai Baba this morning.

Journal Entry/Real Time

On the 29th I went to work out and could not hold the weight. My hands feel arthritic as do my elbows and shoulders. Doubt and inadequacy keep coming up. . . I am writing a letter to the Pope advising him how to reorganize the Catholic Church. The depth of my hearts knowing of the changes that need to occur within this institution that was to be built upon the edifice of Yeshua's consciousness yet continues to perpetuate separation saddens me. They are breaking the heart of God.

December 06, 2001 Journal Entry/Real Time

Feeling annoyed and restless as to what it all means. Letting go of my old self is the struggle. Spending the night at Gabriel's a couple of days ago, I left my Garabandal rosary on the night stand. He called and told me to come get it because he had been sick throwing up blood most of the day after. When I arrived he handed it to me on the end of a pencil. He wouldn't touch it. My brain is attuned to his mental flow. We communicate telepathically, and I feel when he leaves town and when he returns.

December 09, 2001 Dreamtime

Anastasia, Dubhlainn and I were in Los Angeles at a party at the Beverly Hills Country Club, which was on the beach. The whole shoreline of homes were lighted with perfectly placed garlands of gold and white bulbs and everybody was having fun. I won the drawing for a sail boat along with a sliver and carnelian necklace. The next day we were looking out over the sky and the clouds began to bleed. Drops of the clouds fell from the bottom of the cloud cover in the distance. They turned red as the drops turned to bloodlines all the way to the earth. I walked by a television airing a show about war. It was showing black and white footage of a man wearing war garb in the trenches and in the background. No one had ever noticed the clouds were bleeding then. I felt/ heard they were tears from Mother Mary, tears from heaven.

December 10, 2001 Journal Entry / Realtime

Trying to let go of Gabriel, knowing he is not good for me. Giving it more space and need to stay away.

December 12, 2001 Dreamtime

I was in India at Sai Baba's ashram talking to Katerina on the phone as a man and boy were chasing a rattlesnake to catch it. The snake was huge and by the back kitchen door. It was scared and needed direction. I had seen a woman get off her white horse because the horse was spooking. The horse was more like a pony, dwarfed almost. I was talking about my Sai Baba cards and how they were supposed to be humorous. The deck I had was someone else's deck, negative and serious and I pulled the death card three times in a row. A young boy and Anastasia were off playing, then walking down a hallway, the young boy passed me, went into his room and hopped into his wooden crib to take a nap. I told Katerina how I felt at home there and was not homesick. This is my third dream of Sai Baba's ashram.

December 13, 2001 Dreamtime

Dubhlainn and I were invited to Anthony Hopkin's house in Los Angeles. It was huge, like a palace, with very tight security. I was invited because Anthony wished me to become one of his concubines. As we walked toward the house, I saw a huge private jet to my right that was broken in two pieces. We had to use a phone to speak with security. The number was #1516 for the proper extension. Sathya Sai Baba was there that day and hundreds of people were gathered to see him. The size of the house was unreal. Dubhlainn and I walked through the wing of the house where the gathering was taking place, and I stopped. I told Dubhlainn that I wanted to meet Sai Baba and how rare it was that anybody could do that. I walked up past the whole group that was gathered, through a room, then a hallway with lit candles and into a room with flower petals up the steps. At the foot of the steps were four others and I knelt down. Sai Baba came out and spoke to each one of us. He came to me, reached out his hands, cupped mine and said, "You will be speaking and meeting many people." He gave me a book and told me that I would meet a woman and that it would be for her. He instructed me to keep it in a rose box

with gold leaf. Then I left and had lunch with Anthony.

The new year began with the best effort to let Gabriel go. Seeing him much less, I worked on freeing our energies on all levels and gave more attention to my spiritual projects. Our energy drew us together with each of us striving to integrate the other, and we pulled ourselves apart not seeing it was our own inner conflict. We were so much alike in the best ways that I chose to focus on those positive aspects and consciously ignore the rest.

Creating space and allowing more for myself than the pull of Gabriel, I accepted an invitation to a talk given by Grandfather Cachora, a respected elder and spiritual leader of the Yaqui nation of Sonora, Mexico. Cachora was referred to as "Don Juan" through the books of Carlos Castaneda. He embodied the knowledge and medicine of some four thousand plants passed down through his lineage, spending most of his days teaching apprentices and gathering and studying plants in the Sonoran Desert.

Cachora appeared intense at first, his eyes shaded from the light by his black wide brimmed hat.

"The hat was formed with a humble downturned brim, crowned with a single golden eagle feather set in the right side of the woven band. He stood straight and strong through his talk, his hands joined in front of his solar plexus, above his red tunic and behind his deer hide vest embroidered with golden scorpions and edged with cowry shells. Chief Golden Eagle opened the circle of the teachings with a song honoring Cachora and all chiefs that serve the sacred hoop."

-Obit, Dec 7, 2002 (blog post)

It was two days before Cachora's eighty-eighth birthday and he looked younger than most men in their sixties. I was introduced to Chief Golden Light Eagle of the Yankton Lakota Sioux who hosted the event. In our introduction, when I mentioned my logo was the golden butterfly, I saw the heights of his soul in his eyes as his energy responded to my words. Our meeting was brief and I was whisked away, ushered to sit in the row behind the cameras as the lights were dimmed. I felt Cachora's deep connection to the earth via a pulse emanating from his aura that felt like the beat of a low steady drum. Though he spoke with an interpreter, the waves of his wisdom resonated with my soul.

Our evening ended with some interesting insights accompanied by an inner knowing that I would be invited to the sweat lodge ceremony slated over the weekend, but had no idea how that would unfold. Rising from a good night's sleep and a dream of a hawk flying through my house, I was aware of the messenger and knew word was on its way. A sister named Red Moon later called to indeed extend the invitation from the Chief and give me directions.

I prepared food to bring as one of my offerings, gathered up Anastasia, packed the 4 Runner and drove up to Chimayo. My mind wandered on the drive, noting that I had visited South Dakota so many years before and had felt a connection to the land and the people there. Driving onto the property, part of me felt it had come home. Children ran around happily playing games and the women all wearing skirts managed the inflow of food for the feast preceding the ceremony. The sweat lodge, built to all sacred specs, was obviously a permanent fixture on the land of this humble adobe home. Preparation of the stones for ceremony began and those of us who were aware responded reverently to the shifting energy and the consecration taking place.

The children were left in the care of the women who opted to stay outside, and we gathered at the entrance to take off our jewelry and make an offering before entering the lodge. Smudged as we entered, we took our places, men on one side and women on the other. The hot stones were passed from keeper to keeper via deer antlers and placed in the pit, then sprinkled with cedar.

Sitting on my towel, pulling myself inward, listening to the songs led by the Chief and the Medicine Man, I allowed the heat to consume me. We passed the pipe and prayed. Chief Golden Eagle asked me to speak for Archangel Michael, and I spoke from the truth of his sword. The songs pulled me from the ground of the lodge to a more expansive place within my soul. I experienced no roof above me but a vast sky with visible planets and bright twinkling stars. Teetering on the edge of what began to feel like internal combustion, I stayed with the heat it until I broke through to the other side. We concluded our lodge as ceremoniously as we began, and cooled off in the air of the evening, changed clothes and reconvened for dinner. Driving home that night, I felt beauty and abundance, having been blessed by the whole experience and by Chief Golden Light Eagle who gave me the native name Kimimila Zizi Waste Win (Golden Butterfly Woman).

I later received an invitation to celebrate Cachora's birthday in Eldorado on Monday night and gratefully accepted. Tuning inward to this connection to my new friends, I asked myself what kind of cake Cachora would want for his celebration. Pumpkin cheese cake with toasted pinion came to my mind, and so it was. Molded in nine-inch round, three-inch deep springform pan, with toasted pinyon crust, garnished with a rust and gold colored Gerbera daisy and a sprinkle of confectioner's sugar, it was the grande finale of the feast.

Arriving Monday afternoon, I found the women busy in their too-small-to-include-me kitchen, and the children played among the *choya* and juniper on the expansive dusty terrain. The dogs relaxed in the shade cast by the table tops at the feet of the men that sat around them. I sat indoors in a room with a single massive chunk of amethyst crystal points listening to the wise, humorous and poignant stories of a Blackfoot Medicine Man.

When dinner was ready, everyone gathered to bless the food that covered the top of the long rustic wooden table. The drum beat as the Chiefs carried our hearts on the joyous waves of their reverent tones with a ceremony lasting twenty minutes. The blessing came to a close with the last beat of the drum striking the soft deer hide stretched tightly across the strong wooden frame. Receiving a call from Gabriel, I took myself outside the circle and into an empty room to connect, then collected my things and went to see him before I made my way home for the night.

Not seeing I was tearing myself between the two worlds of the old and the new, I created more conflict playing both sides not integrated enough to hold myself strongly in the middle. My body wasn't all, Gabriel wanted my soul and here is where the battle line was drawn. Something in him wanted to possess me and sunk hooks deep inside my psyche as well as my emotional and physical bodies. We were enmeshed; at times I felt I was him reaching for a puff off of his cigarette. Consciously I wondered what would happen if I did as it had been so many years since I had touched a cigarette; at the same time I was wondering why it was happening at all. I would wake in the middle of the night feeling the movement of his body having sex somewhere else, giving me information about his whereabouts I didn't care to know. Other times I woke in the middle of the night, struggling to stand on the way to the bathroom, feeling as if I had no arms, falling to the ground, perspiring heavily and nearly passing out. Breathless and weak I would call to my housemate for help getting back in bed.

Journal Entry / Realtime

I lay in bed an entire day, not able to move, feeling wounded on my left side as life carried on in the rest of the house. The next day my body felt the strength of ten thousand men and I was off to the gym; other days I am a physical wreck. I manifested extremely sharp pain and aches through my forehead and eyes all the way down to my upper gums, and do not understand what is happening.

Dolores and Rachel, witnessed my physical struggle and dire need for rest while dismissing it not sure what any of it really meant.

Objects like reading glasses flew across the room at will when I was in the company of other men. Sensitives would ask me who the man was standing in my aura matching Gabriel's description. Seeing a semblance of his body appear in places where he was especially attached was common for me, and the more I tried to let go, the bigger his presence became in my life. I felt there may be a chance for love if he could change through my love for him and my acceptance of all of his behavior. Not seeing it as control, though subtle and unintentional, my desire that he come to love was enough to keep our energies entwined.

My dreams were many throughout 2002, overlapping, multidimensional and intense. Unfinished business in relationships, premonitions, core issues, reminders of my loving entourage and facets of my deepest feelings blew through my dream space and scrawled into my journals. Day to day, I enjoyed the overall fun of living in Santa Fe and acting on my endless creative inspirations.

February 02, 2002 Dreamtime

I was at a massive dark angel gathering. One of the guys was wearing a black vestment. Standing in front, he began to say black mass. He mumbled incantations, consecrating the brown "host." It was coiled bread in a spiral. Finishing his words, he passed it around for all to partake. He said specifically not to pray to God because this mass was for the devil. As the host was being passed, a group of men all in black satin robes performed hand gestures in a circle facing each other and again began reciting incantations. The bread made its way around the crowd and each person tore a piece off and ate it. Taking a piece and eating it, I prayed to God and my wings felt as if they had grown considerably in size. I bit the host, becoming full of golden light, and felt my being become light, ascending with wings. I was surprisingly welcome among the dark angels, they were respectful and all knew who I was. To prevent me from leaving, a group of women came over to introduce themselves. They all shook my hand with the look and feeling of intimidation. Not feeling threatened, I told them I wanted to see Archangel Michael as he was the only angel I ever wanted to be with. I explained that I loved him so much that I would have died for him and walked away to leave when my cell phone beeped saying that I hadn't paid my bill. It threatened to run out of charge within minutes. Recalling I had paid the bill, it befuddled me and I was worried I could not reach Anastasia if she needed me. Getting in the car, it slowed to a stop sign with a long road ahead.

In my daily meditations, a light being began showing up lying on a cross on the ground from a side view. He would turn his head and come up off of the cross, looking at me with huge distinctive blue eyes, though the rest of his form was vague. At times there was no cross, just those huge blue eyes looking straight at me. They were intense, though not in an intimidating way; they were unique, just looking at me. After a couple of months, I began asking in my heart "who are you?" and with no immediate response, I let it be and gave it no resistance.

February 03, 2002 Dreamtime

I dreamed of a man with long blonde hair . . .he was my mate and his last name was "doro." He had a ton of energy and had been living with men most of his life.

February 04, 2002 Dreamtime

Anastasia and I were in East West Bookshop looking around. Two men we knew said "you should stick around, there is a special man coming here tonight." We were hanging out when he walked in people were all around him all I saw was his beautiful face, dark hair and great smile. His name was Krishna Murtthi. A big man, he exuded unconditional love and everybody wanted to be near him. Being near him was magic. His energy enabled me to dance Indian dances and move my hands effortlessly. I saw myself dancing in my magenta sari. He asked if we wanted a healing and we said yes. We went and laid down. My body fell into stasis, motionless and peaceful. Through the beaming of his hands I saw images of my issues flashing all around me like movie clips. Later we were sitting around chatting about who would be his companion. I thought I was the best for him, but told him "I was not made to sit at the foot of a man, but there I was"!

March 01, 2002 Dreamtime

I left for town with Anastasia and visited a local bath house. There were many outdoor small one-man wooden tubs inscribed on the sides with pastel colored symbols and words about the town and a Shaman "Solomon" who could cast out the witch in people. There were people soaking in the tubs with essential oils and sea salts. The town was pure, simple and healing.

March 03, 2002 Dreamtime

Golden Light Eagle came over. We were holding hands and being close. He told me he tried to bring some people over for counseling, but I wasn't home.

March 03, 2002 Dreamtime

Anastasia and I drove home past a house where some really wealthy people lived. Their front lawn was the size of a park and had a holographic projection of Beauty and the Beast enacting itself in light and color all over the lawn. It was really dark, but a beautiful night. Out of nowhere, Marius called me on my cell. He sounded and looked funny. (I could see his face as we spoke). It was like he was in a dead sleep and suddenly woke to call me to ask if everything was ok. He had the feeling I might be in trouble of some kind.

March 28, 2002 Dreamtime

I was four months pregnant and the paper indicated it was a boy. I told my sister Sara it was impossible because I was having my period. She told me it happened all the time.

May 16, 2002 Dreamtime

I was putting together a wedding ceremony to unwed myself from Dubhlainn. There were two goblets- chalices. The crystal one held milk & the other held whiskey. I was frustrated and didn't want us to share the milk because it was what held us together. It was the nourishment.

July 28, 2002 Dreamtime

I was visiting my brothers and sisters in the mountains somewhere. My dad was there and he was smothering and controlling like Dubhlainn. I kept trying to leave. He burned holes in me with his eyes, his glare was so strong. His eyes were blue in this dream. He would physically try to stop me and become more intimidating. I am awake now and it is 4 a.m. It feels like Dubhlainn. The town was a place I had never felt before, dreamed of or visited. There were three streets mentioned at some point. One was "Independence Ave" I said that I liked that one and the gal said, "well that is in Chicago."

August 13, 2002 Dreamtime

My grandma called me on a cell phone from heaven. The connection and conversation was very clear. I was so happy, I told everyone that there are cell phones in the afterlife. Grandma and I spoke for about half an hour, then the line went dead. Typical cell phone behavior, I thought.

Also dreamed myself as a three year old child was kidnapped. We searched and searched and eventually found her unharmed. She was happy to see me, her shoes were on the wrong feet and she was not really in her body.

August 14, 2002 Dreamtime

I was in the South managing a class for Mrs. Wilkinson. The boys broke five shelves of half gallon bottles of booze onto the floor of a large store room. The cops were called and they came. It seemed as though it took forever. We all formed two single file lines and the kids turned into adults. We were sloppy leaving the building. All of a sudden our surroundings turned into a military-like facility. The woman at the desk made us get back in line to exit the building. Before we could exit, we were put in a room and sprayed us with something trying to get us to conform. I felt something briefly in my head and was screaming "NO WAY!!" A HUGE wind came up that was really loud. Thunder and massive cracks of lightning broke out above our heads and a HUGE tornado was forming gaining momentum moving toward us. Everybody scrambled. The military personnel had shelter under ground, but we were left to figure it out on our own. Some men ran to the river; it was dark and kind of cold. I ran to the left up a road lined with houses, white wooden houses. I was asking God to help me; I didn't know where it would be safe because the twister was erratic. I was running and praying, asking and searching, looking for a church, thinking "it is always mobile home parks that get destroyed." Looking up, I realized I was running in the eye of the tornado. I saw the light of the sun above me; it was a beautiful day in the eye. The dark gray murky clouds swirled around me, but it was still and silent in the center. I just kept following the lead and kept in step with the center, we seemed to be in a dance.

August 10, 2002 Dreamtime

I was on my way to the big city and had to go through the wilderness to get there. I didn't have a problem with that. There was a bear that was being attacked by coyotes and a lion. I arrived at a Greek woman's house -a B&B. She was great and I loved her energy. I was changing clothes in the bathroom & caught the image of a small Jewish man in a skinny closet looking at me. I said something like "that better be the laundry." Then popping out, feeling busted, he hurriedly danced out of the room. I was getting ready to go out. I was in some kind of parade sitting on the top of the back seat of a'65 Lincoln in a classic dress and glasses, waving to people and we passed by two of the Kennedy boys, John Fitzgerald and Ted. I remarked "hey those are the Kennedys, I love the Kennedys."

October 10, 2002 Dreamtime

Gabriel and I were at his house. I was baking and cleaning, he had friends over and he was ungrounded. Somehow we were on our way to Hawaii and the planes were rolling through the streets that were set up as runways. The home owners thought it was cool. A beautiful, huge white and light brown and gold spotted owl with big gold eyes was gently floating overhead looking at us. She was like an umbrella.

Also dreamed Thanasis was having problems with his mom, same as me, after marrying his second wife Cassandra. He felt full of despair and was crying.

216

November 03, 2002 Dreamtime

Katerina and I were watching a game show on television displaying several different gems. One of the questions was about the gem that Yeshua wore. I guessed "the pearl" correctly, and I won the pearl necklace from Galilee. Looking over at Katerina, I said "what do you think?" She said she was not just envious but jealous.

Writing my dreams down was all the attention I paid them outside of getting back to my unending inner work and juggling all the joys and demands of family, home and business as a single mother. My self-confidence that was once so strong began to erode as no project I completed seemed to take root. I began taking the changes in the economy personally, as my clients scrambled from what became the Silicon Valley in the wake of the dot com crash and then 9/11.

Downsizing became my focus as I rummaged through my walk-in and roam around closet. I purged suits, dresses, coats, capes, furs and costumes I was still wearing after twenty-three years, consciously letting them go with every man attached to them.

I failed to see my self esteem was suffering from how I learned to identify myself through the ego of my mate, never being rooted deeply enough in the spirit of myself. I was so used to having men take care of me in my 50's style devotion to the ego, that I didn't believe enough in myself to keep doubt from taking over. Overwhelmed with the power play of my emotions, I shrank into my self-imposed limitation and led myself from a place of fear, instead of looking clearly at my options.

Searching for a smaller place closer to town, I drove by a "for rent" sign on the side of the road and decided to give the place a look. The place was a house behind a house, down a small curved gravel driveway to the back and half the size of the Eldorado house. I met the landlord's son Ricardo. He seemed humble, rather quiet with classic Spanish features of pale skin, dark hair with a touch of gray, and round Spanish eyes. He showed me the place and noted he lived in the front house with his parents and his sister. He asked me what I did for a living and who would be occupying the house. Telling him I was a spiritual counselor and a single mother, I handed him a brochure with a description of all my work. He handed me the application and I brought it back to his parents as he requested.

Arriving at the parents' home, feeling good about the place for many reasons, I stepped into their sparsely furnished living room that was strewn about with empty boxes and a life-sized baby Yeshua in a cradle from a manger scene. A little over the top, I thought, but I had seen stranger things, and then caught a glimpse of the daughter's shadow crossing into another room down the hallway to the right. We had a great conversation about Padre Pio and she gave me relic from his robe. Speaking to her about my love of northern Spain, I thought we found common ground and that it would be a positive front house / back house situation.

December felt cold and empty, like the hole in my heart that I continually tried to repair with the putty of man's illusion. Christmas was busy but uneventful. We had to part with our beloved cat Lucia to move into our new space, though fortunate we had a dear friend who joyfully provided her a great home. We let go and looked forward to the new beginning in 2003. Moving in January, I quickly got the house set up. Everything I didn't sell or put in storage fit and the place looked beautiful. The fireplace was huge in the middle of the house, which was all open and down a few beautiful brick steps from the front door and the narrow kitchen into a large sunken living room. I was thrilled the house would be easy to keep warm and cozy and anticipated the snow and the silent beauty of winter.

Weekly meditations were part of my schtick, and I let the front house know that every Thursday evening there would be cars arriving for the event. There did not seem to be a problem. No one voiced any opposition but I could feel-hear the energy of resistance building behind the scene like hurricane winds pounding my energy field. As the projection of negative energy became stronger from the front house, so appeared a myriad of cards with pictures of the saints and crosses in their back windows facing our home. Gabriel was keeping my emotions baited and I was not finding the strength required to let go.

January 10, 2003 Dreamtime

I was following a man who was walking down in the "hood." He felt comfortable there and as I glided feeling safe and protected, I walked unheeded as a spirit through the neighborhood, seeing the tragic destination of many souls.

January 29, 2003 Dreamtime

The night before I flew to Scottsdale to meet Gabriel to see the Rolling Stones, I dreamed of Mick Jagger for the first time in almost a decade. He sat there silently, looking at me, wearing a long sleeve black shirt, and smoking a cigarette. The smoke moved slowly around and in front of him but the air surrounding him was perfectly still. He faded to black and disappeared completely, like my $400 Matsuda sunglasses my sister gifted me that I left on my seat at the airport coming home.

January 30, 2003 Dreamtime

Second night in the house after the Stones concert, I saw an owl fly through the house. It was flying fast & gracefully but felt as if it were limited by an invisible boundary. The owl felt like me with brown and white stripes.

January 31, 2003 Journal Entry

Two different times in my new bedroom, I felt a woman watching me wanting me to leave. Last night in twilight consciousness, I saw her faceless, wearing a brown hooded Franciscan robe with a rosary dangling from the wrist, to the right and overhead poised to cut me up with an axe. I saw and felt without pain what it would be like to have my arm chopped off and separated and then feel my body sectioned piece by piece until I died. Gee whiz, all the things to realize! I asked Archangel Michael to lead her away; he did and I went back to sleep.

The energy from the front house got so strong, I had to deflect it with a major Feng Shui cure just to get some peace. Jennifer, in our conversation, asked me if I had heard of a healer in Brazil named Joao de Deus or John-of-God. I took a moment and I felt the energy of the "casa," remarking that it was the largest vortex I had ever felt anywhere on earth and I sensed the man himself as a healer to be for real. She mentioned she and Gary were taking a client down for a few weeks and asked if I wanted to present my photo with Anastasia's to the "entities" to get some herbs. I had no idea what it all meant, just that it would be healing, so I sent my photo down with Anastasia's, plus a donation.

I set my intentions with my Feng Shui cure around the property parameter and was either directly or indirectly observed by the front house. I was aware of their obscure posts of observation and the resistance created from "their side," and strange things began to occur as the energy escalated. A completely unopened double wax sealed bottle of bright apple green bath soap I used as a decoration for years turned completely white over night. Perplexed at how this could have possibly happened, I could not come up with any logical explanation. There was the smell of sulphur or egg yolk every morning in the bathroom, whose window opened out front in the direction of the septic tank. The landlord checked it out, finding nothing wrong with the lines or the tank itself, it remained puzzling. I was working at home all day with the fire crackling, except to drive to school and shop. I kept busy beautifying my home and cooking not finding much energy to do anything else, and talked to my friends about how deeply I was sleeping at night.

February 03, 2003 Dreamtime

Gabriel was sitting on a settee kissing some girl he had just met. My hairdresser was sitting nearby with two other beautiful women, watching Gabriel...

I woke up at 3:00 a.m. sweating and realized what a shitty example I was being for Anastasia and that part of me had given up and that is why. Hopelessness.

In real time, that moment, I called Gabriel and asked him to leave me alone. I MUST let go and believe in MYSELF!

I also dreamed a woman named "Merchant" hired some hippy guy to kill me. I was sitting in an old model black Cadillac.

In my strip of a "New York" kitchen as I referred to it, there was a door that I never bothered to look behind, and on several occasions it popped open. Without giving it any thought, I closed it, passing it off as a quirk of the house. The door continued opening over the next few weeks, requiring more of my attention as it happened more frequently. Then I noticed the door wasn't popping open-the handle was without question turning by itself and the door was then opening. Never feeling the presence of spirits in that home except in twilight or dreamtime, I thought oh great, something else (a ghost) I have to deal with. Resisting, I let it continue until one day on the phone with my girlfriend Candelora, I stood in front of the door, and saw the knob turn itself and the door pop open. I shared with her what was happening, knowing it was time to face it, and asked the angels what the signs were trying to tell me.

That was all it took to bring me to my answer: after the second stoking of the fire the following day, once again the handle turned and opened the door. I finally looked behind the mysterious door into what turned out to be a filthy closet housing a single old boiler. An appointment with an inspector shut the boiler off within minutes. The boiler was red-tagged as it was emitting off- the-chart levels of carbon monoxide gas. It was almost the middle of March and I had had the heat and fire cranking for a solid two and one half months sucking down carbon monoxide all day at home while Anastasia was in school. The only reason I speculate we did not die in our sleep was divine intervention. With that resolved, the only thing left to do was let go of Gabriel and cleaning up the closet of energy within me that matched this part of his. Until then, it remained a door unopened within my otherwise beautiful home.

March 04, 2003 Dreamtime

I was driving through a town that looked like Colorado with snow as deep as once I recalled when visiting Mount Shasta. I made a right turn only to be heading very fast down a very steep road, toward exactly what I was not sure. The snow was deep and I drove right through an embankment that seemed to never end. I expected to feel scared but found it interesting that I couldn't. I let the car go, not driving or steering anymore. I was thinking that I could hit a wall, tree, car or something, wondering if I should cover my face to protect it from the impact. Instead, I called Archangel Michael and asked him to take care of it and not let me get hurt. The car then came to an abrupt stop. I did not hit anyone or anything. The snow cleared from the windows completely. I looked outside and noticed the road was clear all the way behind me and was wondering how to turn the car around to head back up the road.

March 07, 2003 Journal entry / Real time

I saw Gabriel at the club who told me his sister was in town. Having met his children and best friends, I asked him to give her my number and he didn't. I was really restless tonight. Was going to go see a movie but the choices were too depressing. I dropped into my favorite cafe, and was shocked to see Gabriel's sister sitting at the bar. She was easy to pick out. She looked exactly like Gabriel with a different nose, tall and with Gabriel's shoulders. She had long black hair and the distinctive eyes shared among the members of Gabriel's family. I introduced myself and we chatted for a little while through the end of a light meal before I bid her a good evening and left.

March 07, 2003 Dreamtime

I dreamed Gabriel's sister and I were close friends. We ran around Santa Fe as a couple and I felt I loved her. I woke up with my energy feeling raw and saw her all day in my head. I studied her face in my mind.

March 09, 2003 Dreamtime

Gabriel was ill mentally and physically, lying and deceitful, bouncing around from place to place. His mother was desperate, telling me to go to him. He was being elusive. I went to his house to find out from his housekeeper that he was on a trip. He had been several other places, including Venezuela. She sounded like she was lying for him. I went to his closet-a huge room with racks of clothes and a necklace I had left there. The clothes were dry-cleaned. I noticed a picture of me on top of a shelf. There were clothes that had been left by hundreds of girls and women. There was a recurring size - it was 14. The woman they belonged to was obviously big, had big breasts & money. Her clothes were great designs, raw silks, colorful and well made. I started taking them off of the racks and throwing them on the floor. I was going to throw them out, but there were more than I thought. Then a toy metal '40s or '50s police car about the size of a Barbie car came out of nowhere toward the door of the room from the outside, lights and siren on moving slowly. I remember thinking it was the clothes police. I picked up the car and broke it in half and then again. As I went to put it in the garbage, a young dark-haired thin girl was struggling in a hurry to get her key to work in her apartment door so she could get in and get away from me quickly. She was afraid.

Awareness and hope were not enough to break the hold of the spell in my mind. I meditated everyday, kept my home life running smoothly and thanked God for the gift of Yeshua's love and integration that kept me afloat on the river, while the sharks swam right below the undercurrent of my ignorance.

My work day came to a close on March 13th running into Gabriel at the La Pousada gathering with other professionals of the community for a mixer. Very tired and with little patience observing his ego in action around the room, I tried to ignore him. I met some nice people, enjoyed a glass of wine and shook a few hands while exchanging business cards. Sitting next to the fire in an over-sized high back leather chair, I decided not to get too comfortable, and go home instead. Passing the hallway where he was entering the mens room on my way out, I acknowledged him with a slight nod as I continued to walk into the foyer and handed the valet my ticket. Driving home, I contemplated some exit strategies, leaving Gabriel in my mind through veils of disempowered frustration. At home I tried to wash my face clean of the disappointment and anger, pretending it whirled down the drain with the remnants of my winter shade of lipstick and my lash lengthening mascara. I kissed my sleeping Anastasia, tucked her in and went to bed.

An hour had passed before my determination to end the relationship caught up with my thoughts that I could not shut off to fall asleep. My intention was to gather my belongings from Gabriel's house and be done with it. Putting on my cotton two-piece pajamas, "Rocky" my full length mink coat, and my leopard print slippers, I grabbed my keys and wallet and drove slowly down the driveway. With only my parking lights on, I turned right onto the well-lit road adjusted my coat, turned on the headlamps and shifted gears. Approximately thirty feet down the pavement I was spotlighted by a cop that must have been sitting somewhere on the roadside.

Providing all requested documents, he told me I entered the road with my headlights off and that was a violation. He noted my eyes were red and asked me if I had been drinking. I told him yes, that I had wine a couple of hours earlier and he asked me to step out of my vehicle. He ran me through the various sobriety tests, while I was weighted by a substantial fur coat and house slippers. Surprised myself that my balance was off, I removed my slippers. My head was clear but my feet were freezing, the gravel hurt and that helped even less. Asking me if I would take a breath test he implied I had a choice and I declined. He informed me if I didn't take one I was going to jail, and when I took one and failed he cuffed me anyway.

He placed me in the holding tank for a solid hour in my fur coat with no place to sit; I was exhausted. Slipping the cellphone from my pocket I called Dolores, told her the situation and she went by the house to pick up Anastasia. Soon after that, a seriously drunk prostitute was thrown in the tank with me. I prayed for her, ignoring her drama as she wobbled on four inch heels in a torn tight-fitting dress. Within minutes, she leaned on the wall and melted down to the floor, passing out through an inaudible plea of justification.

They took me out for booking, and handed me a red jumpsuit. I figured the color red to be a "New Mexico proud" thing, thinking they were orange on television. My visit with the jailhouse doctor was brief. I answered all of her questions, to which she replied " you do not seem intoxicated to me."

I was placed in a large cell with twelve other women. The others congregated below so I staked my claim climbing to the top bunk. It was all so surreal; the jail was old, dirty and run down. The faces on the women around me were in varying degrees of separation; two particularly were the most out of touch and fully aligned with the roughest energy of the game in that world. As they paired up and ran the room, I watched and listened from above as they spoke to each one of the girls, sizing them up over the next five hours. Some were unresponsive, detached, despondent; one was curled up blanket over her head trying to escape the situation. Another girl spilled her never ending story, giving me a chance to catch a one-eyed rest.

My turn came as I sat up at the sound of a someone pushing a huge cart stacked with hard plastic trays of what some called breakfast. The "interrogator" looked up at me with her pale white face of Hispanic origin, penciled-on eyebrows and slicked back hair, extending her amply tattooed arm and offering me a cigarette. I assume she was trying to reel me in, thinking I would be in line with them in the future, and I graciously declined her overture, stating I was on a DUI hold and pending release. Dolores soon came to pick me up and I was summoned for release.

In court with my license taken away, they ran me through a weekly AA meeting, a DUI class and a million hours of community service. The common denominator at the bottom of every pile was "revenue" and I paid in every way.

My boiler had been shut down just days before the offense and the fact I had not been feeling well for weeks inspired me to a certified industrial hygienist. He came by the house to assess my situation. His conclusion to the more than likely cause of my impairment, was based on the location of the boiler in conjunction with the fireplace, the extreme levels of carbon monoxide pulled into the main living area and my prolonged exposure. I approached my lawyer, handing him the paperwork with his scientific findings. He simply stated half laughing that if I had $20,000 he would fight the case. Having no more energy to expend, I stopped resisting, let it go and focused on feeling blessed it was not a felony.

Gary and Jennifer drove through New Mexico to drop off our herbs from Brazil and the timing could not have been more perfect. The herbs were one hundred percent passion flower, individually infused with energy specific to our healing requests, and they altered my entire reality. Anastasia's photo was returned with an "X" indicating it would be best for her to go to Brazil for a divine intervention, and I began asking for guidance so it could happen. My meditations were longer, deeper and more nurturing than I had experienced for some time. The chair that I always sat in to meditate felt like it had disappeared and I was rocked in a formless energy, weightless and above the ground. The golden light poured into my head and revealed a strip that was "clear" in the right side of my brain, and I watched as it was removed. Unapparent to me in thousands of internal scans of my physical and emotional bodies, I marveled at its stealthy nature. An adept at locating vibrations of slower moving energy within my form using color, anything "clear" had been until then off of my radar. It was an important revelation in my inner work and I began noticing even more subtle levels.

April 24, 2003 Dreamtime

Anastasia and I stayed at Gabriel's to clean it as a surprise. The house was old, dark and small. I found his phonebook with many girl's names in it. Each name was decorated to indicate how he felt about each girl. They were colorful in colored pencil, and my name had two full pages and was decorated with hearts. It felt too small to be all of his conquests, and I felt it may have been his favorites. The rooms were messy and unclean. Outside on his wall I found an old, dirty, tapestry purse, a "smoking hags purse," I thought. We were watching television when some people looking for a party that was next door walked into the house and looked around, commenting on how they had always thought the house was empty because it was so dark. A young man was touching something of Gabriel's in one of the rooms. I ordered him to stop and threw him out into the living room. They left and I began to feel Gabriel would be on his way soon, so I called his cell phone and stalled him.

April 28, 2003 Dreamtime

Gary and I were at a place with an indoor pool. Chief Golden Light Eagle was there, but he wasn't well. The people were mostly Gary's clients gathered around the pool. The Chief announced to the crowd that I worked with the earth and elements in a very "native" interpretation segueing into the golden light work that I really do. He was sick, and after he spoke he entered a room and lay down to sleep. I began to speak to the group about the work with the levels I do, and the talk was received well. Gary started making comments to me, saying that his people did not want to hear what I had to say, and making reference to something being wrong with me physically. He was looking at my back as I was walking away from him, saying to the guy standing next to him "she doesn't know, she is totally oblivious" and shaking his head.

May 05, 2003 Dreamtime

I was around a group of people who gave their power away to a wizard. He had a daughter and other people he controlled with his magic. He was dressed for ceremony and walking up the hill. His father told me to stand in the middle and hold him up because I loved him. I didn't, and as a result he was trampled under foot. He looked *embarrassed and angry. At the ceremony, I began my part of the prayer opening the circle in golden light. The wizard was pissed off and looked toward me and I said I forgot. So in my mind I used golden light and called in Archangel Michael. Some of us lost consciousness for a while and I woke up I feeling a little bit different. My eyes felt heavy and I saw black symbols in them. Some around me were scared because they were afraid for me. I was not afraid. I knew Archangel Michael and the golden light would prevail. Sitting across from the wizard I leaned over and kissed him on his lips. Not afraid, not angry. My eyes had changed back and I knew we were done. He and his magic were based in fear as was I. I could now love and accept him as part of myself. This understanding in the moment seemed to transcend it all.*

May 16, 2003 Dreamtime

I lived in a town where several masters lived and was rolling incense doing a poor job with it. I finally figured out how to get the Sai Baba powder to adhere to the resin on the stick. Marie came over and I told her that Paramahansa Yogananda lived here in this town physically. She said he declared himself dead years ago, but he was still there.

Invited by Chief Golden Light Eagle to attend the 11:11 Star Knowledge conference in Colorado, I packed up the 4-Runner, preparing to spend a few days in the company of the Chief. Anastasia said she was ready to part with the desk I painted her with Native images, so I drove it to the gathering to give it to Zasquin, a young native girl from the Rez. As I drove to Colorado, my mind took me back to when I had met her months earlier when she was traveling with the elders when Cochora came through town. She visited my home one afternoon drawing huge pictures of the stars and the sacred spiral. Rooted in her artist connection, she proudly traveled with her easel, paper and vast array of colored pens drawing pictures for people who happily gave her donations. Moved by much about the Sioux way of life, I found the encouragement of her innate gifts and the honoring of her soul from everyone around her beautiful, organic, and the essence of what had been lost in most schools of modern education.

Pulling into the muddy grounds of the conference center, I was greeted by the Chief who helped me back into my spot in front of his cabin to unload. The Chief's cabin is naturally the busiest. I entered the house, walking past many people while the he instructed to put my things in his room as he led the way. His room was the only one with any privacy and we slipped in for a moment to speak. Men, women and children were in and out of what should have been a revolving door. Some watched movies and relaxed on the couch; women slow-cooked elk in the ovens while coffee brewed, the sink overflowed with undone dishes, and the countertops were cluttered with perishables brought for everyone to share.

People slept in the back rooms, men came in to speak with the Chief, and others gathered in the dining room chatting amongst themselves. One bathroom sustained it all, and I got to cleaning it almost immediately. The conference featured many speakers with different voices. Pounding drums of ceremonial songs filled the air and resonated with the beat of our hearts, sealing the circle with our intentions before we dispersed for evening supper.

In the few hours we shared alone, Chief spoke to me of the stars, identifying every constellation that gleamed above our heads while we soaked in the hot tub outside in the cold Colorado spring night. He knew them all and the stories behind them, being a soul from the stars that "walked in" to the form of what used to be Standing Elk some years before.

Lying still between our flannel sheets, embraced by his arm and surrounded by his warmth, I noticed the walls were waves and not really solid at all. His energy kept me in a place between sleep and awareness all night, although I was not tired when I woke fully into the golden sunbeams of the early morning light. With the sun, his energy rose to enliven the room. I lay there watching the mostly blue and white and gold light swirls move like ribbons in and around what I once believed were walls. Spending some time in that wonderful feeling of what I imagined to be the Andromeda galaxy, it took everything I had to get up and go make coffee. The experience carried me on the wings of appreciation on my long drive back to Santa Fe, and I smiled when I saw the bear he told me to watch out for while driving home.

Back to more concrete reality, inspiration began to take hold of me as I worked through the last of my John-of -God herbs and changes began to flourish. Trading in my 4-Runner for a new gold Honda Accord, it felt wonderful driving a vehicle that was soft and feminine again. I decided to go back to work and even though I worked at a spa, having a secular job for the first time in years not focused entirely on my vocation, was strange. When I wasn't on the clock at work, Anastasia and I were there soaking up the gift of the amenities with all the hot water, Yuzu body wash and cucumber water our cells could absorb. My mind began switching gears and rewiring itself to become acclimated to the world of work again, resurrecting my feelings of unworthiness. Unable to say no to the needs of clients, I continued to serve them as was expected of me. For the first time, the exchange of my service felt like an obligation instead of an extension of the heart. Summer came to a close and we breathed the fresh air of what would be the last fall we would spend in New Mexico.

August 07, 2003 Dreamtime

There was a bird in a tree that flew down to my arm. I felt the weight of the bird as he landed. He had an over-layer of black shining Raven feathers which I peeled off of him like a cape to reveal a soft brown bird. Startled, I offered to replace them. He said it was fine that way, but the black feathers were no longer necessary.

The snow fell and the days passed in all of life's normal beauty and the impetus to be where I could streamline life and make a better living pulled me to the West.

Chapter IX

Plagued

Plagued

Having sold off the last of my beautiful Santa Fe style home, I began stripping down even more, putting my remaining things in storage with a plan to leave the Southwest January 01, 2004 on purpose.

Anastasia and I stayed for two weeks in Sedona to see if that is where we wanted to set up camp, but there was no doubt Sedona was not for us.

We drove all the way to the California cliffs of the Pacific Ocean and stayed the night at the Seal Cove Inn at Moss Beach and felt right at home. We showered and dressed for complementary cheese and wine socializing with the guests in the dim light and small crackling fire in the parlor of the English manor. Picking a movie from the inn library and retiring for the night, we climbed the staircases giggling with happiness. After an amazing breakfast of French toast and coffee served on beautiful china, Anastasia and I walked the misty coastline of the cove. She picked up two abalone shells with deep cups lined with lustrous swirling patterns of iridescent colors. We smiled and marveled at yet another gift and sign that we were on the right track and were where we needed to be.

With a job in the pipeline and an offer to stay at a client's house while that was unfolding, we drove down to the South Bay and reconnected with more clients and friends. Within a week, a student had contacted me who had visited John-of-God and had brought back his blessed water. She had the time of her life and could not adequately express the levels of love and appreciation she felt for her experiences there. She handed me a quart-sized bottle of blessed water and a rose quartz rosary that I placed by my bedside.

February 02, 2004 Dreamtime

I was lying in bed and a doctor cut into my solar plexus and there were two huge lines of white powder on both sides of the incision. I took the white, powder put it in a pan and lit it on fire. It did not destroy it completely but attracted the attention of the fire department (Joao and the entities), because It reduced itself to a clear chemical toxic liquid and started to smoke. I saw it as a metaphor for all the work that I have done that has obliterated most of my garbage (energy left by drugs) in its recognizable state. Now it is residual, clear, harder to identify or see and in need of professionals who know what to do with the rest. I heard myself say "Thank you God for your grace in getting me to this point. Give me the courage to surrender my identity as I have known it and become who I was intended to be."

After a few weeks rest, I flew Anastasia back to Santa Fe to stay with Dolores and finish out her school year, and I rested, dreamed and healed until I was to begin work.

When you are one with Spirit your conditions do not affect you. Alignment in Spirit is the cure for all suffering.

- Siobhan Nicolaou, The Sword of Truth

May 04, 2004 Dreamtime

Many of us gathered in a rural place with a huge horse arena. Chief Golden Eagle was to be married to a girl named Christina. At first everyone there was entranced in a meditative state; a lot of energy work was being done. The garments we wore were all white. Mother Mary helped me get through the line. I was the last one remaining in meditation when I opened my eyes. I walked over and was looking at the inside of my physical body. The doctor said my heart was fine. (My heart was my concern- the layer of fat around it). Most of the people left before the ceremony began, including myself. I went back to the ceremony and it was over. The Chief was happily unwrapping gifts. Christina had beautiful energy. It was soft. Her only service this life was to him and thus his people were served. I walked through the remaining crowd, silently wishing them both well. Some man looked at me and watched me walk, as he remarked "I wonder what would be if he married who he truly loved?" I replied that he had choices, got on my horse and rode away.

May 06, 2004 Dreamtime

We were at a first communion for Gabriel's girls. Three of them began singing. Then it switched to Gabriel in his coffin. He was dead, ready to be buried. At his father's coffin, there were pictures of his dad from movie star looks to old age. They told me Gabriel's back gave way and he died instantly that his spine rotted and snapped. I said, "I knew he was going to die, he knew he was going to die." Walking through the line twice, I reached for something of Gabriel's. My sister said, "what are you doing?" She knew that if I touched something of his, the energy would be activated again. I could feel the vibration of the object as my hand got closer. I walked past a tomb on the way to watch Gabriel and two others being buried, and saw a death's head on his coffin, like Aleister Crowley's, and said in my mind that "the black knight was buried at the foot of the king instead of the good son." I thought this had put Gabriel's life in motion somehow. As I passed the coffin, I remarked "That is what the hierophant wanted" and it all made sense to me. I began crying, releasing the energy bound to his.

My job came through at the same time as our one bedroom apartment in Palo Alto. I moved in with a bed, a coffee cup, a fork, spoon and a box of incense. Working double shifts four days in a five-day week until school ended, I flew out to New Mexico to pick up my daughter, load the truck and drive my life home. It was so good to be back in the loving embrace of California, I felt more at ease with the opportunity to build and prosper again. Within a month of Anastasia's return, the answers came to me in regard to her "X" marked photo from the Casa. I got permission to be her surrogate knowing that it was not possible for both of us to go. I set my intention and in that declaration everything began to change in a positive way to support my journey. I planned my trip for September, and money began coming out of nowhere to cover the expenses.

September 08, 2004 Dreamtime

I was at Michael Genzmer's house in the country. Some kids jumped over the fence via a truck with hay stacked on it that made it easy for them to get over it. They were mean and trying to get into the house. I picked up the phone to call for help but they cut the wires. Many white Christian people headed from the town to the property. I was out front trying to break a black man's neck after he unsuccessfully tried to strangle me with a piano wire. I was not quite strong enough, so I shoved his head into a wall instead. At that time, another black man, a preacher, said to me "aren't you the one who can stop all this? Aren't you the one they sent from the bible?" Then the white men were chanting in ceremony with the kids about what they hated. They referred to the women, blacks and heathens as "pig sucking" somethings even though the women were their wives; they hated women. The women, silent and scared, retreated to the kitchen to cook choosing to remain subservient and in complete denial.

My trip to Brazil was soon underway. The deepest part of me knew how healing it would be for both of us, and my desire to know my wholeness moved me forward in such grace. Darren a friend that lives in Sao Paolo, sent his driver to fetch me from the airport to bring me to the financial district to have lunch before we went to the Clube Hipico de Santo Amaro. The cardboard and plywood houses along the muddy hills in the forefront of my view were shrouded in the shade cast by the enormity of the skyscrapers that towered in the background. Lunch was fantastic and light, matching the view we enjoyed out the dinning room window from high above the city. Topped off with the strongest coffee I could possibly order, I was refreshed and ready for our next driving adventure across Sao Paolo on the way to the club.

We relaxed at the club, watching the riders jump their beasts of elegant equestrian blood lines, while sipping a Caipirinha. Sitting in an outdoor lounge on oversized wicker chairs surrounded by lush foliage breathing the air of unlimited abundance, I felt this must be what it is like somewhere in Buenos Aires, imagining the addition of slow turning ceiling fans. We walked the grounds to the stables where I met his polo ponies with a kiss and a carrot. Time passed all too quickly and pecking cheek to cheek, I was off with the driver to the domestic airport. The drive through Sao Paolo seemed to go on forever slowed by the insane amount of traffic that made the worst day on the 101 in Silicon Valley's heyday feel like a leisurely stroll through Central Park.

I caught my TAM flight successfully after intuiting my way to the gate having given up entirely on my ability to effectively interpret Brazilian Portuguese. After a short flight to Brasilia, my driver Arturo was waiting outside the building with an open door and smile. I tossed my suitcase in the trunk and we drove to Abadiania. The road took us one and one half hours through rural lands void of skyscrapers and backseat to backseat traffic.

Exhausted from a thirty- hour journey with scant sleep and half a cocktail, I looked out the window in a daze while images scrolled across my eyeball screens like a movie without my giving any attention to what was or was not going on. Blinking once the entire drive at the image of a dead horse along side the road, bloated and decaying, being devoured by flies, I found it unusual that the people milling in its vicinity didn't seem to care.

Arturo pulled into the Pousada Luz Divina where I hung my hat for what turned out to be the most transformational two weeks I had yet spent on this earth.

After taking a shower and grabbing a nap, I met everyone at dinner in the common space. While acclimating to the pousada and the vibrations of the air, I opted to be quiet and retired to my room after supper. At around 8 p.m., I woke to the laughter and joy of a birthday celebration with a beautiful cake alight with candles. We sang and ate cake under the clear obsidian sky, and I retreated shortly after.

Scouting about early the next morning, "Fruittis" turned out to be my favorite cafe right around the corner. It wasn't possible to drink enough coffee to counteract my jet lag or the depth of relaxation I was feeling. Infused with the energy of the Casa, all I could do was eat, sleep and pray. Orientation was later that night where we were all given the low down on Casa protocol. I went to sleep, prepared to proceed as Anastasia's surrogate the following morning.

Journal Entry / Realtime

Closing my eyes, overcome instantly by twilight sleep, I saw the room around me spinning. My bed remained still, as everything else twirled in a huge invisible tornado swirling faster and faster. The energy took up the dust from the floor and my bed, caught up in the movement, lifted off of the floor and begin to turn. The light from my open door got brighter and I said, "wait for me"! feeling somehow I would be left behind; then I blacked out. Some time lapsed or maybe none at all, half in and half out of sleep, three white light beings with an aura of light blue stood on the right side of my bed and beamed a huge light into me that was so intense and so bright I could audibly hear the vibration. The light penetrated deeply into the entire lower torso of my body, from underneath my breasts to my pubic bone.

Waking up early the next day with my "guts" sore and tender, I found that standing erect was not possible and it hurt to walk. Talking to Catherine (the owner of the pousada) of my pain, she told me to use some blessed water to saturate a cotton ball and dab the area where I was experiencing discomfort, then place the cotton ball on my third eye and call upon Dom Ignacio and it would subside. Finding myself in much less pain and able to stand almost completely upright, I made an appearance for coffee before walking happily over to the Casa.

Those of us there for surrogate intervention were ushered in first and we walked into the "current room" where hundreds sat all in white in silent mediation. Music played and the current moved in and through me as I walked in the line on the way to see Joao in entity. Stepping up to Joao, I saw the huge distinct blue eyes that had visited me in my meditations off and on since 2002. My heart broke open in absolute reverence and appreciation as I paused for further instruction.

The entities asked me to sit in the room to the left, and I did so until guided by a man to go into another room. The intervention was in a separate room with many others. Sitting with my right hand over my heart, eyes closed, Joao came into the room resounding a few words in Portuguese that to this day I can feel throughout my body and mind. The vibration of his voice rippled through my cells from head to toe and much to my surprise it was done. Opening my eyes and jumping up to leave, I saw people collapse, then moved to stretchers for recovery. I exited into the sunshine and advised on the way out to pick up my herbs and water immediately and take a cab that was waiting to drive me back to the pousada. Staying alone out of the bright sun for a twenty-four hour period, I lounged inside and outdoors, slept, ate and slept.

Friday morning I went back to the Casa and meditated in the entity's room until the break where we all enjoyed the blessed soup before regrouping for afternoon session. I remained meditating in current until the Casa closed that day, then rested and healed until the following Wednesday.

Wednesday morning about 5 a.m. my invisible stitches were removed and I went before the entities for a revision. All was well and I stayed at the Casa meditating in the entity's room for most of the day.

Thursday I woke receiving the inspiration to take my 8 1/2 X 11 photo of Sathya Sai Baba through the line. I held it in my hands, thinking "really?" but did what was being asked of me. Baba told me to present his photo and to let Joao know he would accept herbs if offered. Speaking to Catherine, telling her what I was receiving, we laughed at the joy we felt in this request, and at how silly it seemed as we walked it through the line. I gave the message to the interpreter and presented the photo to Joao. He paused and looked at me with those massive eyes and said in Portuguese "do you know who this is?" I said "yes and he said he would accept herbs if offered." The entity said, "no, I will talk to him later" and told me to meditate in the entity's room for the morning session; then we were off to the sacred waterfall.

Friday morning, I asked the entity for intervention for myself, and followed instructions again, to rest alone for 24 hours. I woke in the middle of the night, my body extremely hot, and my kidneys pulsing with a smoldering burn that were the indications of my own physical healing. Laying low until Friday night, I packed and readied myself for my next day flight to Sao Paolo. Meditating one more time before leaving late Saturday morning, I thanked my lovely hosts and the Angels of Pousada Luz Divina, got into my cab and left for Brasilia.

After an uneventful flight and drive to the Ceasare Park in Sao Paolo, my body tender and healing, I followed instructions for my herbal medicine and thanked God for the comfort of my accommodations.

Darren's wife picked me up the next morning and we lounged at the golf club drinking coconut water from young green coconuts. Resting back at the hotel until dinner and out of the Casa energy field, my body began feeling every place the entities had worked on me.

Dining later with Darren at a beautiful restaurant in Sao Paolo, he enjoyed a bottle of wine without me. The city was balmy and the narrow streets inclined as we approached the entrance to his fabulous apartment, that had been in his family for generations. He showed me familial pictures as we sat on his couches chatting about how he was born from an English father, a Brazilian mother, schooled in England and how he loved to ride his polo ponies. Darren made sure I got back to the hotel safely and I went upstairs to take a hot bath. I made a phone call and rooted through the mini bar to see if I missed anything out of the ordinary and passed out.

Not really understanding the depth of healing that had taken place, I was careful lifting things but carried on with my usual exuberance. Arriving home, feeling guilty about taking the time off of work, I resumed my normal schedule two days after returning. Overwhelmed and out of touch with my body's dire need of rest and integration, I nearly collapsed at work. Taking myself home immediately, I lay in bed for five days barely able to move and sent my friend Rachel out for a pot of chicken soup. With each day I got stronger and managed to work my schedule through the herbal regimen, I found myself more open and happy. I rented space in Los Altos and held a weekly meditation. Dolores had moved back to California shortly after I had and like always showed up every week, but I could not feel the drive to get back into holding the space for others. Dolores was there for reasons other than the desire to do the work herself, and I kept seeing the face of Marilyn Manson to the right above her head. Tired of dealing with whatever that was all about, I told her that she knew what to do to continue her work without me and I let her go.

Dubhlainn brought some fun to our lives, spending time with Anastasia, enjoying an occasional dinner at the Sundance and handing over the keys to the Mercedes so we could have some California fun zipping around with the top down. Internally I was not rolling very well with the weight of the financial burden that was now mine alone to carry, my focus became more about money rather than grace.

Although it was great to be beautifying our apartment as a joyful creative endeavor, my self esteem continued to suffer.

October 02, 2004 Dreamtime

I dreamed I was wearing a long black dress with an Empire waist at a huge "spiritual night club" with rows of seats from ceiling to floor and an entrance hall. Two men and a short girl came in. She did not want to follow some rule and I told her "It was for her own comfort, and things were the way they were." She started to act out, so the guys took her outside before I called security. There were men all around with woman entranced, with huge pointed tops on some of the "monks" hoods they wore. The entranced women were chanting "stormeee" (stormy). Anastasia came by me and said" I do not like what these men are doing." I replied "They are letting it happen."

247

Continuing to go about life as I had always expected it to remain, I was tired, and not being firm enough in myself to move in any particular direction, I was looking for a partner to fill the void. Smiles filled the seats at the neighborhood cafe and I kept working in the grind. Manifesting prosperity was effortless, yet my perception kept me narrowing the flow of it to my hard work at the cafe. I was in fear, staying in "more" and "lack" instead of "thank you" trying to satisfy my ego's addiction to illusion, failing to make conscious the extension of God in the abundance raining down around me.

Tired of having my bedroom in the living room, I put it out to manifest a cottage somewhere in downtown Palo Alto, and through a guest at the cafe, we did. The move-in date lined up with the end of our lease and we moved into a cottage closer to everything. I down sized to a twin bed, and got busy.

Planting herbs and trellising sweet peas, I bought slate rock and created a pathway with stairs and an area to put my garden table and chairs. The finishing touches were my Balinese rock water bowl and massive three piece *vongole i cherubini* planter from Sylvestri overflowing with Baccopa and La dolce Vita geraniums.

I picked up a gorgeous over stuffed deep comfortable Italian brocade love seat proportioned to fit in a living room the size of the entire front house, and it worked beautifully as a couch for us. Inspired to paint the kitchen molding and cupboards in the MacKensie Childs "Courtly Check" pattern, it made my kitchen fanciful and the colors of my dishes pop enlivening my soul. After buying a faux marble toilet seat for the bathroom and painting gold Fleur de lis on the ceiling molding of my room, life felt more expansive.

Anastasia was busier than ever with high school and riding her bicycle to the cafe to work as a cashier on the weekends. I worked nights which gave her plenty of time to study and decompress in her own space.

My desire to have my life change and a man to create my stability must have made the airwaves sizzle, as quite unexpectedly, in 2007 I received a call from Gabriel. Out of the blue he apologized with the most sincere pleas for forgiveness and burning desire to make it up to me. I listened, jaw on the floor, with the willingness to give him the benefit of the doubt. I accepted the plane ticket to Santa Fe ready to reunite and curious to see what would unfold.

The first of three trips seemed like always, except we seemed more connected with our hearts. He now lived in his dream home built on the land I helped consecrate on his birthday years previously, tenting a birthday lunch on a Persian carpet with velvet and silk pillows, billowing pyres of incense statues of angels, a magnum and a half of champagne and *insalata gamberoni*, much to his surprise.

The house suited me very well down to the bocce ball court off the back terrace and I felt right at home.

Part of me suspected things were not as they appeared, and I felt around and paid attention. He flew out to California and we spent time going to Fleet Week in the city, to dinner at the Moss Beach Distillery on our way back down the coast. I had never let Anastasia spend any time with him before then; I kept our relationship out of her sight and mind. As a investor, Gabriel was very good and very connected in the real estate world. He had numerous offers in exotic places he was considering taking during this time, and when Anastasia and I discussed all the possibilities of how it could all unfold so positively, we became excited about the expansion.

He proposed to me in Santa Fe in front of all his friends, and I looked into his eyes trying to detect any discrepancies between his words and the gesture. I accepted reluctantly and spent the next few days visiting friend's houses, playing pool in their lounges, discussing the finest in Italian coffee makers. We spent time with his children and grandchildren, and the more time we spent together the more holes began to form in his performance. Gabriel was preoccupied with cigar bars in the afternoon and never seemed to be as focused on work. I assumed he had successfully accomplished his financial goals after so many years and was enjoying semi-retirement.

At home Anastasia and I were busy buying dresses for the wedding and having the dressmaker create a long coat from an old pattern I had of electric blue velvet with French cuffs of white silk and Fleur de lis buttons to wear over the strapless white dress of noble European design.

One more trip to Santa Fe would prove to be my last, as Gabriel and I spent time with his family and the dynamic seemed over the top and a little too high.

Excusing myself to the bathroom to get some space and listen to what I was feeling, I reached to turn the knob of the bide, and noticed a bindle on the floor. Picking it up, I brought it to his attention making it clear that drugs were not negotiable. I drew the line, as did his brother who chopped a pile on the marble counter and handed Gabriel the straw that broke the camel's back.

I packed and slept restlessly on the couch that night, refusing to join him in the bedroom. Remaining calm but firm, I contemplated everything on the flight home. It felt mostly contrived and seemed even more so after I learned he played a role in a movie shot in Santa Fe a few months later. My mind toyed with the notion it was all an act to impress his friends that surrounded us who were artists and Hollywood producers. This pattern to try to love a man in spite of his demons, reflected much for me in regard to the true meaning of love, and what it means when love doesn't seem to be enough. I walked away and never looked back.

Anastasia shifted into over-drive becoming preoccupied with college preparation, realizing she could and wanted to graduate a whole year early from high school. Within months, I manifested fibroid tumors the size of an orange, and made arrangements to see Joao at the Omega Institute in Rhinebeck NewYork. Achieving outstanding results, my stomach was flat again, I was doing another round of herbs and on the mend.

College was becoming a reality faster than ever. I was healing, working, busy and drinking three Peet's lattes besides my morning Bialetti just to get me through each day. Allowing the grieving process to begin early in hopes of having greater emotional stability at crunch time, I held Anastasia's face within my heart during my meditations as I connected the dots to the parts of myself that I was truly grieving.

The tumors began to grow again and I was bleeding profusely at times. I contemplated surgery and how I would be able to afford downtime from work to heal before graduation. With her departure for college quickly approaching and so much to juggle, I decided to wait until Anastasia was on the East Coast to take any medical action.

Anastasia and I met with Dubhlainn for lunch and he informed us he was moving back to Ireland to be with his family. We were happy for him but saddened at the same time. He turned the Mercedes over to us and was gone without warning within a month. We kept the car in the garage and drove it occasionally to the coast. Ceremoniously, we put the top down and drove to our last Mother's day outing at Filoli Gardens for a champagne brunch before putting her up for sale. Spring arrived that day with the unfurling of the daffodils golden yellow splendor, sporadically brightening the emerald grass along highway 280.

The mid-morning sun warmed our faces, opening our hearts as we cherished our time together over smoked salmon and champagne, chicken artichoke crepes with marsala cream, assorted fresh berries dipped in dark and white chocolate and strong, hot coffee for le grande finale. The gardens of Filoli embraced us with abundance of her nurturing beauty and held my heart in the gift of motherhood.

Soon the brake released from any lull time and summer got busy with sorting and packing. The announcement that the landlord was putting the property on the market added to the stress having to search for another place for me to live. Having never lived without a family member or a husband I had no idea what was out there, and had never entertained the thought of leaving my Palo Alto bubble.

After searching for months to upgrade my job, I landed a great position at the first green restaurant on the San Francisco peninsula. The whole place was divinity in action. The food, wine and liquor were the purest and most thoughtfully prepared and plated anywhere. I worked for a woman I greatly admired who held a vision I aligned with that enlivened every cell of my being.

Things got off to a great start. I found a place to live in Mountain View renting a wing from a woman who worked a 9 to 5. The place was not up to my standard of living and I spent days cleaning, painting and working Feng Shui magic to make it warm and beautiful before my move-in day. Anastasia and I flew to Boston, moved her into her dorm, walking through all parental activities and the picnic on the lawn. I spent one last night with her in Brookline and flew out the next day.

Streamlining into my new place, I familiarized myself with the kitchen and laundry and noticed Dawn kept the house cold. She was beyond frugal, mostly depressed, obsessed with the news, bottled beer and the hype surrounding Obama as election day drew near. She sat watching the debates and news programs alone, getting vocal and interactive with the screen.

Having my own entrance and bathroom, I minded my own business, a little upset she was so rigid about the heat. Offering to pick up the difference of the normal bill, she resisted and instead tried to get me to conform. With no energy to give her, I focused on getting into a rhythm before I left for New York to see Joao again two weeks later. The experience at the Omega was remarkable and helped my body get through the months that followed. Being warm and productive were my focus. I was happy to have a place where I intended to pull it all together, feeling weary but good.

Connecting with my housemate on the weekend while making coffee, I observed her peculiar eating habits and found out she was taking prozac. She was still distraught over a relationship she had with a young woman she rescued from her third world reality once she arrived in the US from El Salvador. Overwhelmed with her thoughts and feelings, mine turned to "sweet mother of God," and I sat on the wooden deck in the sunshine, contemplating urns with flowers and hummingbirds staying out of her way. My new-found sense of freedom from toxic relationships had brought back positive "can do anything" attitude. The lightning-fast transformation of my space was unsettling to the energy as I brought continual upgrades of eye-catching beauty and it flung her right over the edge.

Dawn's face became shaded with judgment, glaring from the stance of her proud- to-be earthy sandals, equating my reflection of refined feminine beauty with excess and superficiality. Her closets, partially opened in the hallway near the washer and dryer, were packed tightly from ceiling to floor with clothes, papers, dirt and shoe boxes. The plants in her house were mostly alive, bringing some credibility to the hand-carved heavy bottomed, earth goddess figures with large saggy breasts and big fat bellies sitting on the nearby dusty shelves. Tip-toeing around so as not to touch anything beyond what was necessary, I managed my laundry and took it to my room to fold. I caught something small and black springing from my peripheral vision, but did not think about it and got ready for work.

2009 Dreamtime

I was attending church . . . there were disrespectful hooligans everywhere. People were waiting for mass, talking and smoking pot. Upset from getting a contact high in the process, I told them they should not smoke that crap, and how I was exposed and did not appreciate it now that I was high. The church was packed. I was in a light-colored dress and they kind of laughed at me. A man said to me that he wanted to bend me over something and have sex with me. He was detailed and rude. I told him to take his comment into his dreams this life and the next, because it would never happen.

Later I was brought to a jailhouse to be shown where this man hung himself because of my rejection.

In custody of an Italian priest who also spoke English, I was wearing black now too. I tried to tell him these people were in Yeshua's house being disrespectful and it was like going to a brother's house and not even asking if it was all right to smoke, but he didn't want to hear it. He acted like he did not speak the language and disappeared. I was sent back inside the church to be exorcised by three old ladies who took salt and placed it to their eyes, ears and mouths (see, hear, speak no evil), and tossed the salt on me as I exited the church. I was before the entire congregation and the church was even more packed. I tried to speak again and no one would listen so I hastily moved thru the crowd and left out the front door feeling sure I would be shot in the back on the way out. I passed a Jewish man in a white ketonef *who stayed close to me and followed me up the hill to a lean-to. By this time all the people in red and black clothes from the church started to run out to find me. The Italian priest pulled them back and instead sent a drinking glass eight feet tall filled with some ice cubes and flammable liquid, instructing me to kick it. In that moment I uttered "Yeshua, Yeshua, Yeshua" and he told me, knowing it would explode as it was, said, "no wait, if you wait until the ice melts enough at the bottom you can kick it and it will not explode." So I waited and kicked the glass when he had suggested. When it did not explode, the Italian priest and his mob came to find me. I ran for the pasture and laid down in the grass next to a fawn-colored cow that was grazing. Somehow I was camouflaged by that. The priest laid down in the dead grass next to a black bull and I could see his eyes. They were demonic and squinted. He was chewing on a single stalk of dead grass, contemplating his next move.*

Garbage day came and, offering to help, I was informed the location of the cans was alongside the house by the gate. I walked around the yard, which was largely unkempt with tall grasses and completely enclosed. I saw old rolled-up carpeting outside my bedroom window that ran along the side of the house to the gate that could barely be opened because it was blocked with objects that needed to be hauled to the dump. I offered to garden a bit and was led through a narrow passage in her overstuffed garage to where I could find her tools.

Sliding one morning from feather comforters into slippers and robe, I made my way to coffee and into my office to sit on my Italian love seat to catch the morning sun. Looking down at the sleeve of my soft and warm light blue chenille robe, a brown shiny bug was weaving its way in and out of the fabric. Thinking it may be a lost beetle of sorts that needed to be put outside, I focused more on the sleeve to grab ahold of it and realized it was more than one bug. My robe was dotted with these bugs, and having no point of reference, it took me a minute to get it was fleas. In shock and horrified, I began looking around my room, thinking I kept my robe at the end of my bed and slept with my socks on because of the temperature, and could that be how they got in my bed? I brought it to Dawn's attention and she had no comment.

Immediately checking the mattresses and bedding and beneath all of my sheets and feather topper I saw that there were fleas popping around. I began stripping, vacuuming, washing and bombing my two rooms, but it was way beyond that. The lack of heat kept them down, but they were everywhere: on the linoleum in my bathroom, in my wool rugs, couch, and even the car, clinging to my pant legs and getting in the mats. The next couple of months I spent an enormous amount of money cleaning all of my feathers, wool rugs, clothes, brocades, silks and detailing my car. I threw "Rocky" away in my last moments of freaking out and wanting to be done with it all. I was emotionally traumatized, having intermittent bouts of tears, wondering if they were finally gone and staying on top of it with all the methods of prevention taking care with disposal of things like the vacuum cleaner bags. I was in the nightmare of plague, expelling the energy of such persistence that was bringing my attention to the details of my reality and my levels of resistance that needed to change.

By Christmas I put my belongings in storage and stayed with friends who gave me their guest room after seeing what I had been through and how badly I needed a healthy place to rest. My tumors were growing depleting my body of life force, and what I had left I brought to work and turned it into the most positive experience ever. My immediate boss was very intimidated by me, being new to her job in so many ways. Instead of feeling or appreciating the levels of sophistication and experience I brought to the restaurant, she projected the part of myself to me that felt incapable of ever being good enough and hit me repeatedly with the hammer of resentment.

Praying for all of us, I vowed not to think negative thoughts or meet her on the levels of myself she was showing me. Needing my job, I prayed for the timing to be on my side should she decide to fire me.

Keeping to myself and nurturing my body, resting and finding a doctor were my focus. I was referred to a doctor and made my first appointment in preparation for surgery.

December 03, 2009 Dreamtime

Sleeping on my stomach for the first time in decades, I woke to find Marius' energy mounting me from behind. Shaking him off, he lifted by wings. I thought him a coward for not facing me and was kind of surprised he found a way into my energy.

A few months passed and spirit had me taking care of only what I was guided to do beyond work and resting. As late spring showed signs of emergence, it was time to make other plans and leave my friends who so lovingly gave me a clean, safe and resistance-free environment to live in while I regrouped.

Making an inspired move to find a spiritually-based household, I rented a furnished room from a woman at the Ananda community in Palo Alto. I worked, meditated and tried to make friends with her ill-mannered Beagle. Working at a restaurant where knowing organic wine and spirits were the nature of our business, I came home on several occasions smelling foreign to her environment, no doubt raising eyebrows. It felt great to be in a bubble of Paramahansa Yogananda and I loved so much about the experience overall.

Three months later, the woman made plans to move into a house outside of the community, and a neighbor needed a house sitter for a month post-surgery. My mind was calm and body ready; I requested the time off of work to have surgery and heal.

Anastasia and her boyfriend brought me to the hospital and I waited to be called. I was led into large warehouse style surgery bay with a linoleum floor sectioned off with cloth curtains and various metal stands with instruments. My anesthesiologist tubed me in case I needed a blood transfusion and administered my anesthesia. As my body began responding to the drug, I prayed to the Casa entities of light to guide the hands of the surgeon. In the operating room, the doctor explained the lights above the operating table as I was fading. My last thought was remembering I had to sign a waiver giving them permission to take anything they saw fit, I prayed I would wake up with both of my lungs and kidneys.

Comfortably numb post-op in my stellar hospital situation, all seemed fine until my body responded by shutting itself down when it was time to get up and use the bathroom on my own. The pain was unbearable for blocks of time; my intestines burned and it took a while for everything to calm back down. Like a cat with every hair attached to a forest of nerve endings, my body felt every subtle ripple. My stay was extended as my body strived to adjust to the brutality of the surgery and subsequent removal of my female reproductive organs. Given the suggestion of a blood transfusion, I refused, knowing I could build my blood with nutritional support and gave it a pass.

Convalescing at holy woman's flat, feeding and playing with Tabbitha the house-trained rabbit, I took my meds and laid low. After one relapse and a trip to the emergency room, my body finally adjusted and I was back to work in four weeks and looking for another place to live.

Finding a large room in a blind man's home large enough it had an elevator, I would occupy the garden level floor next to the billiards room. My floors and bathroom were all marble accept the walk in and down closet and dressing room. I had a garden entrance too, so I would be able to keep to myself and focus on finding another job. Three people rented rooms on three other floors and I never met the two men who occupied them and frequently traveled. I got my bedroom set up, Feng Shui'ed the space and everything fit beautifully with my furnishings matching the Mediterranean elegance of the home.

Unrolling my wool rugs that were hand washed for flea removal, I settled in and tried to relax.

In my first week coming home from work, I met the young woman who was responsible for the smell of grilled cheese sandwiches that lingered in the air most noticeably between the fourth and fifth floors. Descending the wide four level circular staircase to my space, I paused to make a cup of tea and introduced myself.

Skin of translucent alabaster, red brown hair, blue eyes and slim fit build encased this fragile soul named Gwen. She would pace the length of the floor engaged in passionate discussions with Fred, the blind owner about what is wrong with America. Her strong Australian accent suited her debate as she often slammed her right palm with her left fist.

Fred, a wealthy businessman, sat with his sunglasses wired with a Borg-looking device, slightly smiling and entertained, rebutting with moments of conjecture while swilling copious amounts of red wine. I witnessed him pass out without warning, falling straight off the side of his chair and onto the floor. My eyes widened as red wine flowed from his plastic cup onto the white carpet, matching the other stains surrounding his feet, and the plastic cup suddenly made sense. Even with her audience out cold, Gwen continued to rant as I bid goodnight and made a speedy exit with my tea.

The difference in the energy between floors was tremendous, and so fragmented on hers that I wondered how it all would turn out. Gwen was lost, bound to Fred through a marriage to a family member of his in her past. Her torn mind anchored to the planet with the calming affects of cigarettes and psychotropics, she wandered the house that was not quite large enough to dilute the extent of her wreckage. With hardly the capacity to get up and face each day, she muttered while making her tea and sandwiches, managing to share enough of her story that I knew it was just a matter of time until I would be moving again.

Within a week, my wool rugs showed signs of residual fleas, and through tears of emotional distress, disbelief and hopelessness, I called the rug people again and ran all my bedding to the cleaners.

Spending time downtown led me to a wellness center to have a look around. Feeling it a place for me to get a meditation group gathered, I inquired, and with the owner's blessing hung out my shingle.

Regina advertised for me in her newsletter and a group gathered each week and things felt like they were moving forward. Barely a month passed, and I had again expressed an interest living around more conscious people. Regina mentioned she had a wing of her house she would rent to me, and that is all I needed to hear.

I gave thanks that my body was holding up and reached for the strength to move again. Cleansing was the game and going through the boxes at another level, my collection of *Bon Appetit* magazines dating back to 1983 had to make an exit. The remaining French bakeware I lugged around for decades creating beauty and joy for my family and friends had somehow lost its luster and I donated it to Yogananda's kitchen at the Ananda community. Sathya Sai Baba's Gayatri Mantra looped for hours, calming my mind from emotional stress and narrowing my focus to the task at hand. Fred kept reminding me in a threatening tone how lucky I was that someone else was lined up to rent the space that I so briefly occupied, and I prayed for strength.

Regina's house was an original English Tudor, immaculately refurbished, with my own entrance adjoining the parlor that had a fireplace and a baby grand. Gifted a Wolff futon mattress for my twin sleigh, it sat on the cold wooden floor on plastic awaiting the delivery of a boxspring, making the perspective from my mattress dramatic as the head and foot boards of the sleigh towered over me.

When the boxspring arrived, I was startled at the puddle of water that manifested between the plastic and the mattress and racked my brain trying to come up with a logical explanation as I dried it with a hair dryer. The room was always colder than the rest of the house, and Regina gave me a portable radiator to use. No matter how long it ran, it failed to produce adequate heat, so longer hotter showers became the short-term remedy in my narrow yellow tiled bathroom.

Appreciating my new dwelling and the European gardens surrounding the home, I lovingly got them in shape discovering the numerous plants, hedges and flowers that made it so special. After they were trimmed, I enjoyed the birds and revitalized plants while relaxing in the hot tub that faced the fire pit across the stone patio.

Anastasia and her boyfriend made plans to stay a night or two over Thanksgiving per Regina saying she would not be around, but her plans changed so Regina and her daughter ended up being home, feeling a little awkward. Inviting them to partake in the feast and festivities, dinner was perfection from turkey to wine, gracing the long wooden table in the original dining room. Board games ensued in the living room with laughter, brandy, coffee and pie while some of the guests consumed the remaining bottles of wine too good to leave unfinished.

Daily meditations brought the image of a woman, svelte in stature, wearing a gray wool dress from the turn of the 19th century. She would stand in the front window of my room gazing onto the front lawn. I could feel her loneliness and in communing with her, knew her yearning to be at peace. Informing Regina of what occurred to me, she confirmed the original owner of the house was a single woman who lived in San Francisco and built the home as a summer country getaway during that time-period.

Once conscious contact was made, things began to change. The back door was found open after being locked for the night, and the alarm went off randomly and the dogs were upset. The energy was releasing from the structure and this angered Regina more than once in her resistance to what was happening. Clearing the space, the woman's energy finally let go along with the pumpkin orange walls in my room that I transformed to French Vanilla.

Somehow I missed the part of our verbal agreement that Regina only wanted a tenant through January. I was beginning to wonder if it was becoming my job to move around clear and beautify energetically ruined homes. I called my sister Marie who lived in the foothills at my wits end and gave notice to leave my job.

Marie graciously moved me into the spare room of her house and I began searching the area for jobs.

Marie, always having a big heart thanked me in advance for the healing she knew would take place, and we gave it the o'l college try while finding it extremely challenging. Her home, full of altars consecrated to the departed souls of family and friends, African dolls, purposeful candles, bird wings, horse teeth, Native American masks, and other assorted trinkets. The energy was dense and moving backwards in some places. Tiptoeing in gratitude for having a place to stay, I tried to be supportive and not focus on or judge any of it. I kept my energy small, hoping nothing would notice my light so as not to attract attention.

Setting up my room with my angel artwork, rugs and French Napoleon bedding, I felt I finally had a space. I got focused and spent hours drinking coffee as I shredded enough files from the past to fill six large Hefty bags. I worked out at the gym for the first time in years, focusing on my abs to prevent adhesions, and cooked for my brother in law who loves good Italian food. I drove all around the area trying to get a feel for a place to work that matched my level of refinement, and it occurred to me I wasn't going to find one.

The roaming soul of my sister Stephania made herself known to me after I had a conversation about my past which called her forth while sipping scotch whiskey. I found myself speaking from her energy as I told my story and it scared the bejesus out of Marie's husband who was very upset telling me it was the first time he was frightened in his own home. Not being consciously aware of myself as a medium, I would have known to ground and not to open up in a living mausoleum. In my meditations I was guided to help pass all of the souls to the other side and things began to shift quickly.

Meanwhile in Boston, Anastasia was having problems with a very unhealthy dorm room situation, and I saw stress like I had never experienced before from her. Anastasia, a focused and intentional student juggling two jobs and sixteen units, needed my support. Always feeling and appreciating Anastasia as a God-given gift whose care was entrusted to me, I proposed the idea of moving to Boston and began my research into the city's chefs and best restaurants, looking for a place to work.

Finishing up some business in San Francisco, I received a call from Danielle requesting my help around her home in Scottsdale for about a month after she had surgery, and I agreed. Knowing I would be moving again, I gifted my sister what I was guided to leave behind and put my other things in storage. Going with the flow was the only name of the game, and I let Spirit guide me all the way.

Anastasia was looking for apartments in Brookline, a beautiful neighborhood on the edge of Boston, and informed me her boyfriend Aaron would also be moving out from California as part of the deal. Knowing he was a good young man with loads of potential, I agreed, making my only request that the apartment have a particular floor plan. The apartment that suited us would not be available until May. My month in Scottsdale held me until March, leaving two months to settle somewhere and find work.

Danielle's house was large and always comfortable. She rented a bed for my stay in the spare room and we shopped, going over details before she was admitted. Her husband William was in charge of the two elderly purebred Shih Tzu males I had known and loved since puppy-hood and I would cook and tend to the schedule of her post-surgery care.

Danielle had buried her mother the previous year, two years beyond her father's passing after moving them out from New York some six years prior. Gambling and unhealed pain held her aging parents together to the end, and for the first time I saw the same pattern within Danielle's.

In my 360 degree vision, I saw energy take the form of scorpions on the floor and checked in to feel what the images were telling me. Informing Danielle of what I was seeing, she mentioned her mother was a Scorpio and that she had lived for months in the house before she died. That conversation brought us to her closet where she showed me the ashes of both parents still in their cremation boxes. In meditation, I cleared the energy from her home and with little resistance the images disappeared.

Danielle's surgery was a great success, and William and I devoted round the clock post-op care. Obstinate and controlling, Danielle was unable to relax when out of her medication-induced coma and scoffed at blessed water from John of God I gave to her for healing. William and I bonded over Johnny Walker Green before dinner and sighed when we got time to relax. William bowed to Danielle's every demand, complaint and criticism, commenting in a circular way how it was easier to make her happy than to argue. Sorry to see my friends in this way, I gratefully shared with an open heart and got her well on her feet and continued to get my things organized for my move to Boston.

Chapter X

Redemption

"God said to our father Abraham, 'Go from your land...' and Abraham went on, journeying southward, began the process of 'birurim' -- of extracting the sparks of holiness that are scattered throughout the universe and buried within the material existence... By the decree of Divine providence, a person wanders about in his travels to those places where the sparks that are to be extracted by him await their redemption..."

– Rabbi Sholom DovBer of Lubavitch

Redemption

I excitedly boarded my one-way Virgin flight to Beantown, where I was met by Anastasia with open arms and a game plan. There was a good foot of snow on the ground and the winter Olympics dominated the airwaves. We sat on the warm double-bed at the Longwood Inn in Brookline, giggling after a hot shower, eating an assorted salumi platter. Anastasia gave me a beautiful arrangement of roses with a hand made card welcoming me to Boston and we opened the curtains to watch the snowflakes fall in the night as we drifted off to sleep.

Not knowing where I was going to stay past the first few nights, I was referred to a pensione on Beacon Street in Brookline three blocks from where our future apartment was located. A brownstone with shared bathrooms on every floor, I stayed there getting my bearings and looking for work. Climbing down eighty-one stairs top to bottom helped me build strength to get around the city without a car and I embraced the new adventure of public transportation.

Interviewing was fun and informative, showing me very clearly how much Bostonians promote mostly from the inside and take care of their own. Enduring derogatory remarks for being Californian and not looking plain enough to make the women around me feel better about themselves, my attempt to work in fine dining on Park St. fell flat.

Taking a server position at an extremely popular local seafood chain on the water front, I introduced myself to the average Bostonian palate. Lobster overflowed from tanks and the tops of buns tossed in a little mayo commonly referred to as a "Lobster roll." Bountiful shellfish were prepared every way you can imagine and the wine list had a French twist like the wine lists of California in the '80s. The clock rolled back about thirty years, when California was much simpler, and things felt reminiscent of days gone by. The snow melted by April, giving way to a remarkable spring where the honey bees gathered in greater numbers on the crocus blossoms than I had seen in years.

We moved into our apartment and I rented a double-bed, bought a set of sheets and a couple of feather pillows. Setting up a photo of Sathya Sai Baba in the corner, I burned Nag Champa and meditated before taking the train to work everyday.

Coming into high season for tourists on the waterfront, the patio tables were set up bringing the total number of seats to about six hundred. The work ethic was so different on the east coast, that I waited tables sometimes for fifteen hours a day, with some shifts back-to-back and never on a set schedule. It was not unusual to have thirty plus servers on the floor on any given day, bottlenecking through a small kitchen space with no room to stand. I lived primarily on seaweed salad, french fries and chowda the first four months, just to keep things simple while I integrated all the information I was downloading about my new life.

My co-workers were from all cultures and rungs of life: Italians from the North End, Southie Irish, Jewish kids, folks from Revere, kitchen staff from Morocco, the Dominican Republic, tons of college kids from everywhere else, and everybody had a hustle. I learned quickly not to trust anyone. There were always thieves among us, and I had to pull out my bag of street smarts. It astonished me the lengths the company had to go to prevent the crew from robbing the place blind.

It was every man for himself, with rampant lack-based thinking, favoritism and competition. The belief in scarcity and the promise of rewards drove competition, generating more sales, so it was not only acceptable, it was encouraged. We were the flagship restaurant in the company, with a track record for holding the #1 spot in every category. Reminded our job could be terminated at any time, we were always being threatened about the consequences of not reaching minimum sales goals.

Management seemed to get a kick out of watching the servers act as they knew they would, knowing their programming in childhood. Like throwing a bone to a pack of starving wolves, in the end there would be a single one standing while the others limped about growling and licking their wounds. Heads banged and tempers ran hot from long work hours, too much caffeine, lack of sleep and dehydration. The line "cover your ass" blinked like a neon sign in my mind throughout my time at the fish shack. I kept my eyes open, paid attention and shared very little about my true self.

The enormity of the restaurant gave me a complete workout carrying standard heavy restaurant plates back and forth from the ends of the earth all day. Getting my food dialed, I started bringing yoghurt, blueberries, bananas and nuts to work. The company forbade us to keep our own food anywhere so I stashed my yoghurt in the fridge behind the butter until the Chef started tossing it out. Stuffing bananas and nuts behind the cappuccino machine worked longer, but he got hip to that too. The large steel elevator was where we were allowed to eat during our shift, riding it to the basement and back until the door opened again on the ground floor. The elevator, used to schlepp thousands of pounds of fish each week, rarely got a break except the five hours between closing time and deliveries and always felt slimy. Sometimes the basement flooded from high tide, adding to ambiance and smell of a true New England fishing dock.

Trying to get my head around the psychology of their practices, I considered the corporate think-tank that came up with the psychological test I had to take as part of the application process. I imagined who they referred to as test subjects while creating their model for business concerning people in the lower ranks. Putting on my evil genius cap, *Arbeitslager* came to mind, but I sucked it up, kept my eyes on the goal, cried at home when no one was looking, and got up each day to make the donuts.

Making no exceptions to the rule of meditating before work, I stuck with it, streaming devotional songs through my mind to remain connected to myself while on the floor. Getting distance from the chaotic energy of the morning crew, I stood alone asking if I was really supposed to be where I was. Turning around, my eye caught a glimpse of something sparkling on the carpet across the room. I picked it up to find a small platinum and diamond earring in the shape of an angel's wing and I knew for some reason it was perfect. Feeling like I had a "get out of jail free card" with no inundation of energy to clear, hot water for days and outstanding climate control in the apartment, I was keeping my head down, my faith strong and feeling better at work.

With a greater sense of stability and assuredness getting around the city, I opened up more of my California light. The "C" train always carried fewer cars on a Sunday, making the ride a little more crowded than usual. The sun was bright, the air fresh, and being organized for my long shift I was relaxed, casual and hanging on like everybody else. Quickly scanning the people around the train, my eyes paused on the blank face of a woman standing in front and facing me. Opening my heart, I smiled a warm smile to say good morning. The blank look changed. Her eyes became shaded with a dark personality that affixed to my eyes and responded by saying in a surprisingly low tone, " don't you smile at me, don't you be looking at me." The tone of her words frightened me, catching me completely off guard. I closed my heart, moved down the train and her face returned to blank.

Nine weeks into our new place as I stood waiting at our elevator, a dark shadowy image smeared around the edges appeared down the hallway to the left and disappeared through the apartment door to its right. I had never seen it down our hallway before. I stopped, grounded, and asked if it had anything to do with me. The answer being "no" confirmed it wasn't, so I hoped to avoid it and ignored it every time I saw it in the days that turned into weeks.

Our entrance faced the hallway inside the building where all the windows were screened and closed. I found it curious that black flies were buzzing around the windows looking for a way out. I asked the kids how that could be, and no one had an answer.

Listening to my phone messages on the way home from work, Anastasia explained that I should come up the stairs instead of using the elevator as the coroner's office and crew were removing the dead body of a young woman. Anastasia called in an effort to prepare me for the smell

273

and drama, but nothing can quite prepare you for that. Awful was an understatement, her body being in an advanced state of decay having lain dead on the living room floor for weeks until someone reported the smell. The shadowy figure of her soul had tried to show me something, and I had chosen to ignore what could have led to her discovery sooner.

Men in hazmat suits brought large sheets of plastic and what was left of her body and anything considered evidence were sealed, stacked and carted down our elevator. Becoming a possible crime scene, the drama unfolded for days and nights with yellow tape while investigators removed countless boxes of her belongings. The saddest part was that in all that time no one had called or reported her missing- not her family, friends or her work.

The smell, overpowering us initially, was masked with wintergreen and some sort of air filters. They gutted her apartment, taking out everything including the kitchen cabinets. The reverberating sound of the jack hammer breaking up her cement floor for removal affirmed how long she laid there dissolving in the sweltering heat of her apartment. The renovation continued into fall as the students returned for the school year with a more somber tone than usual.

New England began reflecting the angry emotions I had yet to integrate from the previous six years, being too busy to keep up with myself effectively. The noise was constant especially about the time I was getting home from work which was after midnight most nights and later on the weekend. The university kids came over in buses from the clubs downtown and attended parties already in full swing all around the building.

Trying to tune it out I showered immediately, and popped Benadryl trying to shut down my over-stimulated mind so

I could grab five hours sleep before getting up at 7a.m. to work the next day. It was rare to sleep all the way through the night with the constant loud noise. My eyes felt gritty and my adrenaline stayed spiked to deal with the physical and mental demands of my job. My mind over rode my feelings of rage, with physically trembling hands of emotional distress and after months of trying to adjust, and I had no choice but to transmute my inner feelings at the end of my meditations. I just couldn't transmute fast enough to exact the shift at the rate I wanted to bring it about.

Tornado warnings were a first for me when the television news streamed live footage of a huge black funnel cloud on its way from the west to the downtown water front. Jumping on the "T" to go home, I felt safe underground until I emerged to street level at St Mary's. The wind whipped the trolley and the trees that lined the streets, the sky became darker, branches broke and the leaves kicked up in swirling patterns from the sidewalks. I raced home on foot from Trader Joe's carrying a bottle of Chardonnay and ingredients for chicken piccata, staying ahead of the six funnel clouds threatening the commonwealth. One touched down to rip apart Springfield eighty five miles west of us and kept moving east.

Safe in my neighborhood, surrounded by the vibration of my beloved King Solomon, Anastasia, Aaron and I watched the sky churn, releasing its black thunder with a lightning storm for the records. For a solid two hours we sat with the curtains drawn, drinking wine and having dinner watching torrential rain and lightning streak in sheets and bolts in awe of its intensity.

Suppressed emotions of fear and anger were within each of us in our home and like always, I felt it all. Being aware of it, I dealt with my part under the conditions and met the new challenge.

Aaron, content in his new space, anchored himself to his chair with more tenacity than any barrel clinging to the bottom of Lake Michigan. No matter what time, day or night, the scene remained unchanged except at his random meal times when a pizza box, or a foil wrapped "food tube" added more crap to the landscape of the entire left corner of the living room that he occupied. In front of his large computer screen wearing full sized head phones, he played expensive interactive war games for up to twelve hours at a time.

Aaron's fear sat like a boulder in his aura spawning a resistance that stemmed from an illness he had outgrown of at the onset of puberty, and I tried to be compassionate. Honestly, I was more often annoyed knowing he was aware of his stuff, holding a degree in psychology and consciously not engaging in the work required to free himself from what was holding him so solidly in this pattern. Though he looked for jobs, he couldn't seem to find one that met his criteria so I encouraged him to volunteer at a psych clinic to be with people and projects aligned with his field. A bright and capable young man, he pulled it off like I knew he could and got out of the apartment a few days a week working on some research projects.

Feelings of pulsing inner rage surfaced as I recalled the lazy, angry, spineless jelly fish of a man my inner child felt my father was. Aaron's reflection gave me plenty of inner work when I had time to deal with it, but the mounting frustration exacerbated by the unending music and noise around our apartment made my blood simmer on high.

The holidays came and went with Anastasia preparing a great Thanksgiving feast. My plan moving forward was to remain detached and allowed those two to figure out their own lives. I stayed in my wing when I was at home, consciously deciding not to stew. A new year was upon me and I was ready to make changes and focus more on my joy. I knew Anastasia would be graduating in another year and did not know what that all meant. Scrolling through Craigslist religiously, I looked for a place to work that was better suited to my skill set and quality of life. My breaking point was drawing near with my work schedule and lack of adequate down time. I turned inward for a connection to something loving and light and hung on knowing my prayers were being answered.

Feeling something in the left lower side of my colon, I called Gary asking him to tune in. "a small spot" he pointed out over the phone, right in the area I felt it. The insight he gave me about the emotional energy creating the dis-ease made me cry with hopelessness. Healing it solely with the inner work of transmutation wasn't the whole answer managing every molecule of energy I had left after work to stay on top of the necessary details of life.

Inspired to seek the help of a surrogate in Abadiania, I got the green light from the Casa and set up the time and date. The ability to have an intervention while in Boston from Abadiania was a saving grace to my whole being and my energy field shifted dramatically. I faithfully took my herbs and tried to focus at work. My body relaxed. I meditated more and felt happy and relieved. The kids and I talked about moving to get away from the noise, but I made the decision not to put myself through another upheaval, and we stayed. We got more clever at dealing with the kids on our own, and the building management team was forced to deal with the endless problems as the mounting threat of a law suit was no doubt hanging over their heads.

Stretching myself beyond the familiar, I answered an ad for a waiter at a long established restaurant on Beacon Hill and got off the trolley at Arlington Station for the second time since my move to Boston.

It was the most beautiful part of the city. The air put a spring in my step as I crossed the street to the Public Garden.

Sunlight streamed through the tall standing trees and the long willow branches hanging over the waters edge swayed gently in the morning breeze. The ducks were floating peacefully before the onslaught of spring tourists flooded the garden. Looking down at my feet, my clothes in my minds eye transformed to a black Spanish theatre cloak with two black tassels hanging from the neck line bouncing on and off the chest with each step. The words "Jack the Ripper" entered my mind, translating the feeling of the image. He was wearing a top hat, strolling through the park after a performance on a cold and clear night.

My feet sensed a familiarity crossing Beacon Street and walking in the footsteps of so many of my favorite politicians, artists and authors. More than the hand cut granite curbs or the bricks, was the New England charm that like a melody carried my every step to the front door of the building.

Entering the restaurant of dark wood and Italian tile, I asked the handsome light-eyed Italian manager for an application, admiring his classic old world features, medium height, stocky stature, broad shoulders and the curls of his light brown hair. I imagined his suit an ornate leather breast plate with an imperial blue cloak fastened to his shoulders and draped behind him. I smiled, took the paper from his hand and as I turned to sit at the bar, my mind flashed to a scene from another time on the beach somewhere in Mediterranean watching some ships in the distance sail closer to the shore.

Flashing back to real time, I turned, taking a seat at the bar and shifted my focus from whatever world that was to filling out the basic information on the simple job application. As I began to write, a large swirling force of energy swept up behind me, moved through the left side of my body and erased my mind. Staring straight at the page, I tried to focus, but was a bit stunned and suddenly not able to remember my address or phone number. Trying not to appear obvious, I wondered what had just happened. After a couple of minutes passed, I regained the use of my mind, finished the application, thanked him and left. Since it was not unusual for me to be affected by another's energy, I assumed it was the princepe, not making the connection to what I saw and felt in my walk across the garden just minutes before.

When I was hired, joy bubbled in my heart with the knowing it was where I belonged, among fellow Italians and all male management team with impeccable professional standards. My first ascent from the basement to the ground floor was a déja vu, as if in that moment I was walking the stairs looking through a window of the past.

Every day that vortex of energy swirled around the restaurant undetected by most people and was never made conscious by those I observed obviously caught up in the rush of the swirl. I would witness them feeling something, then with a strange look on their face, quickly disregard it. One lamp fixture of six would swing in the dining room, and when I pointed it out to a coworker one day, he remarked saying "that was a first."

The energy among the staff was somewhat emotional and oppressive. The servers expressed their upset at not being sent home in the middle of the afternoon lull between lunch and dinner service on a double shift. There was an obvious cloud of energy affecting some people more than others and it was fascinating to witness. One gal had such a creepy energy attached to her that whenever she moved toward me and tried to engage in conversation, I had to immediately walk away. When I looked at her face I saw "Nurse Ratched" in my mind. She was currently training to manage children in a vulnerable mental capacity with an internship at an institution and it all made sense in that discovery. My solar plexus wrenched when she spoke about training for placing patients in straight jackets and I prayed for guidance in handling the layers of antiquated toxicity coating everything and almost everyone.

Another guy was very sensitive, was smart and quirky who knew the menu inside and out. He had been there for many years and was brilliant at delivering an excessively memorized- and forgetful- performance at the table due to his minuscule people skills and lack of an open hearted approach. Each day he reiterated his loathing for our clientele, sitting behind a large wooden beam during "family meal" ruminating on the negative thoughts he couldn't block from is mind.

Misplaced in life, frustrated in knowing he was more than he had deemed himself worthy, he was bitter from being excluded from his family's money and continually compared himself to his brothers. He placed everyone on the pedestal of success, and always argued for his limitation. He worked like a machine, moving very quickly as if it would somehow shorten the time he had to be there. Keeping to himself and famous for mumbling under his breath, he was a very thorough employee who executed his tasks with Germanic perfection, who trained me well and who I left alone.

The rest of the girls were Italian or Irish, steeped in sports, drama, alcohol and generations of unhealed familial programming. I saw in their behavior old patterns from my own family that I had left long ago. They clung tightly together with my arrival on their scene. My presence rocked their world as I stood out in ways that forced them to reflect on their personal and professional standards, making it awkward at times and every gesture insincere. They whispered among themselves, told me nothing, introduced me to no one and prayed I would leave. Regardless of how I was treated, I also knew what it was like to be where they stood, and how uncomfortable the face of awakening can be. We all made a great team, when all pain was put aside, and loving everything about this establishment, I got it working for me by keeping my eyes on the goal and being professional. The management team seemed to like me well enough, and I jumped in with both feet and focused on the new menu and company formalities.

Downstairs taking my menu exam, I lost time and it seemed like it took hours to complete. My head was reeling as the energy smeared the information I was recalling in my brain. Leaving the room completely altered and in need of some fresh air, I knew something was definitely off. It wouldn't be long before it all revealed itself.

The same vortex of this mysterious energy constantly assaulted my body, leaving my brain to cross-up transactions on the computer, making interesting one-of-a-kind, never before seen mistakes that perplexed my managers. I could see by the looks on their faces they could not figure out how these incidents were related to me, but knew somehow they were, and I remained an enigma.

The story unravelled in my mind a little more each week as I polished the crystal wine glasses, readying my tables for Beacon Hill's finest. I constantly heard a woman screaming in my mind, I saw the image of her partially clothed body lying on the ground held up by a man behind her as he finally cut her throat, putting a stop to the chaos and struggle which both were fighting to end. "Can't anybody hear me?" was the thought that was going through her mind while being terrorized. Then the scene went silent in the bloody aftermath of her brutal attack.

The screams and images continued in my mind, trying to get my full attention, and I found myself doing very well in spite of being constantly distracted. Knowing it was a murder unresolved, perhaps a skeleton yet to be discovered beneath the basement floor, I ran the address through the internet trying to dig up a story, but to no avail. This was the first time that energy was requesting my help but with no way to communicate what was happening with the business or building owners. It left me deliberating how I could perform the ritual I had used for many years on various properties and homes around the country without anyone knowing. The solution occurred to me in meditation guiding me on how to perform the ritual remotely, in my mind and heart anchoring a new vibrational pattern for the building. I worked everyday for almost two years with the Archangels in meditation and watched the changes continue as two hundred years worth of tormented souls let go of the building.

Almost immediately after I was hired we began experiencing fire alarms going off without human error, although the manager was looking for someone to blame. The first couple of times everyone was upstairs and busy, but the fire department insisted it was the fire alarm downstairs near the pantry. I just kept my mouth shut knowing what was happening having witnessed this many times before.

In the beginning, the unreasonable demand of my schedule, insufficient rest, constant negative energy and the drama unfolding in my mind got me a sit-down with the bosses. I explained my irritability stemmed from lack of a regular schedule without two days off in a row. Grateful when they complied with my request, it gave them the hours they wanted and the time my body and mind required for healing and integration.

Life fell into a rhythm and everything ran more smoothly. I was clearer and able to give my best in all areas of life which rolled over into even more offerings of homemade *cantuccini* and other various biscotti for the bosses and the staff.

The young woman's soul found peace and moved on because someone finally heard her cries and brought the Angels to end her suffering. The response from the astral imprint of the masculine energy was aggressive, and took much longer to settle down. Slowly and over some time, the entity refrained from assaulting me when I was working, but continued to let me know it was still there. It jumped around on the light fixtures and wreaked havoc on what the bosses always believed was the clumsiness of the waiters when glasses broke in numerous ways and all the time.

Stepping out onto the cobblestones after work one night, closing the heavy metal door behind me, I felt the entity's presence watching me from a short distance down the alley. The energy compelled me to turn around, I turned and peered into the dark shadows looking for a form. Telepathically I let it know I was aware and not afraid; then I turned my back and walked down the narrow alley toward the street.

The gaslight lamps would "breathe" when I walked by them, going from extreme bright to dim and back, so I turned around to feel and observe. It was then I became aware the energy was not confined to the restaurant, but seemed to roam outside the building onto Charles St.

One morning as I was polishing glasses while people-watching on Charles St, a coworker came up beside and me pointed to a second-story window directly across the narrow street. He said, "Did you know that is where the Boston Strangler killed his last victim?" I had no idea until that moment, but it made me wonder if I was intuiting that murder given how the energy seemed to roam.

The more energy work I did on myself, the more things happened at the restaurant. Whole shelves of olive oil fell to the floor without provocation; the music turned itself up and down. I noticed The refrigerator behind the bar went out after I went through energetic adjustments and wondered if any of it happened when I wasn't there.

The most jaded personalities among the staff condensing in the presence of an ever-increasing, cleansing vibration, began to display greater verbal dissatisfaction concerning the work environment, and quietly I knew what it was all leading to for them. The angry mumbling waiter left quite emotionally in the middle of his shift, storming out the front door and never returned. "Nurse Ratched" gave notice and was let go on the spot, and other negative personalities among the staff gave notice in the months that followed, some with and some without incident. The energy began to blend, and the leaves about the hill burst into color.

November's first snow dusted the bare dark branches of the trees in the Public Garden, and I left work that night with great enthusiasm readying myself for a new inspirational perspective of a place I was falling in love with more every season. My nose paused at the entrance, catching the scent of a sweet flower nowhere in bloom, and with no one else around. Stepping into the garden that looked like a three-dimensional snow globe of an Ansel Adams photograph, the contrast was stark, the silence was welcoming and the soft golden lamp light guided me quietly on the path across the garden to my exit.

The opposing energy in the restaurant waned, reducing itself to a small presence clinging with a distinct sensation to the back side of my right shoulder that felt like a goblin. Making it clear to this energy it could stay but the light wasn't going anywhere, I gave it a choice to hang around and succumb to love or move along and the energy surrendered. Then one day I awakened realizing how long it had been since I had felt it.

The energy completely shifted at the restaurant the night I had returned to work after being on retreat for a week and visiting the John-of-God current room in Sedona. Later that night, a huge 3/4 inch glass divider shattered in the middle of the night with no one around. The camera pointing right at it recorded the incident and left the bosses scratching their heads. Things were much more mellow after that, and always proportionate to the energy I was processing within my emotional and physical bodies. The vibration of love gained a greater foothold everywhere at work as I ceremoniously held this intention in my heart and in my mind every day. Opening my heart onto the tables of our guests, I showered them with warmth and compassion as I had the building and it souls for so long. The new hires were different than the souls they replaced and I watched my example of healthy living influence theirs.

Writing and meditating more, I pondered at times the determination of the murderous energy I had been loving into submission since before the previous spring. On a glorious New England morning in February, with its clear blue sky, my hands wrapped around a steaming mug of hot coffee, all the notes of my soul's score began harmonizing and everything fell into place. My mind became integrated enough that I was able to experience darkness as the illusion it truly is, rather than knowing it and still resisting it cries for love. Its pertinacious pursuit to keep my attention forced me to reconcile it or be consumed by it. Love more, judge not, be compassion instead of resistance, and more light and integration is all that is required to eventually return to wholeness. The illusion of darkness or "evil" that tormented me unceasingly throughout my life was suddenly powerless compared to my ability to love completely. I witnessed that love can be reborn within anything because it is the essence of everything, absolutely everything, and that some energies especially unworthiness take longer than others to transmute.

Spring was a lot brighter this year, life was more abundant than ever and I settled happily into my soul's greater expansion. Summer came upon us gently and I strolled into my wonderful job, grateful to work for the most stellar people at one of the best restaurants in Boston. I made coffee, always arriving early to be grounded and prepared before the deluge of European tourists this time of year. I knelt down to adjust the levelers on the table for lunch service, turning my head to the side while spinning the hardware to the proper height. I observed a news crew setting up their equipment on the sidewalk, lights on, cameras rolling. The newscaster went on to announce that authorities had solved the case of the Boston Strangler, pointing up to the window, proving with a DNA test that De Salvo was definitely the perpetrator and closing the case. The murders I cleared in and around this location appeared in my mind to be much older than the De Salvo murders, but the vibrational interpretation of the energy reveals itself in images and sounds that represent the density of the vibration and emotions of the players. De Salvo was without a doubt the Jack the Ripper of New England.

Work continued to get easier with the complete integration of the energy, but with my real job here being finished and my vibration continuing to increase, Spirit moved my feet again, pointing my toes toward the west.

The images of my reality began changing as I looked in the direction that my feet had turned. Spirit showed me new views from different angles of the city as I "accidentally" and frequently got turned around on my commute. The new perspective was fresh and beautiful, yet felt limited to the height of Boston's magnificent buildings. Unable to see the limitless possibilities yet to be revealed, I made the decision to move back to California. I packed my things along with some residual energies and manifested new opportunities there that forced me to surrender every last breath of my resistance until that too was overcome.

It is only in the condition of non-resistance you find love, and only in love that you will find the absence of evil.

ABOUT THE AUTHOR

photo credit:

Siobhan Nicolaou is an emissary of Truth, expressing her spirit as a powerful voice for the evolution of human consciousness. An expert in the field of Alchemical Transmutation, she encourages a sovereign approach to spiritual development. Siobhan offers talks and Soul Readings around the globe.

SiobhanNicolaou.com